Negotiating the Sacred

Blasphemy and Sacrilege in a Multicultural Society

Negotiating the Sacred

Blasphemy and Sacrilege in a Multicultural Society

ELIZABETH BURNS COLEMAN AND KEVIN WHITE (EDITORS)

ANU

THE AUSTRALIAN NATIONAL UNIVERSITY

E PRESS

ANU

E PRESS

Published by ANU E Press
The Australian National University
Canberra ACT 0200, Australia
Email: anuepress@anu.edu.au
Web: http://epress.anu.edu.au

National Library of Australia
Cataloguing-in-Publication entry

Negotiating the sacred : blasphemy and sacrilege in a
multicultural society.

ISBN 1 920942 47 5.

1. Religion and sociology. 2. Offenses against religion.
3. Blasphemy. 4. Sacrilege. I. Coleman, Elizabeth Burns,
1961- . II. White, Kevin.

306.6

Indexed by John Owen.
Cover design by ANU E Press.
Art work by Elizabeth Burns Coleman.

Table of Contents

List of Tables

Contributors

Dr Veronica Brady

Veronica Brady is Honorary Senior Research Fellow (previously an Associate Professor) in the Department of English, University of Western Australia. She is also a Roman Catholic nun, and a member of the Institute of the Blessed Virgin Mary (the Loreto Sisters). Her research interests include Australian literature, and social and theological issues. She has a strong commitment to social justice, especially to reconciliation with Aboriginal Australians. Her most recent books are *Shall these Bones Live?*, *Caught in the Draught*, and *South of My Days*. She is currently writing on issues to do with ecology and the sacred.

Dr Elizabeth Burns Coleman

Elizabeth Coleman is Lecturer in Philosophy, La Trobe University. She has held a post-doctoral fellowship in the Centre for Cross-Cultural Research, The Australian National University, and lectured in the Department of Philosophy, School of Humanities, The Australian National University. Her most recent publication is *Aboriginal Art, Identity and Appropriation* (Ashgate Publishing, 2005).

Professor Riaz Hassan

Riaz Hassan is ARC Australian Professorial Fellow and Emeritus Professor in the Department of Sociology, Flinders University. He has published extensively on the sociology of religion, including *Faithlines: Muslim Conceptions of Islam and Society* (Oxford University Press, 2002), 'On being Religious: A Study of Christian and Muslim Piety in Australia', *Australian Religious Studies Review*, 2002, and 'Imagining Religion: Self-Images of Islam', *Asian Studies Review*, 2002.

Professor Ian Hunter

Ian Hunter is a Research Professor in the Centre for the History of European Discourses at the University of Queensland. He specialises in the history of early modern religious, political and philosophical thought. His most recent monograph is *Rival Enlightenments: Civil and Metaphysical Philosophy in Early Modern Germany* (Cambridge 2001). Together with Thomas Ahnert and Frank Grunert he has just finished the first English translation of works by the early German enlightenment thinker, Christian Thomasius, and he is currently completing a book on Thomasius.

Mr Liam Dee

Liam Dee is a PhD student at the Department of Critical and Cultural Studies, Macquarie University. Mr Dee's current research is an examination of the aesthetic, from its origins as an ancient Greek epistemological concept to contemporary trends in the design of lifestyle commodities. Other research interests include the imagination as social critique and the 'culture industry'.

Dr Winifred Wing Han Lamb

Winifred Lamb teaches at Narrabundah College in the Australian Capital Territory and is a visiting fellow in Philosophy at The Australian National University. She has published in philosophy of education and religion. Her most recent book *Living Truth and Truthful Living: Christian Faith and the Scalpel of Suspicion*, 2004 is published by ATF Press.

Ms Dianne McGowan

Dianne McGowan is a PhD candidate at the Centre for Cross-Cultural Research, The Australian National University. Ms McGowan's research project is tracing the historical production, by the West, of the category 'Tibetan Art'.

Mr Colin Noble

Colin Noble is Chaplain and teaches Studies of Religion at William Clarke College. Prior to that he taught Japanese Studies at the University of Sydney for 14 years, after studying and working in Japan for a number of years. He has postgraduate qualifications in Japanese Studies, education and Christian Studies. His areas of publication include church-state conflict in Japan, Japanese Christian thought, and Buddhist-Christian parallels.

Dr Helen Pringle

Helen Pringle is a Senior Lecturer, School of Politics and International Relations, University of New South Wales. Her research is in the areas of the history of political thought, political and social theory, politics and literature, questions of sex, gender and public policy, and in particular pornography and hate speech.

Ms Pauline Ridge

Pauline Ridge is a Senior Lecturer in the Faculty of Law at The Australian National University. Her research interests are in equity and trusts, restitution, and law and religion. In 2001 and 2002 she conducted an empirical study on the receipt of financial benefits by Ministers within the NSW Synod of the Uniting Church in Australia. She has written on the equitable and probate doctrines of undue influence generally, and in the context of religious faith.

Associate Professor Suzanne D. Rutland

Suzanne Rutland is Associate Professor and Chair of the Department of Hebrew, Biblical and Jewish Studies at the University of Sydney and Associate Professor in Jewish Civilisation. Her major publications include *Edge of the Diaspora: Two Centuries of Jewish Settlement in Australia*, Collins, 1988 (1997), and *Pages of History: A Century of the Australian Jewish Press*, 1995. She has held numerous leadership positions within the Jewish and academic communities, including being current president of the Australian Jewish Historical Society, Sydney, and immediate past president of the Australian Association for Jewish Studies.

Mr Kuranda Seyit

Mr Seyit is currently Executive Director of the Forum on Islamic Relations and chief editor of *Australia FAIR*, and is a former editor of *Australian Muslim News*. He is also undertaking postgraduate research at the University of Sydney in Peace and Conflict Studies.

Revd. Eilidh Campbell St John

Eilidh St John is the Unitarian Chaplain at the University of Tasmania. She trained at Manchester College, Oxford, majoring in comparative religion and community development. She served as a minister in England and Northern Ireland where she was active in peace and reconciliation work. She teaches courses on Ideas and Faiths and the Politics of Democratisation – East and West – at the University of Tasmania. Her doctoral thesis on the epistemology of the sacred and its political ramifications in a multifaith society is nearing completion. She is Director of the International Institute for Social Change and Non-Violent Action and is a Global Advisor to Generation Next, a UK Charity working to educate disadvantaged South African children.

Professor Colin Tatz

Colin Tatz is a Visiting Professor of Political Science at The Australian National University, Visiting Research Fellow at the Australian Institute for Aboriginal and Torres Strait Islander Studies, and Director of the Australian Institute for Holocaust and Genocide Research, Shalom Institute, Sydney.

Dr Kevin White

Kevin White is a Reader in the Sociology Department at The Australian National University. He has held appointments at Flinders University in South Australia, Wollongong University, and the Victoria University of Wellington. His most recent publications include (with Frank Lewins and Alastair Greig) *Inequality in Australia*, Cambridge University Press, 2004, and *An Introduction to the Sociology of Health and Illness*, 2002.

Professor Hal Wootten AC, QC

Hal Wootten is a Visiting Professor, Law School, University of NSW. He has been a QC, secretary-general of Lawasia, foundation dean and professor of law at UNSW, foundation president of the first Aboriginal Legal Service, Supreme Court judge, chairman of the Australian Press Council, president of the Australian Conservation Foundation, royal commissioner into Aboriginal Deaths in Custody and Deputy-President of the National Native Title Tribunal. In 1991 he was made a Companion of the Order of Australia for services to human rights, conservation, legal education and the law. He encountered sacrilege issues as

Ministerial rapporteur/mediator on Aboriginal claims for protection of sacred sites threatened by a dam at Alice Springs, mining in SA and Queensland, and water-skiing and grazing in NSW.

Acknowledgements

This book had its origins in a conference, Negotiating the Sacred: Blasphemy and Sacrilege in a Multicultural Society, hosted by the Centre for Cross-Cultural Research, The Australian National University, in May 2004. We are indebted to the Director of the Centre, Professor Howard Morphy and to Ms Anne-Maree O'Brien, Ms Suzanne Groves, Mr Alan Wyburn, and Ms Celia Bridgewater for their assistance. In organising the conference and in selecting papers, the editors were assisted by a planning committee. We are indebted to Mr Roger Garland, National Museum of Australia, Dr Sarah Bachelard, Department of the Senate, and Ms Elizabeth Kentwell, Department of Immigration and Multicultural Affairs. We would also like to acknowledge the support of Professor Adam Shoemaker in his role as Director of the National Institute of the Humanities and Creative Arts, The Australian National University, for financial assistance and ANU E Press for publishing this book.

1. Negotiating the sacred in multicultural societies

Elizabeth Burns Coleman and Kevin White

The social costs of increasing antagonism, fear and social dislocation on the basis of religious persuasion suggest that Australia, as well as other multicultural societies, needs to re-examine the place of religion in society, the causes of social discontent, as well as the various means by which religious differences may be negotiated peaceably. Such an examination requires information from a wide variety of perspectives, and discussion at all levels of society. The purpose of this volume is to make a contribution to this discussion by providing a rich, multifaceted exploration of the issue. It brings together religious and secular perspectives and the insights of scholarship from a wide variety of disciplines. It explores histories of religious conflicts, our assumptions about secularisation, and examples of ways in which people of religious persuasions have, and can, negotiate religious difference. These issues have enormous practical significance in a multicultural society with diverse religious beliefs and cultural practices.

This book offers a unique contribution to this discussion because it attempts to engage with belief, not merely between faiths that can find some area of commonality, but between secular and religious perspectives. Importantly, it introduces new conceptions of blasphemy and sacrilege that explore them as broader, cross-cultural concepts that cannot be defined in terms of religious dogma and sentiment. A second way in which the book brings a unique perspective to bear on the issue of religious conflict is in its focus on negotiation. In political and social philosophy, religious belief is usually examined as a 'problem' of tolerance in a liberal democratic society. This book of essays seeks to move away from these traditional ways of discussing the issue, as they assume that religious commitment is intolerant, and cannot, and should not, be negotiated. The book addresses the issue of the nature of the sacred as part of the cultural reality of individuals' existences, and explores how the sacred has been contested, and negotiated between groups as part of a process in which agents make sense of the world, and seek to create order in it.

Blasphemy and sacrilege in modern societies cannot be considered as relics of the Middle Ages. Neither are they topics only of interest in relation to religious fundamentalism. In a society with a diverse religious and cultural make-up, such as contemporary Australia, there are inevitable clashes between conceptions of the sacred. What is held sacred by one group of people will not be sacred to another. In fact, what is sacred in one religion may be considered sacrilegious to another.

A society's reaction to and management of blasphemy and sacrilege goes to its core, for it defines how it relates to its constituent groups, protecting difference or leaving the vulnerable to cope on their own. Yet we should be wary of assuming that this is an issue best addressed within the rubric of identity politics and the right to culture. For while we might agree that community is necessary for an individual's well-being, claims about religion as a cultural right fail to make a necessary distinction. There is a difference between having an ethnic or cultural identity and having a religious affiliation. While cultural affiliation is not a matter of choice, religious affiliation may be. We can, and often do, change our religious affiliation. Paradoxically, while we may change and adapt our cultural practices reasonably easily, we tend to think of our religious practices, once adopted, as stands that cannot be negotiated.

In this volume we do not set out to construct our present as an enlightened transformation out of the dark ages, nor to construct 'the other'—whether living in other countries or amongst us—as religious zealots and as totalitarian. A secular society risks limiting its understanding of itself if it reduces the terms of its discussion of these issues to the debates about free speech, or to the need to tolerate the irrational and incomprehensible beliefs of others. Neither paradigm provides a sufficiently rich vocabulary to address the content of the claims that are being made by believers. Debates over blasphemy law reduce blasphemy to 'offence'. The debates about toleration that assume religious belief is immune to reason limit our understanding of and interaction with those people who hold religious beliefs. Rather, this volume represents a collection of papers exploring how 'the sacred' is encountered, and negotiated, or fails to be negotiated, in a multicultural society.

Secularisation and secularism

Australia prides itself on its secularism. This does not mean that people do not profess to hold religious views. A sizeable minority of the population, 15.3 per cent, described themselves as non-religious in the 2001 census, however, the majority of Australians are Christians. The census showed that 67.3 per cent of Australians are Christians, and that Buddhism is the second largest religion in Australia, with 1.9 per cent of the population identifying themselves as Buddhist. The third, fourth and fifth largest religious categories are Islam (with 1.5 per cent of the population), Hinduism (0.5 per cent), and Judaism (0.4 per cent). In addition, many Aboriginal and Torres Strait Islander peoples maintain their traditional religious practices, or consider their traditional sacred sites a significant part of their heritage.

Australia may be said to be a secular society in two, quite different, ways. It may be described as a secular society in terms of its embrace of political secularism, which is reflected in the separation of religion from the state in Section 116 in the Constitution[1] and in its embrace of the policy of multiculturalism. The Australian policy of multiculturalism appears to be the legacy of the political ideal of toleration. The basic tenet of toleration was a commitment to freedom of conscience.[2] The ideal of multiculturalism is the respect for different ethnic, cultural and religious groups in society. The state makes a distinction between the roles of public citizens and their private beliefs, and maintains a commitment to freedom of religion. The second way in which Australia may be said to be a secular society is as a result of a social process of secularisation. The process of secularisation involves religious institutions losing public influence, a drop in attendance at religious ceremonies, and the loss of respect for religious symbols and specialists, such as clergy. The world-view of people in a secular society is increasingly rationalised and 'disenchanted'.[3] Australia was secular in this second sense before it adopted a political policy of multiculturalism, and it is this second sense of secularism that is celebrated in its foundation myths of self-sufficient pioneers and working-class larrikins.[4] One price of the process of secularisation is the confusion many people express about 'the place' of the sacred in our public lives. The sacred is held to be something of fundamental importance or value, and it has 'a place' in society to the extent that it is respected in our lives or has status within society. Blasphemy and sacrilege are both affronts to this value: they are acts of disrespect, irreverence, or destruction.

These two senses of secularism have become blurred in Australia's 'institutional norms' in relation to religion: religion is considered 'to be a "low-temperature" matter', not something to get over-enthusiastic about, and certainly not a trumpeted certainty.[5] This institutional norm, or culture of secularism, tends to blind Australia's policy development in relation to cultural and religious diversity. As one social scientist has commented, when social issues are viewed through this perspective, 'religion cannot be a problem because it is, or should be, or shortly will be irrelevant'.[6] Unfortunately, such an attitude has become an unaffordable luxury. As Riaz Hassan demonstrates in this volume there is a complex relationship between modernity and religion, but the bottom line is that religion does not disappear, as social scientists through the 1950s, 60s and 70s predicted.

In contemporary Australia, blasphemy and sacrilege are on the rise as are deliberate assaults on other groups and their belief systems.[7] Suzanne Rutland argues in this volume (chapter 2) that what we are witnessing is a clash of religious extremists, and a resurgence of extreme right-wing movements in Europe, America and Australia that are against both Judaism and Islam. The impact on the Jewish community in Australia has been significant, with five synagogues set fire, a Jewish kindergarten attacked, and bomb threats made against Jewish buildings. As she also points out, the Muslim community has been attacked, mosques set on fire, women's headdress has been pulled off in the street, as well as mosques being attacked and desecrated. The Jewish community's response has been one of increased vigilance, with the impact that this will have on the younger generation who stands guard around synagogues and Jewish buildings—of fear, apprehension and social exclusion.

Understanding blasphemy

In recent years, there has been significant debate about the role of blasphemy law in a multicultural society, and although some governments have considered abolishing elements of existing blasphemy laws, which only protect Christianity, there have also been suggestions that they should be extended to cover all religious groups. At the core of this debate is an important concern: how best to protect and respect religious pluralism, through freedom of speech or through the recognition and extension of blasphemy laws.

Understanding blasphemy poses an enormous challenge, largely because both its definition and our comprehension of its harm are generally understood within a legal framework.[8] Laws against blasphemy and sacrilege are infrequently exercised in most Western democracies. Nonetheless, certain acts elicit strong public reactions and widespread debate. Recent famous cases include the *fatwa* issued against Salmon Rushdie for his novel *Satanic Verses*, and the attack on Andres Serrano's photograph 'Piss Christ' at the National Gallery of Victoria, with the subsequent closure of the exhibition. The extent that a liberal democracy should respect and engage with these religious sentiments presents an ongoing problem for any multicultural society. In law, blasphemy is prohibited as a form of libel within the criminal code. Its origins are from the ecclesiastical courts of the Star Chamber and the Court of High Commission. Since the early twentieth century, when it lost its connection with heresy and sedition under Australian law, blasphemy has been defined as vilification, ridicule and irreverence towards Christianity. As such, it is concerned with the manner rather than the matter (content) of something that is publicly spoken or published. Its primary purpose is understood to be the protection of the sentiments of Christians and the prevention of social disorder.[9] As such, it might be thought that the primary moral wrong of an act of blasphemy involves giving offence.

Interestingly, however, the authors collected here who speak from a religious perspective have resisted interpreting blasphemy in terms protecting religious sentiment. Pringle specifically argues against this interpretation (chapter 3). She notes that it is almost universally agreed that blasphemy laws should be abolished. If their purpose is to protect the public order, and to protect Christians from outrage and insult, then there seems little point in keeping them. Blasphemy has become almost impossible to prove, and it is not clear what it is really protecting. The charge of blasphemy mounted by Bishop George Pell, in Melbourne, against Serrano's Piss Christ, was dismissed because it did not incite social unrest. The case mounted by Mary Whitehouse against *Gay News* for its publication of a poem and illustration of Christ's crucifixion, while in part based on the claim that it offended believers, was also based on the claim that it offended God. Pringle argues a belief in blasphemy ultimately relies on the belief that God can be offended. And she thinks that this is the case. Blasphemy is an offence to God which calls into question the ethical integrity of the world, and which has consequences that resonate through God and the world. Similarly, St John argues that blasphemy, which she develops as a category separate from specific belief systems, is the abandonment of a cardinal virtue common to all human beings, that is, the experience of awe which is central to the subjectivity of all peoples.

Like Pringle, Brady does not think blasphemy is a harm of offence to the believer, but in contrast, sees it as an act of denial (chapter 4). The existence of blasphemy is tied to the existence of the sacred, and where the latter does not exist, or is not accepted by the dominant group in society, then blasphemy occurs in the denial of the sacred as an aspect of human existence. Thus, Brady argues that the experience of the sacred is not tied to organised religion, but the sense of that which extends beyond the known world, *mysterium tremendum et fascinans*, and the failure to recognise this is in itself blasphemous. As Brady argues, contemporary Australia is materialistic, and (growing out of its origins in imperial expansion and domination) has an exploitative and utilitarian orientation to other peoples, the land and the future. As a result, rights, and the dignity of subordinate groups are ignored or denied, and enormous moral harm done both to those who are rejected and to the ethical being of those who reject them. As she puts it 'the growing coarseness, narrow-mindedness and violence, the paranoia and xenophobia evident around us today point to its consequences'.

For Rutland, it is not the agnostic or atheist who blaspheme, but the religious extremists and bigots who foster hatred and destruction. Yet, while there is disagreement between Rutland, Pringle, St John and Brady about which acts constitute blasphemy, all four interpretations seem to share a common theme: blasphemous acts constitute a disruption of 'right relations' in the world and a diminution of what it is to be fully human.

These authors should not be understood as promoting religious orthodoxy. Nor should they be thought of as undermining the political ideals of toleration, the secularisation of the state, or the policy of multiculturalism. Their interpretations of blasphemy operate beyond debates about the relationship between organised religion and the state, because they refuse to align the concept of 'the sacred' with any particular organised religion. Rather, they should be thought of as directing their attack on the culture or process of secularisation that leaves no place for the sacred as an important value that needs to be taken into account in our public and private lives.

Liberals, on the other hand, would like to see religion as a matter for the individual in the private sphere (which they can then comfortably defend) but they do not want it as a public matter in the political sphere. This becomes most problematic when religions—other than individualised Protestantism and Catholicism—enter liberal societies, since often they will take the position that religious adherence is not about the privatised practices of the individual, but about the provision of a total environment in which the religious life can be led. Where the sacred is directly tied to a specific religion, as in Islam, it would appear then that there is less scope to negotiate the sacred. However, as Kuranda Seyit argues, there has been a long history of legitimate dissent within Islam, culminating in attempts by modern Islamic scholars to develop a position that is 'authentically Islamic and effectively modern' (chapter 5). Like Rutland and Lamb, scholars such as Omid Safi and Tariq Ramadan identify fanatic fundamentalists as the real blasphemers, and call for Muslims to wrestle with their faith and to reject traditionalism that is embraced for the sake of traditionalism. Nevertheless, there are strong social tendencies, especially in the Salaf movement, in Indonesia, Afghanistan, Pakistan and Saudi Arabia, which resist critical debate, calling for the strict observance of Shari'a law. Seyit, however, is confident that the history of critical thought within Islam, will prevail over fundamentalism.

Sacrilege and the sacred

To have sacrilege we must have the sacred, and how the sacred is construed will determine how sacrilege is construed. In chapter 6, following Durkheim, we argue that even secular societies, such as Australia, hold some events, places and things sacred, and perceive attacks on them as sacrilegious. Durkheim posed that the state, the individual and property could all be seen as sacred in contemporary societies, in that they are set aside and protected by interdictions. We argue that one way of explaining the profound reaction of the public and the legislature to the theft of the Australian coat of arms from Parliament House is in terms of an affront to the sacred. For Durkheim, those things that are constituted as sacred hold that character by virtue of the power relations of society that act to defend them. In contrast to earlier contributors to this volume, we present the experience of the sacred as a social, rather than personal event, and to the extent that it exists universally, as a characteristic of societies, and not of human beings.

In this vein, Colin Tatz explores the political constructions of the sacred (chapter 7). In particular, he explores the sacrality of the memorials to holocaust victims and to other peoples subjected to ethnic cleansing. In his analysis, sacrilege and blasphemy are irreverence towards persons or places held in high regard as a consequence of horrific acts perpetrated there or on them, and culminate in genocide denial—the attempt to erase from history knowledge of holocausts.

The question of what constitutes sacrilege is also at the heart of Dianne McGowan's paper, which explores historical and cross-cultural variations in the treatment of the dead human body (chapter 8). At this historical juncture the body is 'sacred' in Western societies, though this has not always been the case, nor has it always been the case for all bodies. In the eighteenth and nineteenth centuries the bodies of criminals and of the poverty stricken who could not afford a funeral were used for anatomical experiments in the newly developed medical schools. With the passing of the Anatomy Act of 1832, the West entered the current phase of protecting the body in death. How then to accommodate contemporary cultures where the body in death is, as part of religious practice, dismembered and left to carrion eaters in the open? Could Australia accommodate the use of parts of the body, such as the head (sometimes of people newly dead) in religious ceremonies, as Tibetans do? Moreover, what does it say about Western culture when it exhibits these religious artefacts of Tibetan culture, as art in museums. As McGowan points out, when this occurs, the artefacts are sanitised of their religious function, allowing us to see them in aesthetic ways rather than being offended by them. In a similar way, Liam Dee argues that in capitalist economies the sacred becomes commodified and used as a marketing tool (chapter 9). Indeed some religious leaders, such as the Dalai Lama, are willing sell their religious prestige to multinational companies. The processes of aestheticisation and commodification, which substitute the value of the sacred for more 'acceptable' or profane commercial values, may be considered part of the process and culture of secularisation.

The state and tolerance

Ian Hunter discusses how, in European Catholicism, the sacred is the presence of a transcendental God on earth, whose presence is mediated by specific individuals, practices and places (chapter 10). It is this that makes other places, individuals and practices profane. Sacrilege is the abuse or violation of sacred individuals, places or practices. Crossing the boundary of the sacred and profane is where sacrilege occurs. Where this boundary is also the boundary of a community—of communicants—then sacrilege threatens the community itself and results in violent self-protective responses by the community. In early Modern Europe, Christianity and the political community were one, and the religious and political community was one. Hence sacrilege was both a transgression against God and a crime, enshrined in canon and Roman law across Europe, under the centralised authority of the papacy. Sacrilege was then linked not just to the transgression of the sacred but to heresy, blasphemy and witchcraft. Those outside the community threatened not just the civil survival of the community but also the community's ability to communicate with God.

As Hunter shows, the bloody sectarian conflicts of early Modern Europe were calmed and resolved in different ways across Germany, France and England.

However, there are some features in common that can be identified. There was the gradual acceptance of European public law as the language for negotiating peace. Jurists came to accept the permanency of heresy, notwithstanding the attitude of church leaders. Religious truth was dropped as a criterion for peace in treaties and social peace given priority. This meant that the political domain was secularised. The church was to pursue salvation, the state social peace. This development was backed up by the 'spiritualisation' of religion. In this movement the individual's relationship to God became a matter of their personal spirituality, and not tied to orthodoxy or membership of the church. Hence, with the changing definition of the sacred, the nature of sacrilege changed. The outcome was that individuals could hold and develop a range of *personas*: Christian and citizen, while the state, with no religious objectives of its own, provided a space for voluntary religious association.

However, it does not follow from this that the culture of secularisation is a result of the separation of church and state. We expect the separation of the church and state, and increasing levels of education and industrialisation, will be accompanied by a decrease in religious dogmatism. In short, we expect that the benefits of modernity will lead to greater toleration of religious and ethnic differences, and therefore peace within and between nations. Yet, as Riaz Hassan shows in his contribution to this volume, modernity and the separation of the church and state does not necessarily lead to a decrease in religious commitment and to the secularisation of society (chapter 11). Rather, the secularisation of the state may be accompanied by an increase in private commitment to religious values.[10] Hassan's research, conducted in seven Muslim countries, shows that there are paradoxical relations between religion and modernity. Conventional sociological wisdom, the secularisation thesis, argues that with modernisation comes secularisation and privatisation of religious beliefs, with religion increasingly losing its significance. However Hassan's findings suggest that where religion plays a strong role in the provision of services in modern societies, there may be higher levels of personal religious commitment. This research, if correct, has implications in relation to domestic policy. If modernity and the separation between the state and religion increases rather than decreases people's personal commitment to religious 'truth', the policies of toleration and multiculturalism may create the conditions for the kind of dogmatism and domestic conflict for which they are supposed to be the cure.

A tolerant society?

As a policy, freedom of religion has been understood as providing a 'negative freedom' from interference in religious beliefs or worship.[11] Unsurprisingly, the process of democracy may place pressures on the state to be less tolerant of minority positions or to impose particular views of morality. For example, in recent political debates over gay marriage and abortion, people holding Christian beliefs may be seen as attempting to impose a particular religious conception of the sanctity of marriage and of life on other members of society. However, the structures that maintain a Christian domination of the moral norms of the state may not be explicitly stated in legislation. Wherever the law refers to 'community standards', it appears to refer to Christian values. For example, until recently in the United States of America, it was argued that laws forbidding the use of peyote did not impede religious freedom as drug laws were not laws that were directed towards religion. Such inexplicit domination may regulate the expression of religious belief in all areas of life, and law and social policy may be used as a means of regulating minority religions or sects.[12] The issue here is not merely that the law forbids some kinds of actions. The law must say something. But there is a problem where the law, or its application, unreflectingly fails to respect religious beliefs in areas that it has the capacity to do so, or is used as a form of harassment.[13] Inexplicit domination may reflect a systematic intolerance. Both explicit and inexplicit intolerance may be grounds for criticism of the state, and are one obvious cause of discontent for people belonging to minority religions.

On the surface, religious freedom and tolerance are hallmarks of liberal societies, and often-enshrined in constitutions, and enshrine the state as an arbiter of religious disputes. But it can be shown that the state's tolerance is a tolerance to major religions in the Christian-Judaic tradition and that it will over-ride the impact of believers' views where it regards those views as departing from what it considers community values. In dealing with the disposition of property left in wills, the courts use the standard of the wise and just testator to evaluate the fairness of the way in which an estate is bestowed, particularly where it benefits a religious group over a living relative or dependant. Thus, the principle on which the state operates will most likely disadvantage a minority group's religious convictions.

Pauline Ridge points out that appeals against wills can be carried out under the Family Provision Act 1982, whereby the applicant can challenge the distribution of the estate on the grounds, essentially, of financial need (chapter 12). The test the court applies is whether the disposition of the estate accords, in the court's view, with the judgment of 'a wise and just testator', in effect, in accord with community standards. Ridge shows in her analysis that the courts will over-ride testamentary gifts based on strong religious beliefs, since it will be unlikely for the testator's bequest to be upheld in the face of the normative and idealised model of a testator used by the court. Ridge explains that people who hold strong religious convictions are labelled 'obdurate believers', that is, as believers who are guided by religious conviction to the exclusion of other concerns. This applies not only to minority religions, but, for example, to members of mainstream religions who use their beliefs as a way of disentitling their children. Notwithstanding this, overall the standards of law reflect the dominant religious groups in society. Indeed, as Ridge points out, biblical stories (the prodigal son) have been used in court decisions to justify the overturning of a will. In this case, as she puts it, 'the general community, knowingly or unknowingly, upholds an ideal of parenthood that reflects Christian teaching'. In short, Ridge demonstrates that the courts will accept testamentary gifts motivated by religious belief only if they conform to the model of the wise and just testator, as determined by community standards. Ridge points out that there is far less likelihood of a challenge to religions stemming from Judaism—at least the dominant ones—since they incorporate in their teachings the responsibility of parents to provide for their family and children.

These problems of domination are not exclusive to Australia or Western democracies, as Colin Noble demonstrates in his examination of Catholicism in Japan (chapter 13). Under the Japanese constitution there is a separation of church and state, yet when the Emperor died in 1989, the state spent large sums of public money on his religious funeral. Japanese Christians mounted a legal challenge through the courts as they attempted to prevent the state from defining the realm of the sacred. However, the consequence was the opposite of what they hoped to achieve. In the presence of open hostility and indifference to their claims, Christians experienced further marginalisation, and the state strengthened its hold on the definition of the sacred.

The future—openness and dogmatism

What form can a dialogue between believers and non-believers take? Nietzsche, in his famous critique of Christianity, argued that all religion was a form of self-deception that leads to epistemic closure. Whereas the standard philosophical critique of religion has been, as in Hume, 'evidential atheism', that there is not enough evidence to justify the belief in a god, Nietzsche's critique is based on an 'atheism of suspicion', which questions the possibility of truthfulness in believing, constructing belief as a self-serving lie of a subservient group. Thus, the atheism of suspicion would seem to create an impasse for any dialogue. Yet, Winifred Lamb argues that the atheism of suspicion can be used by believers to check the drift into the support for an organised religion at the expense of the truth, or the slide to idolatry rather than worship (chapter 14). Lamb argues that Nietzsche's critique alerts believers to the easy drift to servility in prayer, prayer that is a form of bargaining with God, rather than the self-surrender that all religious traditions urge that it should be. She argues against a form of faith that she calls a form of 'cheap grace': the certainty that one has found the 'truth'. Rather, against fundamentalists, and drawing on the work of theologians such as Bonhoeffer, Merton and Moltmann, she suggests that applying Nietzsche's thought as a scalpel to one's own beliefs is central to the religious vocation. As she concludes: 'suspicion can provide a creative spur to religious self understanding', taking the philosophy of religion closer to religion.

Similarly, St John argues for a reframing of religion such that the sacred is not identified with any specific set of beliefs, but as an ontological attribute of human beings (chapter 15). This conceptual step moves debates about sacrilege and blasphemy away from problems of cultural relativism towards what she describes as the universal human capacity to experience the holy. Sacrilege and blasphemy are affronts to this capacity to experience awe in the face of existence. A tolerant society is one where this capacity for awe is respected and defended.

As political theorists have pointed out before us, 'respecting diverse beliefs' cannot mean treating people as if their religious beliefs were of no consequence.[14] But respecting beliefs does not mean that a judgment needs to be made about the truth of those beliefs, or that the state needs to enter disputes about religious dogma. Toleration in a multicultural society needs to be understood as more than a negative liberty. If Australia and other multicultural nations are to maintain peaceful societies, the religious values held by individuals and communities must be acknowledged and negotiated as social and political 'realities'. The sacred can literally be negotiated, as Hal Wootten argues (chapter 16). He documents how a secular state can balance the relationship between Aboriginal claims to sacred land with the economic imperatives of white Australians. At the core Wootten suggests that the very fact that the Aboriginal and Torres Strait Islander Heritage Protection Act, 1984, does not use the word sacred (rather it refers to an 'area of particular significance to Aboriginals') has meant that cases could be adjudicated without entering into evaluation of the beliefs of Aboriginals. Wootten also points out that the negotiation of specific claims is not much different from a myriad of choices that people make daily: it is not a special case. The case of land rights involves only a recognition that the Aboriginal group in question holds specific beliefs about that land and that we should recognise the sincerity of those beliefs and respect them. In this, the role of the state is to negotiate the sacred, and it can fulfil this role precisely because it is secular, liberal and committed to protecting cultural identity.

In Australia, the Mabo case, and more recent Native Title legislation, has meant that indigenous religions are not only recognised, but their maintenance is recognised as a human right and is a requirement for land claims. Under the Aboriginal and Torres Strait Islander Heritage Protection Act, 1984, sacred sites are protected as long as groups can show an ongoing connection to the land. As in the Hindmarsh Bridge case, an ongoing connection may be difficult to prove, and hotly contested. Yet overall, this experience provides us with a way of understanding what it might mean to respect religious beliefs and to acknowledge them as being of consequence, without having to accept them as true. In the resolution of such cases, we do not question the truth of Aboriginal beliefs about what is sacred, but acknowledge that such beliefs and values compete with other interests and values, such as public safety or economic development.

Conclusion

Sacrilege and blasphemy are contested concepts, dependent on the definition of the sacred. Within the social sciences, and as the papers in this volume illustrate, the Durkheim-James debate is based on the different constructions of the sacred. This may be either as an individual perception of an overwhelming sense of the existence of God, or as the product of society itself, manifest in beliefs of the existence of the sacred.

What is clear from the contributions to this volume is that religion will remain a central aspect of modern and modernising societies. Whether embedded in the laws of secular states such as Australia, or manifest in more private devotion in the states of south-east Asia, despite the predictions of many early sociologists of religion, it has not, and is not becoming less of a social, political and cultural force. Equally though the implicit assumption of these early works—that religious belief was by definition beyond negotiation and was by definition totalitarian -- has been shown not to be the case. Religious tolerance has been both expressed and practised. Between devout Muslims, Hindus, Jews and Christians there is scope for dialogue, reconciliation and negotiation.

At the same time, the complexity of this debate has to be understood within the paradox of Australian multiculturalism. This, while seeking to foster social cohesion, also promotes cultural uniqueness. Again, as this volume illustrates, contributors from a range of cultural and political backgrounds have demonstrated by their openness, their commitment to dialogue and their understanding of their faith as contributing to a harmonious society, that a space does exist. That negotiation is possible, and a culturally and religiously pluralistic society is a viable option. In short, while there will be no easy resolution of the negotiation of the sacred, nevertheless as the contributors to this volume demonstrate, it can be achieved and it must be constantly sought after.

ENDNOTES

[1] 'The Commonwealth shall not make any law for establishing any religion, or for imposing any religious observance, or for prohibiting the free exercise of any religion, and no religious test shall be required as a qualification for any office or public trust under the Commonwealth'. At the same time the Australian constitution of 1901 is framed in terms of Christianity, 'humbly relying on the blessing of Almighty God'.

[2] King, P. 1976, *Toleration*, London, Allen and Unwin, p. 77.

[3] Maddox, M. 1999-2000, *Indigenous Religion in Secular Australia*, Parliament of Australia, Parliamentary Library Research Paper 11, p. 3.

[4] Maddox, 1999-2000, p. 3.

[5] Bouma, G. 1999, 'Social Justice Issues in the Management of Religious Diversity in Australia', *Social Justice Research*, vol. 12, no. 4, p. 288.

[6] Bouma, 1999, p. 293.

[7] Corr, R. 2000, 'Asians, Muslims and "Authentic Australians": Neoracism Down Under', Paper presented at *Challenges of Immigration and Integration in the European Union and Australia*, Centre for European Studies, The Australian National University.

[8] An exception is Fisher, A. and H. Ramsay, 2000, 'Of Art and Blasphemy', *Ethical Theory and Moral Practice,* vol. 3, pp. 137-67.

[9] New South Wales Law Reform Commission, 1994, Report 74, *Blasphemy,* pp. 9-10.

[10] See also Hassan, Riaz 2003, *Faithlines: Muslim conceptions of Islam and Society,* Karachi, Oxford University Press.

[11] Murphy, Andrew R. 1997, 'The Uneasy Relationship between Social Contract Theory and Religious Toleration', *The Journal of Politics,* vol. 59, no. 2, pp. 368-92, p. 370.

[12] Recent research into the sociology of social control has attempted to theorise the ways in which in-explicit domination occurs, see Richardson, James T. 2004, *Regulating Religion: Case Studies from Around the Globe,* Kluwer Academic Publishers.

[13] For example, Magistrate Gregory Levine suggested that in the removal of children from the Christian Evangelical group, The Family, in 1992, authorities acted against the sect in something like a form of class action. <www.thefamily.org/dossier/legal/australia.htm> viewed January 2005.

[14] Jones, Peter 1990, 'Respecting Beliefs and Rebuking Rushdie', *British Journal of Political Science,* vol. 20, no. 4, pp. 415-37, p. 429.

Section I. Religion, Sacrilege and Blasphemy in Australia

2. Negotiating religious dialogue: A response to the recent increase of anti-Semitism in Australia

Suzanne Rutland

In January 1991 during the first Gulf War, Gerry Levy, Sydney-based president of the New South Wales Jewish Board of Deputies, received an urgent call that the North Shore Temple had been attacked by arson and was on fire. He rushed over to find the synagogue's rabbi standing outside with the Torah scrolls in his arms and one building completely gutted. As a young boy, Levy had been in Germany during *Kristallnacht*, the Nazi pogrom of November 1938, when the synagogue of his home town, Magdeburg, was burnt down and his community violently attacked. In 1991, he felt he was reliving these events and found the experience extremely traumatic.[1]

This chapter will explore the rise of anti-Semitic attacks on the Australian Jewish community, making reference to parallel developments within the Islamic community, a parallel that can be seen in an article published in the *Maitland Mercury* shortly after September 11. This article highlights attacks on the Muslim community in Australia, with its headline 'racial abuse starts to affect Muslim minority' but visually represents the attacks on the Jewish community with the graffiti, 'Victoy [sic] to Islam; Death to the Jews', painted on at least three entrances to the Primus Telecom Building on the corner of King and Collins Streets, Melbourne in September 2001.[2]

I will argue that the problem facing Australia, and indeed the world, is not the question of Samuel Huntington's model of a 'clash of civilisations'[3] but rather of a 'clash within civilisations' between fundamentalists and conciliators. In order to deal with this increasing problem, what is needed is more understanding, education to combat xenophobic, racist attitudes, and a coalition of the moderates across the religions. More dialogue to create better understanding across the major faiths in Australia is important both at the roof level of leadership, and at the grassroots in schools and individual communities. I believe that those who oppose such dialogue create blasphemy and sacrilege in our society and that the religious zealots are, indeed, the ones who create the most serious problems. In saying this, I would like to support Veronica Brady who has argued that a 'blasphemous society is one which refuses to recognise the other' (see chapter 4) which is something which often happens with religious zealots.

With the 1990–1991 Gulf War came a spate of attacks against Jewish institutions across Australia. Over a three-month period in Sydney, arsonists attacked five synagogues, a quarter of the community's synagogues. After the fire at the North Shore Temple on 28 January, there were fires at three Sydney synagogues in February and March, possibly linked. The first occurred on 26 February at the Sephardi Synagogue in Woollahra, when petrol was poured into a rear window and set alight. One week later there was a fire at the Bankstown Memorial Synagogue. The last, on 29 March, was at Kogarah's Illawarra Synagogue; petrol was spread across the synagogue and set alight. A security guard foiled another arson attempt in mid-April at the North Shore Synagogue.[4] A year later, in May 1992, arsonists attacked the Newtown Synagogue, one of the oldest in the city, built in 1918. Fortunately it has been restored, as has the Illawarra Synagogue, but the Bankstown Synagogue was not so lucky. The community was too small and did not have the funds to rebuild it, and decided to close the synagogue.

Synagogues and other Jewish buildings in Melbourne, Canberra and Newcastle were also attacked. The first arson attack occurred on the Jewish kindergarten in Doncaster, Melbourne, while a bomb threat was made against the Palais Theatre, Melbourne, just at the end of a Jewish solidarity rally being held there. Other anti-Jewish manifestations included desecration of Jewish graves; hate letters prophesying the coming of the 'Fourth Reich' in which Jews would be incarcerated in concentration camps like the 'Auschwitz holiday camp'. Bottles and eggs were hurled from passing cars at individuals walking in Melbourne streets. Such events continued after the Gulf War, although at a reduced level, with one of the worst episodes being the desecration of Jewish graves in an Adelaide cemetery in 1995.

With the failure of the 'Oslo Accords' and the outbreak of the al-Aqsa Intifada between Israel and the Palestinians in September 2000, attacks against the Jewish community increased with problems developing one year later, reaching its peak after the historic and horrific attack on the twin towers in New York on 11 September 2001. In September 2000, the synagogue in Rosco Street in Bondi was attacked by arson while anti-Israel graffiti was daubed on the Illawarra Synagogue in Sydney's South. The Canberra Jewish centre was fire-bombed four times between September 2001 and September 2002. Individual Jews, particularly men wearing skullcaps, were physically attacked, while community leaders received death threats. Violence and Jew-hatred manifested themselves in the pro-Palestinian rallies of 2000 and 2001, with the burning of Israeli and US flags. Such outbursts created fear and anxiety amongst Australian Jewry and the wider community. Most recently, the court cases in Perth against Jack Roche, a Muslim convert, and Jack van Tongeren, a far right national extremist, highlighted the danger faced by Jewish institutions and individual Jews in Australia.[5]

To date, no arrests have been made for any of the arson attacks and there is much debate as to whether the cause of these attacks in Australia and elsewhere has been due to radicalised Islamic fundamentalist ideologies and movements, or the resurgence of extreme right-wing movements, such as Hansonism (the right wing, racist movement known as One Nation led by Pauline Hanson), which are both anti-Muslim and anti-Jewish. Arrests in Western Australia in 2004 seem to indicate the attacks come from both groups—Jack Roche, radical Islam, and van Tongeren, far right. Roche was planning to attack Jewish leaders as well as the Israeli embassy. Van Tongeren was arrested for desecrating the Perth Hebrew Congregation's Synagogue in Mount Lawley with swastikas.

The Executive Council of Australian Jewry (ECAJ), through the work of Jeremy Jones, its current president, has monitored the level of anti-Semitism. Since October 1989, annual reports have been compiled documenting incidences, as well as activities of groups and individuals responsible for purveying anti-Semitism in Australia, such as Dr Fredrick Toben of the Adelaide Institute and Olga Scully in Tasmania.[6] These incidents include abusive emails, graffiti such as 'Bomb the Jews', mail and telephone threats, verbal harassment and abuse, including the bullying of Jewish children at school by some Muslim children, and actual physical violence against individuals and institutions. The majority of such attacks are anonymous so it is difficult to determine who is responsible.[7] In his introduction for the 2002–03 survey, Jones notes that there were 'over 500 reports of anti-Jewish violence, vandalism, harassment and intimidation'. He presents a graph, showing that since 11 September 2001, the number of incidents has almost doubled,[8] with 63 per cent of such attacks occurring in New South Wales in 2002–03.[9]

Since 1995, telephone intimidation and hate letters have decreased. However, the phenomenon of hate email has been growing rapidly. In 2003, hate email increased by 20 per cent from the previous year. Indeed, online media, including hate emails and websites, is the area of greatest concern today. As Jones points out, 'individuals with time on their hands are able to reach a variety of audiences quickly and inexpensively'.[10] The medium used by anti-Semites may be new, but their messages are not. They continue to propagate the traditional anti-Jewish stereotypes ranging from 'the international Jewish conspiracy', 'the 'Jewish/Nazi' analogy', via Holocaust denial to 'Mystical Jewish Power' (promoting the myth that Australian Jews influence public policy through their wealth and business connections), and that Jews are 'Un-Christian' and Judaism is 'Anti-Christianity'.[11]

The Australian League of Rights continues to be the longest-running, most influential, as well as best organised and most substantially financed, racist organisation in Australia.[12] Founded in Victoria by Eric Butler, in 1945, it became a national movement in 1960. From the beginning, Butler has been opposed to Israel, attacked the veracity of the Holocaust, and portrayed Jews as dangerous and evil creatures. Through the Heritage Bookshop in Melbourne, he has sold anti-Semitic literature, including the Tsarist forgery, *The Protocols of the Elders of Zion*, which fosters world conspiracy libel against world Jewry. Today, the League is directed by Betty Luks in Adelaide and it continues to publish its weekly newsletter, *On Target*, as well as *New Times* and *Social Creditor*, both of which started in the 1930s. The League has established links with other far right organisations such as the Australian National Action, the Australian National Socialist Movement, National Alliance and members of Pauline Hanson's One Nation, as well as supporting anti-immigration groups and working with Holocaust deniers such as Melbourne lawyer, John Bennett. The Citizens' Electoral Councils, centred in Melbourne, draw on material produced by Lyndon la Rouche, an American anti-Semite and Holocaust denier.[13] There are also a number of small, radical, 'identity' churches which claim to be Christian, but emphasise the idea of white supremacy, and portray Jews as evil. All these groups have increased their use of the internet in recent years to spread their message of hate.[14]

The substantial increase of anti-Jewish verbal and physical attacks in Australia, especially since September 2001, reflects a worldwide phenomenon.[15] Commenting in *The Age*, journalist Peter Fray wrote:

> Incredible as it may seem, barely 60 years after the Holocaust, antisemitism has returned to haunt Western Europe's 1.13 million Jews. Since September 11, there has been an average of 18 attacks a day on Jewish people or their property.[16]

This violence has developed over three main stages, only two of which directly related to Israel. The first stage began with the al-Aqsa Intifada of September 2000. The second stage followed the attack on the twin towers in New York on September 11. The third stage started with the suicide bomber who in March 2002 exploded his bomb on the Passover Seder night at the Park Hotel, Netanya. This attack on the first night of Passover resulted in the Israeli incursion into the West Bank and Gaza and the controversy surrounding Israel's attack on Jenin.[17] It is understandable that both the outbreak of the al-Aqsa Intifada and the operation in Jenin inflamed Muslim feelings against Israel and that these feelings of hatred were extended to Jews in general. However, the link with September 11 is much less obvious and involved a number of elements, including the false claim that the operation was actually planned by the Mossad, the misconception that the increase of anti-Muslim feelings and the decision to go to war against Iraq post-September 11 were a result of the Jewish lobby in the United States, and the belief that the attack on the twin towers was planned because of Jewish connections to high finance.

Following the Park Hotel bombing, at the end of April 2002, attacks took place against Jews and Jewish institutions across Europe, and also in North America and Australasia in what was described as a list 'too long to summarise adequately'.[18] These attacks, including harassment and violence against individuals[19] and vandalism against Jewish institutions, occurred in Britain, France, Belgium, Holland, Denmark, Germany, the Ukraine, Greece and Canada.[20] With this wave of anti-Jewish attacks, the European Monitoring Centre on Racism and Xenophobia (EUMC) in Vienna requested Professor Werner Bergmann and Dr Juliane Wetzel of the Centre of Research on Anti-Semitism in Berlin to undertake a review and analysis of these events. They produced a 105-page synthesis report entitled 'Manifestations of anti-Semitism in the European Union' in February 2003.[21] This report has created significant controversy relating to the definition of anti-Semitism, the issue of anti-Zionism and the role played by the small minority of radical Muslim youth.[22] The report has been placed on the website of the Centre of Research on Anti-Semitism but it has not been published because of the controversy surrounding its findings.

As a result of the violence beginning with the al-Aqsa Intifada in September 2000, Israel's actions were compared with those of Hitler and Nazi Germany. A classic example is Portuguese Nobel Prize winning author, Jose Saramago, who drew parallels between Israel's bombing of Ramalla in 2002 with the Nazi death camp of Auschwitz/Birkenau.[23] Yet, in my view, no comparison can be made with Nazi genocide, which aimed to kill the entire Jewish people. The attacks on Ramalla were Israel's response to the horrific crimes perpetrated by the suicide bombers against innocent civilians and their ramifications in Israel. During the present al-Aqsa Intifada, 3000 Palestinians have been killed but close to 1000 Israelis have also died in suicide bombings and Palestinian attacks.

In 1971, Walter Laqueur published an article entitled 'The Jewish Question Today: Between Old Zionism and New Anti-Semitism', in which he argues that 'the Jewish Question has always been a sensitive barometer' in terms of tolerance and humanity.[24] Laqueur points to the pessimistic conclusions of the German Jewish writer, Jacob Wassermann who in 1921 stated,

> Vain to seek obscurity. They say: The coward. He is creeping into hiding, driven by his evil conscience. Vain to go among them and offer them one's hand. They say: Why does he take such liberties with his Jewish obtrusiveness? Vain to keep faith with them as a comrade in arms or a fellow citizen. They say: He is Proteus, he can assume any shape or form. Vain to help them strip off the chains of slaves. They say: No doubt, he found it profitable. Vain to counteract the poison. They brew new venom.[25]

More than eighty years after Wassermann wrote this pessimistic comment, half a century after Auschwitz and a generation after Laqueur wrote his article, the issue of anti-Jewish feelings and the reasons for the increase in violent attacks on Jews across the Diaspora, as well as in Israel, has moved again into the centre of public and academic debate. Anti-Semitism has proved to be 'Proteus', not only assuming 'any shape or form' but with key concepts such as world conspiracy theories and Holocaust denial being promoted by groups from across the political spectrum determined to attack Israel, the Jewish state, and Jews in general.

Historian Robert Wistrich, world authority on the history of anti-Semitism,[26] points to Muslim anti-Semitism as a decisive factor in the rise of anti-Semitism in the world today. In a booklet entitled *Muslim Anti-Semitism: A Clear and Present Danger*, he argues that the 'vast output of anti-Semitic literature in the Arab and Muslim world' has 'become increasingly apparent as the anti-Semitic virus has taken root in the body politic of Islam to an unprecedented degree'.[27] Other scholars have supported his theme of Muslim anti-Judaism, arguing that recent Islamic writings have drawn on anti-Jewish trends in traditional Islam. These include statements about Jews in the Qur'an, which 'see the Jews as a people who do evil'.[28] The Pact of Omar, thought to have been drawn up in the ninth century, created the concept of the *dhimmi* status, extending protection at first to Christians and afterwards to Jews, based on the payment of special taxes and acceptance of subjugation and inferiority.[29] However, whilst Jews did suffer periods of forced conversions and massacres under Islam, on the whole they enjoyed a more peaceful coexistence in Muslim societies than they did under Christianity.

Since the creation of the State of Israel the situation has changed. Over 600,000 Jews have fled Arab lands since 1948. Today only a tiny minority are left, mainly in Morocco and Iran. The Arab world has fostered Jew-hatred by publishing the *Protocols* and a plethora of anti-Semitic literature. In 2002, the *Protocols* formed the basis of a thirty-part television series produced in Egypt.[30] The Arab media has published anti-Jewish cartoons, with negative images of Jews, and has continued to promote the blood libel accusation that Jews have to use gentile blood for religious festivals such as Pesach and Purim. Leaders of radical Muslim movements such as Hamas and Hizbollah disseminate the idea that Jews wish 'to take vengeance on the whole world for their history of persecution and humiliation'.[31]

Since September 11, Muslim radicals have intensified their attacks on Jews. Some have claimed that the attack on the twin towers in New York was planned by Israel's secret service, the *Mossad*, and that Jewish and Israeli employees were warned about the attack in advance.[32] Another key element of present day radical Islam is the denial of the events of the Holocaust, with the belief that

Jews created the 'hoax of the Holocaust' in order to justify the creation of the state of Israel. One of the most disturbing aspects of recent Muslims attacks on Israel is the equation of Zionism with Nazism and the ongoing accusation that Israel is committing genocide against the Palestinian people.[33] The Jews, who were once the victims, have now become the perpetrators, and they maintain that the war of 1948 or Naqba (disaster), is equated with the *Shoah* (Holocaust). Again, in my view, such comparisons cannot be made. Even some modern Arab scholars have pointed out that in 1948 the Palestinians lost their homes and property; during the Shoah six million European Jews lost their lives.[34]

A number of scholars, both Jewish and Christian, have argued that the 'new anti-Semitism' is directed against the 'Jewish State', whilst the 'old anti-Semitism' was directed against individual Jews.[35] In a well argued article, Brian Klug opposes this view and claims that,

> The underlying hostility towards it [the Jewish state] in the region is not hostility towards the state *as* Jewish but *as* European interloper or *as* American client or *as* non-Arab and non-Muslim—and, in addition, *as* oppressor. Whatever names we may legitimately give these attitudes, "antisemitism" is not one of them.[36]

The conflict between Israel and the Palestinians has led to legitimate criticisms of Israel's policies but the problem is that these criticisms have been taken over by Jew-hatred with images of the traditional anti-Jewish stereotype of the satanic nature of the Jew out to destroy the world. The consequence is that criticism of Israel now nourishes the general hatred of Jews, particularly in the Muslim, Arab world. Klug himself notes that: 'this is not to say that anti-Semitism cannot and does not enter into anti-Zionism in the Arab and Muslim world. Clearly it does. Moreover, the longer Israel is at loggerheads with the rest of the region, the more likely it is that anti-Semitism will take on a life of its own.'[37]

It could be argued that the connection between anti-Zionism and anti-Semitism is not a new phenomenon. During the 1960s, the Soviet government constantly attacked Israel, using traditional anti-Jewish stereotypes in the media.[38] In 1971, four years after the 1967 Israeli conquest of the West Bank and Gaza, Laqueur wrote:

> The establishment of the Israeli state was the greatest turning point in the 2000 years of Jewish history; it had a profound effect on Jewish life all over the world. But while esteem for Jewish determination and prowess has increased, the position of the Jews has not become more secure. In a world where might counts more than right, Jews are still at the mercy of superior forces. Zionism has not changed this...The state created by Zionism thus faces an uphill struggle to be accepted as a fact that can no longer be undone. As long as this struggle continues, the

existence and independence of the state of Israel is no more assured than that of other small countries situated in an area where an expansive super-power has staked its claim.[39]

It is more than thirty years since Laqueur wrote about Zionism and the 'new anti-Semitism', and there have been many important developments, including peace agreements with two of Israel's neighbours, Egypt and Jordan. However, Israel still feels besieged—the al-Aqsa Intifada, which began in 2000 with the constant threat of suicide bombings within Israel and physical violence against individuals and Jewish institutions across the Jewish world, including Australia on the edge of the Diaspora, has added to the Jewish sense of embattlement.

It is important to recognise that in the same period there has also been a substantial increase in attacks on Muslims in Australia and elsewhere. The Muslim migration to Australia is a fairly recent phenomenon. In 1947 there were almost no Muslims in Australia, compared with 32,000 Jews who comprised 0.4 per cent of the population. While the Jewish population has increased to 84,000 in the 2001 census, Jews still only constitute 0.4 per cent of the population. In comparison, the Muslim population increased from 22,000 in 1971, or 0.2 per cent of the Australian population, to 201,000 in 1996, or 1.1 per cent of the population, and further increasing to 282,000 in 2001, or 1.5 per cent of the population.[40] Against the background of these demographic developments, the Muslim Arabs have become a large and visible target of growing xenophobic sentiments endemic in Australian society, which has a history of attacking visible minorities who are 'the last people off the boat'.

The rise of anti-Muslim feeling as part of the general Australian racist xenophobia has been fed by a number of specific events. Already during the Gulf War there were significant attacks on Australian Muslims, with women wearing the *hijab* being the major targets of abuse.[41] In 2001, three events came together to produce strong anti-Muslim feeling in Australia. These were the issue of gang rape in Sydney, the arrival of illegal boat people highlighted by the incident of the *Tampa* when the Australian government refused to allow the 440 refugees who had been on board the capsized boat to land on Australian shores and the events of September 11.

In the weeks after September 11, members of the Arabic community suffered abuse, with hijab-wearing women and children again being a key target of abuse. Women endured verbal abuse, were spat at and some had their veils pulled off.[42] Arabic newspapers and institutions received bomb and death threats and mosques were desecrated and attacked by arsonists. The worst attacks occurred in Queensland, where two Brisbane mosques, in Holland Park,[43] and Kuraby[44] were damaged by fire, and arsonists were apprehended while trying to set fire to another mosque on the Gold Coast. In Perth, the Nooral Islam Mosque had human faeces thrown into its grounds. Schools and pupils were also targets, with a bus carrying Muslim schoolchildren in Brisbane being hit with rocks, bottles and other missiles[45] and the Islamic College of South Australia in Adelaide being vandalised and forced to close after bomb threats.[46] Arabic Churches were targeted with racist graffiti.[47] The viciousness of the anti-Muslim feeling was expressed on talk-back radio and in hate mail such as: 'you are all Muslim fanatic terrorist criminals' and 'you are all marked for death. All Muslims must suffer for this and other terrorist acts'.[48]

The Jewish community responded to the anti-Jewish and anti-Israeli attacks by organising rallies across the world. In Sydney, a major protest rally held in April 2001 attracted between 5–10,000 members of Sydney Jewry. Australian Jewry has been identified by the police as 'number one terrorist target' and has been on high security alert. Young volunteers provide much of this increased security but despite this voluntary approach, professional trainers and some professional security guards are also employed, placing a great financial strain on the community. The Muslim community has also had to increase its security measures and both communities have faced skyrocketing insurance costs, which are difficult to keep up with.

Let me add a personal note. Over the last few years I have developed a new definition of being a Jewish woman—it means having your handbag searched before entering a synagogue, something I would never have imagined as a young girl growing up in Australia. I also wonder what the impact is on our idealistic Jewish young people, our best and brightest, who devote so much of their spare time to guarding Jewish institutions, synagogues and schools. This experience of anti-Semitism has led not only to a sense of threat, but also an awareness of the obligation to combat this rise of xenophobic and racist attacks. As an historian, I realise that Jews on their own are not in a position to defend themselves. They need the support of others.

The commonality of this experience of fear of attack and the need for increased security has led to one positive and important initiative—the creation two years ago of the Australian National Dialogue of Christians, Muslims and Jews, supported by their roof bodies—the National Council of Churches in Australia, the Australian Federation of Islamic Council and the Executive Council of Australian Jewry.

Inter-faith dialogue began in Australia during World War II with the creation of the New South Wales Council of Christians and Jews and, although this initiative petered out after the war, it was later rejuvenated. Over the last five years there have been a number of important initiatives including the New South Wales-based Women's Interfaith Network, the government-sponsored Australian Partnership of Ethnic and Religious Organisations, and the 'Living in Harmony' projects, which are also funded by the federal government to create greater understanding of the cultural diversity in Australia.

The creation of the National Dialogue at the federal level takes these initiatives onto a new level of discussion. This new organisation aims to build bridges and create a better understanding of key issues during this period of increased ethnic and religious tension in Australia. In a recent paper, one member of this dialogue, Peta Pellach, outlines the three main areas of discussion as follows:

> Matters of national importance where a religious perspective is pertinent; matters of theological interest that are of significance to all the partners in the dialogue; religious ideas and practices that are unique to one of the participants in the dialogue and require explanation in order to create understanding.[49]

Relating to national issues, the problems of globalism, dealing with tragedy and foreign policy decisions, especially in relation to the War on Terrorism and Iraq, are the main areas for discussion. In relation to theological issues, the concept of 'Covenant', the meaning of a 'just war', Messiah, peace, medical ethics and educating the next generation of believers are the key areas of concern. Possibly the most challenging of the three discussion areas relates to exploring religious concepts which are unique to one faith group such as Evangelism, the Exodus, the Trinity, Jihad, and the Jewish concepts of Israel and the love of Zion, meaning Jerusalem, which is the basis of modern Zionism.

Developing a wider dialogue between religious groups is an important element in the present crisis facing not just Australia but the whole world. In an editorial published in the American Jewish periodical, *Shofar*, Zev Garber has summarised well-known scholar of Islam, Bernard Lewis' suggestions of ways to overcome the problems as: 'self criticism, interpersonal dialogue, and the need to study and observe the totality of a group's behaviour and not only doctrinal, popular, and journalistic teachings'.[50] To achieve this, Garber has stressed:

> Learning the complexity of the historical, religious, cultural, psychological, and political factors of the Palestinian national movement is imperative for Jews. Similarly, Arabs and Muslims must come to realize that Jewish self-pride as expressed in peoplehood, religion, and the statehood of Israel are answers to Jewish identity, survival and anti-Semitism. Both communities must learn that blatant immoral acts by individuals or states can never be condoned.[51]

Creating a more balanced perspective in both communities is a necessary precursor for any real peace between Israel and the Palestinians, and also in the broader, world scene. However, this needs to take place at a number of different levels. The National Dialogue relates to the religious roof bodies, and as such mainly touches the elite, the top leadership. Efforts to penetrate at the grass roots are also needed, and this can be best achieved through school programs and curricula. The innovative program of 'Goodness and Kindness' run by

Kuranda Seyit and Rabbi Zelman Kastel represents an important innovation in this regard, but such activities need to be extended.

The theory of the 'clash of civilizations' developed by Huntington sought to divide the world into a clash between the Judeo-Christian heritage of the West and Islam.[52] However, Osama bin Laden and other Muslim terrorist leaders do not represent the majority of Muslims, just as the extremist Jewish leader, Rabbi Kahane, did not represent the Jewish people and, indeed, was not permitted to take his seat in the Israeli Knesset because of his extremist views. The divide between the fundamentalists and the conciliators represents what has been called 'a clash within civilizations'. In 2003, in a speech to the Subcommittee on Near East and South Asian Affairs of the United States Senate Committee on Foreign Relations, Knesset member Rabbi Michael Melchior stressed this point. He advocated the need to empower the moderates to be joined in 'a cross-cultural coalition to counter the extremists in each camp'. He stated:

> An imam and a rabbi may disagree over many things. One's God and His Messengers may not be like the other's. But if both agree that neither of their gods and prophets wants us to kill each other, then a partnership can begin...

Melchior argued that the true 'culture clash' will actually be an intra-civilisational fight to change public opinion in the two societies, a clash between the totalitarian extremists (both Muslim and Jewish) on the one side, and the rational moderates (both Muslim and Jewish) on the other. The political leaders of today must do much more than pay lip-service in support of the religious moderates. It must be a top priority for the enlightened world to empower them. We should all applaud the Nobel Peace Prize committee for taking a first step in this direction. The governments of the world must summon all the creativity and resources at their disposal to enable a coalition of moderate religious leaders to change the way their constituents perceive adherents of competing civilisations. The voice of this coalition must be heard overpoweringly in local media, in schools, synagogues and mosques. The media prefer to broadcast fiery radicals, and extremists have a built-in advantage in the competition for public exposure. Moderate religious leaders must be given whatever tools they need to redress this imbalance, and educate their peoples towards realistic moderation, rather than romantic martyrdom. Otherwise, the extremist religious elements will continue to dominate public opinion and fan the flames of violence.[53]

While the 'flames of violence' have been much more horrific in the battle between Israel and the Palestinians, especially since the outbreak of violence with the second Intifada in September 2000, we in distant Australia have not been immune from this religious and racial hatred and violence. I would like to support Rabbi Melchior's suggestion that what is needed to counter this extremism, which breeds division and hatred, is a coalition of the conciliators.

With the creation of the National Dialogue, one step has been taken in this direction over the last two years, but it is too early to assess how significant its impact will be. If we are to ensure that 'sacred' beliefs create harmony and not division, much greater efforts need to be made to ensure that the conciliators triumph, not the extremists on both sides, who have caused so much damage to our society and I would argue are, perhaps, the real blasphemers since all members of their religious groups are tarnished by this brush of extremism and violence. Those who so focus on the importance of the sacred—such as the Jewish settlers in Hebron or organisations such as Hamas—and fail to recognise the rights of others—end up creating the ultimate blasphemy as they create hatred and destruction.

ENDNOTES

[1] Rutland, Suzanne D. and Sophie Caplan, *With One Voice: the History of the New South Wales Jewish Board of Deputies,* Sydney, Australian Jewish Historical Society, 1998, p. 262.

[2] *Maitland Mercury,* 14 September 2001, p. 14.

[3] Huntington, Samuel P., *The clash of civilizations and the remaking of world order*, New York, Simon & Schuster, 1996.

[4] Rutland, Suzanne D., 'The Jewish Experience', in Murray Goot and Rodney Tiffen (eds), *Australia's Gulf War*, Melbourne, Melbourne University Press, 1992, pp. 91-92.

[5] See Daly, Martin 'Trial cut short as Roche admits guilt', 'News', *Sydney Morning Herald*, 29-30 May 2004, p. 4.

[6] The story of the activities of Toben and Scully and the court cases against them is outside the purview of this paper. For a summary see Jones, Jeremy assisted by Landis, Josh October 2002 to September 2003 Report, ECAJ, pp. 57-63.

[7] Jones, Landis October 2002 to September 2003 Report, p. 17.

[8] Jones, Landis October 2002 to September 2003 Report, p. 14, reproduced in Rutland, *The Jews in Australia*, Melbourne, Cambridge University Press, 2005, p.156.

[9] Jones, Landis October 2002 to September 2003 Report, p. 15.

[10] Jones, Landis October 2002 to September 2003 Report, p. 47.

[11] For a more detailed discussion of these concepts, see Jones, Landis October 2002 to September 2003 Report, pp. 7-14.

[12] For a more detailed discussion of the activities of the League see Rutland and Caplan, *With One Voice: the History of the New South Wales Jewish Board of Deputies*, pp. 282-285.

[13] Jones, Landis October 2002 to September 2003 Report, pp. 64-66.

[14] Jones, Landis October 2002 to September 2003 Report, pp. 67-69.

[15] In a report written by the Washington-based Lawyers Committee for Human Rights, *Fire and Broken Glass: The Rise of Antisemitism in Europe*, New York and Washington, DC: Lawyers Committee for Human Rights, 2002, they stated in the foreword that: 'As this report makes clear, there is an alarming rise in anti-Semitic violence in Europe: but it is on the rise in other parts of the world as well'. As cited in Klug, Brian 'The collective Jew: Israel and the new anti-Semitism', *Patterns of Prejudice*, vol. 37, no. 2, 2003, p. 118.

[16] Peter Fray, *The Age*, Melbourne, 22 June 2002.

[17] Gardner, Paul 'The new threat: global antisemitism', *Australian Jewish News*, 16 August 2003, p. 19.

[18] Schoenfeld, Gabriel, Editorial comment, 'Israel and Anti-Semitism', *Commentary*, June 2002.

[19] The worst incident occurred when skinheads stabbed David Rosensweig to death outside a kosher pizza shop in Toronto. Coren, Michael '"Blaming it on the Jews": Antisemitism is an old, never-ending story', *Sun Media* (Toronto), 20 July 2002.

[20] There were a large number of articles about these attacks published in the Australian media in 2002. See for example Evans-Pritchard, Ambrose 'Jews face resurgence of hate in Europe', *The Age* (Melbourne), 31 May 2002; and Fray, Peter 'Europe cultivates the ugly flower of prejudice', *The Age* (Melbourne), 22 June 2002.

[21] Bergmann, Werner and Wetzel, Juliane 'Manifestations of anti-Semitism in the European Union, First Semester 2002', *Synthesis Report, on behalf of the European Monitoring Centre on Racism and Xenophobia*, Vienna, March 2003.

[22] 'Anti-Semitism Study in the Spotlight', Centre of Research on Anti-Semitism, *Newsletter*, no. 26, December 2, 2003.

[23] World Jewish Congress (WJC) Institute, 18 May 2002, in ECAJ files, Sydney.

[24] Laqueur, Walter 'The Jewish Question today: Between Old Zionism and New Anti-Semitism', *Encounter*, vol. XXXVII, no. 2, August 1971, p. 52.

[25] Wassermann, Jacob *Life as a German Jew*, 1921, cited in Laqueur, 'The Jewish Question today: Between Old Zionism and New Anti-Semitism', p. 44.

[26] Wistrich, Robert S. *Antisemitism: The Longest Hatred*, New York, Pantheon, c. 1991.

[27] Wistrich, Robert S. *Muslim Anti-Semitism: A Clear and Present Danger*, The American Jewish Committee, 2002.

[28] Garber, Zev 'America Attacked and Zion Blamed—Old-New Antisemitism: *Fatwa* Against Israel', Editorial Viewpoint, *Shofar*, vol. 20, issue 2, p. 3.

[29] Garber, 'America Attacked and Zion Blamed—Old-New Antisemitism: *Fatwa* Against Israel', p. 3.

[30] Wistrich, p. 3.

[31] Statement of Hizbollah's senior cleric, Sheikh Husyn Fadallah, as cited in Wistrich, p.12.

[32] Wistrich, pp. 19-20.

[33] Wistrich, pp. 37-42.

[34] Based on information provided by Dr Irit Abramsky-Bligh, Yad Vashem Education Department, who has been teaching Holocaust courses to Israeli Arabs in recent years.

[35] Well-known lawyer, human rights activist and Canadian parliamentarian, Irwin Cotler, summed this up as Israel having become 'the collective Jew among the nations' - as cited in Klug, 'The collective Jew: Israel and the new anti-Semitism', p. 120.

[36] Klug, 'The collective Jew: Israel and the new anti-Semitism', p. 134.

[37] Klug, 'The collective Jew: Israel and the new anti-Semitism', p. 134.

[38] Wistrich has written about issues of left-wing antisemitism. In 1985, he published a book entitled *Anti-Zionism as an expression of antisemitism in recent years*, published in Jerusalem by the Shazar Library, Institute of Contemporary Jewry.

[39] Laqueur, 'The Jewish Question today: Between Old Zionism and New Anti-Semitism', p. 49.

[40] Figures from Cahill, Desmond 'Religion and Social Cohesion in Australia: an interim report', presented at the *Academic Colloquium, 'After September 11: Religion, Diversity and Cohesion in the Global Neighbourhood*, 13-14 September 2002, RMIT, Melbourne.

[41] Asmar, Christine 'The Arab-Australian Experience', in Goot and Tiffen, (eds), pp. 57-81.

[42] Attacks on Muslim women were an ongoing problem. See the *Sydney Morning Herald*, 13 September 2001, *The Australian*, 15 September 2001, *The Daily Telegraph*, 26 September 2001, the *Sydney Morning Herald*, 20-21 October 2001, and the *Canberra Times*, 26 November 2001.

[43] *The Australian*, 15 September 2001.

[44] *Sydney Morning Herald* and *The Australian*, 24 September 2001.

[45] *Herald Sun* (Melbourne), 14 September 2001.

[46] *Advertiser* (Adelaide), 14 September 2001.

[47] *The Australian*, 14 September 2001.

[48] *Canberra Times*, 14 September 2001, p. 2.

[49] Pellach, Peta 'Interfaith Dialogue and the Issue of Israel', paper presented at the 16th *Annual Conference of the Australian Association of Jewish Studies*, Melbourne, 16-17 February 2004.

[50] Garber, 'America Attacked and Zion Blamed—Old-New Antisemitism: *Fatwa* Against Israel', p. 4.

[51] Garber, p. 4.

[52] Samuel P. Huntington, *The Clash of Civilizations and the Remaking of World Order*, New York, Simon and Schuster, 1996.

[53] Speech by Knesset member, Rabbi Michael Melchior, to the Subcommittee on Near East and South Asian Affairs of the United States Senate Committee on Foreign Relations, 15 October 2003.

3. Are we capable of offending God? Taking blasphemy seriously

Helen Pringle

Until quite recently there appeared to be a consensus in Western democracies as to the desirability of abolishing the offence of blasphemy and blasphemous libel. Indeed, in 1949, Lord Denning argued that 'the offence of blasphemy is a dead letter'. According to Lord Denning, the basis of the law against blasphemy was the idea that 'a denial of Christianity was liable to shake the fabric of society, which was itself founded upon the Christian religion', a danger that no longer existed.[1] A long series of judicial remarks and government reports, most recently by the House of Lords Select Committee on Religious Offences in 2003,[2] stressed the archaism of the offence, and endorsed some form of proposal to abolish or further confine it. However, in the 1990s, dissenting voices were raised against the consensus, particularly from Muslims who argued that in fact the law should be extended beyond Christianity. Misgivings about the effect of such an extension on the freedom of speech have dogged such proposals, particularly where they have found form in laws against religious vilification.

The offence of blasphemy is often treated as a question of freedom of speech. A frequent argument against the continued vitality of the law of blasphemy is that it is an outmoded imposition on the freedom of speech, as can be seen in the public framing of the two most notorious modern cases: *Gay News*, which concerned the publication of a poem by James Kirkup,[3] and *Choudhury*, concerning Salman Rushdie's *Satanic Verses*.[4]

I do not hold to the position that freedom of speech is an absolute. Moreover, I do not think that it is in general necessary or even useful to treat speech as a class distinct from action, or that expression deserves some different protection over and above other forms of action. Indeed, my argument in this chapter is that the problem with the law of blasphemy has very little to do with the fact that it (largely) targets speech. The central difficulty of the law of blasphemy is not that it deals with speech and its freedom, but that it deals with the place accorded to God, or to different Gods, in human society. The law of blasphemy appears archaic and incoherent today not because it unfairly restricts speech, although it might indeed do so in specific instances. My argument is that the law of blasphemy is incoherent insofar as it has lost its central rationale, the requiting of offence *to God*.

In making this argument, I draw on the story of Thomas Aikenhead, who was the last person executed for blasphemy in Britain. Even in Aikenhead's time, in the late seventeenth century, the law of blasphemy had largely lost its coherence as punishment of affront to God, and had largely been reconstituted in terms of punishment of offence to believers. This shift in the focus of the law destabilised the category of blasphemy, long before widespread liberalisation of views on free speech. A final implication of my chapter is that attempts to recover some of the ground of the law of blasphemy through religious vilification laws are misguided. Religious vilification laws can be defended on other grounds, for example as measures against discrimination, but not as a practical reclamation and extension of the object of the law of blasphemy.

Before I begin, I want to caution that in the course of the chapter I shall be repeating claims that have been prosecuted in law and culture as blasphemous, and my repetition of those claims might be counted as a further transgression, traditionally requiring the tearing of garments. This practice is portrayed in cultural artefacts, from Giotto's *Christ before Caiaphas* through to Mel Gibson's *The Passion of the Christ*, that represent the moment when Jesus is brought before the Sanhedrin and is asked whether he is the Christ (Matthew 25). On Jesus' allegedly blasphemous reply, the high priest Caiaphas tears his robes. Such rending of garments was required even in the presentation of evidence in ancient blasphemy prosecutions. However, I shall take my lead from Rabbi Hiyya, who said that after the destruction of the Second Temple, such rending is no longer required, otherwise we would all be walking around in tatters.[5]

L'affaire Aikenhead

An important milestone in the history of blasphemy concerns a young medical student at the University of Edinburgh in the 1690s called Thomas Aikenhead.[6] Aikenhead engaged in spirited conversations with his friends and fellow students on matters of religion. Accounts by at least five of those friends formed the basis for his indictment before the Scottish Privy Council which alleged that Aikenhead,

> shakeing off all fear of God and regaird to his majesties lawes, have now for more than a twelvemoneth by past...[vented] your wicked blasphemies against God and our Saviour Jesus Christ, and against the holy Scriptures, and all revealled religione...you said and affirmed, that divinity or the doctrine of theologie was a rapsidie of faigned and ill-invented nonsense, patched up partly of the morall doctrine of philosophers, and pairtly of poeticall fictions and extravagant chimeras,...

According to the evidence of his friends, Aikenhead called the Old Testament 'Ezra's fables', and the New Testament 'the History of the Imposter Christ'. Aikenhead had affirmed that Jesus 'learned magick in Egypt, and that coming from Egypt into Judea, he picked up a few ignorant blockish fisher fellows, whom he knew by his skill and [sic] phisognomie, had strong imaginations, and that by the help of exalted imaginatione he play'd his pranks', that is, miracles.

The indictment and evidence in the case present for the most part a consistent account of what Aikenhead had said, and Aikenhead and his counsel seem not to have disputed the reports offered as evidence. The summation of the indictment noted that Aikenhead claimed that he 'preferred Mahomet to the blessed Jesus', and continued with a recital of claims:

> and that you have said that you hoped to see Christianity greatly weakened, and that you are confident that in a short tyme it will be utterly extirpat, and you have been so bold in your forsaid blasphemies, that when you have found yourself cold, you have wished to be in the place that Ezra calls Hell, to warme yourself there'.

This latter remark was made outside the Tron kirk, apparently in August.[7]

The mention of the Prophet is of course a very interesting aspect of Aikenhead's case to us today. I think that too often we assume that multiculturalism and the problems it raises are something new to modernity, and that older societies were more homogeneous in action and belief than was actually the case. Aikenhead was tried at the end of a century of civil conflict and war in England, a conflict which concerned the place of God in civil and political matters and which revolved in part over who wore what on their heads. Aikenhead was allegedly more loyal to the Prophet than to any of the warring Christian dispositions. Patrick Midletoune, a fellow student, testified that Aikenhead had told him that 'Mahomet was both the better airtist and polititian than Jesus'.[8] Although some of the sources of Aikenhead's ideas are clear, it is possible that Aikenhead knew of the extraordinary work by Henry Stubbe, *An Account of the Rise and Progress of Mahometanism*.[9] As Abdal Hakim-Murad notes, the vehemence of some seventeenth century polemics against Islam also suggests that there was more sympathy for Islam within English Dissenter circles at that time than is commonly acknowledged.[10] The minister Robert Wylie hushed the critics of the action against Aikenhead by arguing that 'no man shuld in the face of a people spitefully revile & insult the object of their adoration,' adding that, after all, 'a Christian could not be innocent who should rail at or curse Mahomet at Constantinople'.[11]

Aikenhead was charged under Scotland's two blasphemy acts. The 1661 Act passed by the first Scottish Parliament under Charles II mandated death for one who 'not being distracted in his wits shall rail upon or curse God, or any of the persons of the blessed Trinity'. The 1695 post-Settlement Act upheld the 1661 Act and set out a graduated scale of penalties depending on the obstinacy of the offence by 'whosoever shall in their wryteing or discourse denye, impugne or quarrell, or argue, or reason against the being of God, or any of the persons of the blessed Trinity, or the authority of the holy Scriptures, of the Old and New Testaments, or the Providence of God in the government of the world'.[12]

In November 1696, Aikenhead was summoned to the Scottish Privy Council to be charged, and was sent 'to be tryed for his life' to the courts. Five of the jurors summoned had refused to attend and were fined; while these refusals are seen by some writers as a protest against the action, I am not so sure given the assiduousness with which many people avoid jury duty. Aikenhead was found guilty of cursing and railing against God the Father and the Son, denying the incarnation and the Trinity, and scoffing at the Scriptures. He submitted a petition for leniency at the end of December and again on 7 January, although it has been suggested by Michael Hunter that the 'gushing profession of faith' in these petitions might have been written on Aikenhead's behalf by others.[13] On 8 January 1697, at the age of 20, Thomas was hanged and buried on the road to Leith.

This was the last recorded execution for blasphemy in Britain. Soon after, the Scottish Privy Council began what was to be the last major witch-hunt in Scotland, the affair of the Renfrewshire witches.[14] Macaulay's history later linked the Aikenhead and Renfrewshire prosecutions as actions 'worthy of the tenth century', conducted by men whose 'own understandings were as dark and their own hearts as obdurate as those of the Familiars of the Inquisition at Lisbon'. These men, Macaulay says, 'perpetrated a crime such as has never since polluted the island', executing Aikenhead for nothing more than 'the prate of a forward boy'.[15] The cruelty of the prosecution and sentence certainly did not go unremarked or unprotested at the time either.

Offending the *Ens entrum*...or the beliefs of believers?

I am fascinated by the story of Aikenhead for a number of reasons. An extremely vivid picture of the intellectual life of a young man in late seventeenth century Edinburgh is painted in the documents, particularly in Aikenhead's parting speech and a letter to his friends. In his parting speech, noted on one copy as his *'Cygnea Cantio'*, or swan song, Aikenhead attributes his heterodoxy to an 'insatiable inclination to truth' which led him from an early age to search for a grounding of his faith. Aikenhead says that his doubt led him to the question, 'whether or not man was capable of offending *Ens entrum*'.[16] Aikenhead concludes that we are not capable of such offence, for reasons that I do not explore here. What interests me in Aikenhead's question has more to do with the definition and understanding of blasphemy: what exactly does blasphemy perform, and in particular, whom or what does blasphemy wrong?

Modern answers to these questions are fairly clear on two main counts. First, a long tradition of judicial and political commentary understands blasphemy as an attack of some sort on social or civil order, that is, as closely allied to incivility at one end of the scale, and sedition at the other. The emergence of blasphemy as an offence of civil order can be pegged to around the time of *Taylor's Case* in 1676. John Taylor was accused of uttering 'divers blasphemous expressions, horrible to hear, (viz.) that Jesus Christ was a bastard, a whoremaster, religion was a cheat; and that he neither feared God, the devil, or man.' Sir Matthew Hale held in this case

> that such kind of wicked blasphemous words were not only an offence to God and religion, but a crime against the laws, State and Government, and therefore punishable in this Court. For to say, religion is a cheat, is to dissolve all those obligations whereby the civil societies are preserved, and that Christianity is parcel of the laws of England; and therefore to reproach the Christian religion is to speak in subversion of the law.[17]

The terms of Hale's judgment on Taylor also restricted the scope of blasphemy law to the protection of Christianity, a restriction recently reiterated in *Choudhury,* although it had been questioned by Lord Scarman in *Gay News.*[18]

John Taylor's offence was understood as akin to sedition. Understandings of the wrong of blasphemy as a fomenting of civil disorder underlie much of modern blasphemy law. For example, in the 'Piss Christ' case in Australia, the definition of blasphemy was said to hinge on the risk of such disorder. In 1998, the then Archbishop of Melbourne, George Pell, had sought an injunction to restrain the National Gallery of Victoria from showing a photograph by Andres Serrano. The photograph depicted the crucified Christ immersed in urine. Justice Harper remarked that if the offence of blasphemous libel did exist, it would be necessary to show that the exhibition of the photograph would cause unrest of some sort—and in the absence of that showing, no injunction could be granted. Justice Harper's refusal to grant an injunction in this case was however made on other grounds.[19]

The second important characteristic of modern understandings of the wrong of blasphemy is that it involves an offence to the beliefs of believers. As Lord Scarman noted in the *Gay News* case, the 'true test' of blasphemy is 'whether the words are calculated to outrage and insult the Christian's religious feelings'.[20] At issue in the case was the publication by the magazine *Gay News* of James Kirkup's poem entitled 'The Love that Dares to Speak Its Name', alongside a somewhat lurid illustration by Tony Reeves. Prior to this case, blasphemy seems not to have been successfully prosecuted in the United Kingdom since 1921, when John William Gott was sentenced to nine months in prison for publishing pamphlets that suggested that Christ looked like a clown as he entered Jerusalem on a donkey.[21]

The action against *Gay News* was a private prosecution by Mrs Mary Whitehouse, the Secretary of the National Viewers and Listeners Association. She explained the grounds of her case in the course of an interview by saying, 'The blasphemy law is to protect the feelings of people rather than Christianity. Its purpose is to implement one of the three basic civil rights set out by the Geneva Convention that people shall not be offended on the grounds of race, class or religion.' However, it had *not* in fact been the claim of the prosecution deposition that Kirkup's poem offended the feelings of Christians, but rather that the poem 'vilified Christ in His death, His life and his Crucifixion'.[22]

In the same interview, Mrs Whitehouse noted that, 'When the poem arrived on my desk and I read it, I had one overwhelming feeling that this was the recrucifixion of Christ with 20th century weapons—with words, with obscenities, and if I sat there and did nothing I would be a traitor. It was just as simple as that'.[23] As many people at the time of the trial reminded Mrs Whitehouse, in principle it would have been quite possible for her to bring an action for obscene libel, rather than for blasphemy, given the character of the poem and illustration at issue. What is striking however is the notion of traitor that Mrs Whitehouse invokes. There is nothing to suggest that Mrs Whitehouse has in mind being a traitor to herself if she 'did nothing'. She uses the word 'traitor' with its connotations of betrayal of trust, falsity, and failure in allegiance in such a way that indicates that she is thinking about being a traitor *to God* by not avenging his honour. So while Mrs Whitehouse certainly thinks, like Lord Scarman, that blasphemy is an attack on the sincere religious *beliefs* of *believers*, she also voices a sense of blasphemy as violence to God. That is, Mrs Whitehouse thinks that we are entirely capable of offending God—and, I think, that God is entirely capable of being offended by us. But she has not quite settled on one of these alternatives—offence to beliefs of believers, or to God—as constituting the central wrong of blasphemy.

The confusion of Mrs Whitehouse about what blasphemy performs is more general, and it is not confined only to the modern world. In Aikenhead's time, there was a similar lack of clarity as to what blasphemy does and to whom it does it. While it would be tempting to see Aikenhead's trial and execution as the last gasp of older ways of understanding and of addressing blasphemy, I do not think it is quite that simple. Blasphemy has been a difficult thing to define at least since it was set loose from enforcement by the ecclesiastical courts. In regard to Aikenhead's prosecution, many of his contemporaries thought that he had done something wrong, but that it wasn't blasphemy. For example, James Johnstoun wrote to the philosopher John Locke,

> It's plain Aikenhead must have died by the first Act of 1661, since it was his first fault as he himself pleads in his petition, and that he did retract, which delivers him from the second article of the first act. Now the words of the first article being *railing* and *cursing*, no evidence except that of Mr Mungo Craigs (in which he is said to have called Christ an

imposture) seems to answer the meaning of those words, and as to this Craig Aikenhead in his speech in which he owns other things, denies his evidence and no doubt he is the decoy who gave him the books and made him speak as he did, and whose name is not put in the copy of the petition to the Justiciary sent to you, because the writer would spare Craig.

The age of the witnesses is observable and that none of them pretend, nor is it laid in the Indictment that Aikenhead made it his bussines to seduce any man. Laws long in dessuetude should be gently put in Execution and the first example made of one in circumstances that deserve no compassion, whereas here there is youth, Levity, docility, and no designe upon others.[24]

In other words, Aikenhead was simply speculating and bantering, and lacked intention either to outrage the feelings of believers or to incite disorder.

The perspective taken by Johnstoun and others on Aikenhead's case came to flower in 1883, when Lord Coleridge argued that 'if the decencies of controversy are observed, even the fundamentals of religion may be attacked without the writer being guilty of blasphemy'.[25] Lord Coleridge was echoing Lord Denman's remark in the 1841 case of *Hetherington*, that blasphemy lies not merely in what is said, but in how it is said. Lord Denman had argued that, even in regard to the fundamentals of Christian religion,

If they be carried on in a sober and temperate and decent style, even those discussions may be tolerated, and may take place without criminality attaching to them; but that, if the tone and spirit is that of offence, and insult, and ridicule, which leaves the judgment really not free to act, and, therefore, cannot be truly called an appeal to the judgment, but an appeal to the wild and improper feelings of the human mind, more particularly in the younger part of the community, in that case the jury will hardly feel it possible to say that such opinions so expressed, do not deserve the character [of blasphemy] affixed to them...[26]

Again, this approach to blasphemy as necessarily including incitement to wildness or impropriety has received wide and continuing legal approval.

However, if the 'decencies of controversy', and not the particular content of the utterance, is what counts in defining the width of the offence of blasphemy, then it becomes difficult to argue that religious utterances should have any particular protection over and above any other utterance. Blasphemy is not a facially neutral category in a way that, say, the category of obscenity is. Whatever else they do, laws against blasphemy do not protect the beliefs and/or feelings of unbelievers. As Mary Whitehouse noted in answer to the question of why the beliefs of humanists are not protected by laws against blasphemy: 'Well, if they are non-religious, they can't be offended in their religious feelings, can they?'.[27] In *Gay News*, however, Lord Diplock voiced the rather cryptic note on this point that 'the poem and accompanying drawing were likely to shock and arouse resentment among believing Christians and indeed many unbelievers', which echoed Lord Trevethin's remarks in *Gott* that the libel then at issue was 'offensive to anyone in sympathy with the Christian religion, whether he be a strong Christian or a lukewarm Christian, or merely a person sympathising with their ideals'.[28]

To use the language of Cass Sunstein, why maintain the asymmetry of a special category for blasphemy, if it is possible to address its performances and effects in terms of such neighbouring categories as sedition, obscenity, or defamation? The distinctiveness of blasphemy as an offence is difficult to uphold if its focus is offence to the beliefs of believers. Even in Aikenhead's time, it was not clear to many people what constituted the exact difference between blasphemy and atheism, apostasy, idolatry, irreligion, etc. Aikenhead himself felt impelled to say that while he might have blasphemed, he certainly did not practise magic or converse with devils.

When the Privy Council said that they would grant Aikenhead a reprieve, the Church of Scotland refused, on the basis that it was necessary to put an end to 'the abounding of impiety and profanity in this land'.[29] In 1696, the Scottish Privy Council had ordered that search be made of Edinburgh booksellers for 'atheistical, erroneous or profane or vicious' works, and John Frazer was gaoled and put in sackcloth for reading deist works. Tacked on at the end of the *State Trials* report on Aikenhead is the story of Francis Borthwick, a convert to Judaism, who was declared 'outlaw and fugitive, and all his goods and gear to be brought in for his majesty's use, for his contemption and disobedience; which was pronounced for doom'. At this time too, University of Edinburgh students were in the habit of pelting Catholics coming out of Mass.[30] Blasphemy was not the only available category into which religious offences could fall, and other forms of religious insult to the beliefs of believers were matters of lively controversy. But what was becoming ambiguous was the sense of blasphemy as a specific wrong entitled to a specific remedy.

Conclusion

Some, perhaps even many, people in Thomas Aikenhead's time held the view that it is possible to offend God, and that dire consequences would follow from such offence. For example, the informer Mungo Craig argued in his first pamphlet against Aikenhead that the magistrates should 'attone with Blood, th'affronts of heav'n's offended throne'.[31] Although the category into which a particular form of speech or action fell might be unclear, God in the view of Craig and others was certainly capable of being offended, and (civil) persons were capable of avenging the affront and restoring divine order. Moreover, they had a *duty* to respond on God's behalf. In concluding, I want to suggest that understandings of blasphemy changed decisively not when we became secular, and devoted to free speech, but at some point much earlier, when understandings of God began to shift radically, such that God was understood as incapable of being offended.

Some fragments of the earlier understandings can still be glimpsed in other than Christian religious traditions. For example, in a remarkable reflection on Rabbi Hayim Volozhiner's *Nefesh ha'Hayyim*, Emmanuel Levinas argues that our acts, words and thoughts condition the association of God with the world(s). Levinas quotes Volozhiner:

> Let nobody in Israel—God forbid! ask himself, 'what am I, and what can my humble acts achieve in the world?'. Let him rather understand this, that he may know it and fix it in his thoughts: not one detail of his acts, of his words, and of his thoughts is ever lost. Each one leads back to its origin, where it takes effect in the height of heights, in the worlds...The man of intelligence who understands this in its truth will be fearful at heart and will tremble as he thinks how far his bad acts reach and what corruption and destruction even a small misdeed may cause.[32]

In this view of God and his demands, blasphemy is perhaps best understood as the opposite of prayer, or rather of the moment of offering and grace in the benediction. Levinas argues that in prayer we make possible the association of God with the worlds in a creating and sustaining association. In contrast, blasphemy is something like a violent infidelity to God which shakes the foundations of the world by destroying its ethical intelligibility, not just by disturbing the social or political order by insulting believers. What flows on from blasphemy in this view is the malediction, not of God's punishment, but simply of the breach between God and the world.

According to such older views, few remnants of which survive today, the verb 'to blaspheme' is transitive, and the object of the verb is God. Hence it was possible to claim that someone had 'blasphemed God', or to claim like St Paul to have been 'blasphemed'. In older understandings of blasphemy, there was still the difficulty of whether we *as citizens* are capable of repairing the violence to God accomplished by the blasphemer, that is, whether the faithful have *standing* to apply for a *civil* remedy of wrong to the deity. Such a difficulty aside, the coherence of the position rests centrally on acceptance of blasphemy as constituted by affront to God, not to fellow believers.

One of the more interesting recent developments in regard to the offence of blasphemy are attempts to salvage what is still alive in the offence by substituting the category of religious vilification for that of blasphemy. For example, the

Victorian *Racial and Religious Tolerance Act* of 2001 makes unlawful the incitement of hatred, contempt, revulsion or severe ridicule on the grounds of religious belief or activity.[33] Rather than being explicitly targeted against discrimination, the Act is linked to the promotion of tolerance. In this way, I would argue, the Act understands vilification as akin to blasphemy, by construing the issue as involving offence to believers and as a matter of public order. Hence, I would argue, the Act does not avoid the problems of modern blasphemy law, and still does not grapple with the problem of offence to God.

ENDNOTES

[1] Lord Denning, *Freedom Under the Law*, Hamlyn Lectures 1st series, London, 1949, p. 46.

[2] House of Lords Select Committee on Religious Offences, *Religious Offences in England and Wales – First Report* [HL Paper 95-I, Session 2002-03], <http:www.parliament.the-stationery-office.co.uk/pa/ld200203/ldselect/ldrelof/95/9501.htm>, viewed 11 August 2005. In Australia, see esp. New South Wales Law Reform Commission 1992, *Discussion Paper: Blasphemy*. <http://www.lawlink.nsw.gov.au/lrc.nsf/pages/DP24TOC>, and 1994, *Report: Blasphemy*, <http://www.lawlink.nsw.gov.au/lrc.nsf/pages/r74toc>, viewed 11 August 2005.

[3] *Whitehouse v Gay News, Whitehouse v Lemon* [1979] AC 617; [1979] 2 WLR 281; [1979] 1 All ER 898 (HL), and *Gay News Ltd. and Lemon v United Kingdom* [Eur Comm HR] 5 EHRR 123 (1982).

[4] *R v Chief Metropolitan Magistrate, ex parte Choudhury* [1991] 1 QB 429.

[5] Sanhedrin 60a. I use the Soncino edition of the Talmud.

[6] The primary documents on Aikenhead are printed in 'Proceedings against Thomas Aikenhead, for Blasphemy, 8 William III. A.D. 1696', in Cobbett W. and T. B. Howell et al. (eds), *A Complete Collection of State Trials*, 34 vols., London, 1809-1828, [State Trials], vol. 13, cols. 917-940, and Hugo Arnot (ed.),1785, *A Collection and Abridgement of Celebrated Criminal Trials in Scotland*, Edinburgh, pp. 324-7. The documents printed in State Trials are from the records of the Justiciary in Edinburgh, and from a collection of manuscripts in the property of Lord King, now kept in the Lovelace Collection of Locke's papers in the Bodleian Library at MS Locke b.4, ff 86-106. Michael Hunter notes that 'an early 19th-century commentator on Locke's Aikenhead material described it as being 'In a bundle of MSS. On the subject of Toleration': Francis Horner, 1843, *Memoirs and Correspondence*, Leonard Horner (ed.), 2 vols, London, i. 487'; see Hunter, Michael 1992, '"Aikenhead the Atheist": The Context and Consequences of Articulate Irreligion in the Late Seventeenth Century', in Michael Hunter and David Wootton,(eds), *Atheism from the Reformation to the Enlightenment*, Oxford, Clarendon Press, p. 231, fn. 27.

[7] State Trials, vol. 13, p. 919.

[8] State Trials, vol. 13, p. 925.

[9] E. Hafiz Mahmud Khan Shairani (ed.) 1954, *An Account of the Rise and Progress of Mahometanism, with the Life of Mahomet, And a Vindication of him and his Religion from the Calumnies of the Christians*, Lahore, Orientalia. I was led to Stubbe by a passing reference in a talk by Sheikh Hamza Yusuf, and found that no library in Australia holds a copy of the work.

[10] Hakim-Murad acknowledges Stubbe and his influence in 'British and Muslim?', lecture given to a conference of British converts to Islam, 17 September 1997, <http://www.masud.co.uk/ISLAM/ahm/british.htm>, viewed 11 August 2005.

[11] Hunter, '"Aikenhead the Atheist"', p. 238, quoting letter from Wylie to William Hamilton, 16 June 1697.

[12] Printed in Thomson, T. and C. Innes (eds), *The Acts of the Parliament of Scotland*, 12 vols, Edinburgh, 1814-1975, vol. 7, pp. 202-3 and vol. 9, pp. 386-7.

[13] Hunter, 1992, p. 228.

[14] See especially Larner, Christina 1981, *Enemies of God: The Witch-hunt in Scotland*, London, Chatto & Windus, and Larner, Christina 1984, 'The Crime of Witchcraft in Scotland' in Alan Macfarlane Larner (ed.) *Witchcraft and Religion: The Politics of Popular Belief*, New York, Blackwell. The bundle of documents on Aikenhead in Locke's manuscripts also includes material relating to the Renfrewshire incident.

[15] Macaulay, T. B. Firth, 1915, Charles Harding (ed.) *The History of England, from the Accession of James the Second*, 6 vols, London, Macmillan, vol. 6, pp. 2698-9. In the context of blasphemy, recall that Ma-

caulay had sponsored the Indian Criminal Code, which penalised religious incitement, though not in quite those terms—and which has sometimes been put forward as a model for addressing religious affronts. See Lord Scarman's mention of Macaulay's reform in *R v Lemon* [1979] 2 WLR 281 (HL), at 308.

[16] 'Thomas Aikenhead's Paper', in State Trials, vol. 13, p. 931. Also 'Thomas Aikenhead his Cygnea Cantio', Harleian MS 6846, ff 400-101, as noted in Hunter, 1992, p. 229, fn. 25.

[17] Taylor's Case (1676) 1 Vent. 293 (KB), 86 ER 189.

[18] *R v Chief Metropolitan Magistrate, ex parte Choudhury* [1991] 1 QB 429.

[19] *Pell v National Gallery of Victoria* [1998] 2 VR 391.

[20] *R v Lemon* [1979] 2 WLR 281, at 312 per Lord Scarman.

[21] *R v Gott* (1922) 16 Cr App R 86.

[22] See Anderson, Ingrid and Pamela Rose, 1978, '"Who the Hell Does She Think She Is?"', interview with Mary Whitehouse, *Poly Law Review*, vol. 3, no. 2, p. 13.

[23] Anderson and Rose, 1978, p. 15. The interviewers present the interview in order 'to demonstrate that the watchdog of this country's moral welfare appears to have no coherent philosophy of law or morality'.

[24] [James Johnstoun?] to [Locke?], 27 February 1697, BL MS Locke b4 ff 86-87, enclosures 92-7, reprinted in de Beer, E. S. (ed.), 1981, *The Correspondence of John Locke*, 8 vols, Oxford, Clarendon Press, vol. 6, 19. No record remains of a reply by Locke to Johnstoun on this matter.

[25] *R v Regina and Foote* 15 Cox CC 231 (1883), 238.

[26] *R v Hetherington* (1841) 4, State Trials ns. 563, at 590-1.

[27] Anderson and Rose, 1978, p. 13.

[28] *R v Gott* (1922) 16 Cr App R 86, 89-90 per Trevethin LCJ.

[29] See Macaulay's accounts of the period, and Hunter, 1992, p. 239-41.

[30] Case of David Mowbray, 'Of Tumult within Burgh', in Hugo Arnot (ed.), 1785, *A Collection and Abridgement of Celebrated Criminal Trials in Scotland*, p. 270.

[31] Craig, Mungo 1696, *A Satyr against Atheistical Deism*, Edinburgh, quoted in Hunter, 1992, p. 233.

[32] Levinas, Emmanuel 1984, 'Prayer without Demand', trans. Sarah Richmond, in Seán Hand (ed.) 1989, *The Levinas Reader*, Oxford, Basil Blackwell, p. 230.

[33] See *Racial and Religious Tolerance Act 2001* (Victoria), <http://www.austlii.edu.au/au/legis/vic/con-sol_act/rarta2001265/>. The act was tested in the Catch the Fire case: see *Islamic Council of Victoria Inc. v Catch the Fire Ministries Inc* [2003] VCAT 1753 (21 October 2003), <http://www.austlii.edu.au/cgi-bin/disp.pl/au/cases/vic/VCAT/2003/1753.html>, *Islamic Council of Victoria v Catch the Fire Ministries Inc* (Final) [2004] VCAT 2510 (22 December 2004), <http://www.aust-lii.edu.au/au/cases/vic/VCAT/2004/2510.html>, and *Islamic Council of Victoria v Catch the Fire Ministries Inc* (Anti Discrimination – Remedy) [2005] VCAT 1159 (22 June 2005), <http://www.austlii.edu.au/cgi-bin/disp.pl/au/cases/vic/VCAT/2005/1159.html>, all viewed 11 August 2005.

4. A flaw in the nation-building process: Negotiating the sacred in our multicultural society

Veronica Brady

In a way our topic is strangely anachronistic: blasphemy is a problematic notion in a professedly secular society like ours. It is true, of course, that laws against it are still on the books in most states and territories. But they are laws inherited from the English legal system, designed to protect the established religion of the Church of England which was 'part and parcel of the laws of England' and the monarch, 'the defender of the faith'. In that, these laws against blasphemy served to protect the social fabric rather than any particular theological position. Australia, however, has never had an established Church, and even if we had there is little danger that speaking out against it or any other Christian Church or indeed other religion would shake the foundations of the state. Indeed, I sometimes think that speaking in its favour might be more likely to do so.

The current suspicion of Islam is perhaps a case in point, especially in the inadequacies it reveals in our notions of multiculturalism. The suspicion is probably more political than religious, fuelled by fear of the terrorism associated—not always accurately—with Islam in the popular imagination. By and large, Australians are not interested in theological matters—and sometimes, it seems in questions of right and wrong, at the public level at least—and our society is self-consciously and often self-congratulatorily secular, which is understandable in the light of the divisive nature of the sectarian squabbles of the nineteenth century. In the early days of Federation A. G. Stephens, the literary editor of *The Bulletin*, associated the suspicion of religion with 'mental enlightenment'[1] and even today the general belief is still that the open and tolerant society which we like to think we live in depends on the exclusion of religion—often a source of conflict in the past—from the public sphere. I want, however, to argue to the contrary, that a multicultural society like ours badly needs to recover a sense of the sacred as a kind of canopy under which people of different cultures and beliefs can live together with mutual respect. Before we go any further, however, a crucial point needs to be clarified. I do not want to identify the sacred only with organised religion. Rather, I see it as the product of the world view William James describes in *The Varieties Of Religious Experience,* a sense that the 'so-called order of nature, which constitutes this world's experience, is only one portion of the total universe and…[that] there stretches beyond this visible world an unseen world of which we know nothing positive, but in its relation to which the true significance of our present mundane life consists'.[2]

It is, that is to say, a sense of the sacred, of some ultimate mystery which fascinates us yet fills us with awe and demands our respect and obedience. Although, as the New South Wales Law Reform Commission noted in its report on the subject, blasphemy means different things to different people in our society, it has, I would argue, a core meaning, the profanation of this sacred reality. Most cultures throughout history have had some such sense of an unseen world which claims our obedience and respect. By and large, however, as I have argued, most Australians have fixed their attention on the visible and material, giving priority to them. As Stephens saw it, 'there is in the developing Australian character a sceptical and utilitarian spirit that values the present hour and refuses to sacrifice the present for any visionary future lacking a rational guarantee'.[3] This is perhaps not surprising in a settler society facing a difficult environment. But it has led to an emphasis on the short term. Especially as far as our use of the land is concerned this has led to problems. But this is true also, and perhaps especially, in our relations with Aboriginal Australians whose cultures are imbued with a deep sense of the sacred and the obligation to honour its claims. Where for most of us, however, the claims of economic development are paramount so that this obligation, in this instance to protect sacred sites, leads them to see as blasphemy what many, if not most, of us, would see as good business.

I would argue, however, that in the long run this indifference to the claims of the sacred may prove politically and socially destructive and would also contend that it represents an ontological and epistemological mistake. In fact there are 'more things in heaven and earth' than are dreamed of in a merely pragmatic and utilitarian culture. This is especially the case as far as human relations and their extension, politics are concerned. There questions of right and wrong eventually have an effect. As Raymond Gaita argues, 'Even in politics we are, inescapably, moral beings. No adequate concept of our interests or of our well-being should ignore or diminish that fact'.[4] Certainly the evidence suggests that the current lack of concern for justice and truth in public life has affected the tone and quality of our public life. Self-interest does not provide a proper base for social coherence.

Indifference to the sacred has also made national identity a problematic matter. Since the self lacks a sense of an authority beyond itself, identity is often equated with conformity. Hence Australian identity has often been defined in exclusionary terms: if we are not entirely clear who we are, we can at least say that we are not like 'those others'. The Constitution excluded Aboriginal Australians from citizenship, for example, on the grounds of 'difference'—which implicitly meant that they were 'inferior' to us. Similarly the so-called 'White

Australia Policy' was for many years directed against non-Caucasian migrants on similar grounds. According to Lisa Strelien, in an essay discussing the apparent inability of the Howard government to contemplate a treaty with Aboriginal Australians, this failure to develop a comprehensive notion of humanity represents a fundamental 'flaw in the nation-building process'.[5] It is also becoming increasingly clear that it creates problems in our relations with people and cultures different from ours.

For our present purposes it is useful to reflect on the historical causes of this 'flaw'. Like most settler societies, in the nineteenth century especially, Australia is the product of the history of empire, a history, Karl Jaspers suggests, which has arrogated to itself a 'grandeur...stolen from God' and has presented itself as fate, a 'grand triumphal march' through the world of certain people, who as the spearhead of civilisation are destined to rule the world.[6] As Luiz Carlos Susin points out, it thus becomes a 'form of critical understanding which identifies and distinguishes good and evil in a very particular way, based on itself, on its glorious position as basis and referent of the whole of reality spread out at its feet'.[7] This helps to explain our present government's self-confidence and apparent lack of self-interrogation in its dealings not only with asylum seekers, Aboriginal Australians and those less successful in economic, social or intellectual terms but also with our Asian neighbours.

But ultimately, I would argue, it is disabling since it locks us into a 'closed circle around sameness'[8] which prevents us from coming to terms with our actual, as distinct from our imagined, situation. Susin suggests that imperial identity is based on the model of Ulysses who left home and travelled through strange places but always intended to return home. By and large, this was true of the first free settlers in Australia who were determined, if they were not able to return home, to make the new place the equivalent of home, a 'new Britannia in another world', as W. C. Wentworth put it.[9] British values, purposes, names and architecture were imposed on a very different environment so that our culture was post-modern *avant la lettre*, resting on 'the exaltation of signs based on the denial of the reality of things'.[10]

Enclosed in our own imaginary world in many ways we failed to recognise the reality and power of the land, seeing it as *terra nullius*, empty and useless until our arrival. We were thus unaware of the long history of the place and the knowledge of it built up over thousands of years by its First Peoples. To borrow Wittgenstein's image, our own story held us captive so that we were merely tracing round its frame when we looked at the new world opening out before us rather than coming to terms with the realities which confronted us.[11] The ecstatic description of nineteenth century Melbourne in the colonial romance, *The Recollections of Geoffry Hamlyn*, is a good example of this self-enclosure:

[T]wenty-two years ago the Yarra rolled its clear waters to the sea through the unbroken solitude of a primeval forest. Now there stands a noble city, with crowded wharves, containing with its suburbs not less than 20,000 inhabitants . . . and through the low sandy heads that close the great port towards the sea *thirteen millions sterling* of exports is carried away each year.[12]

There is little sense of the past here. What matters is the future, the transformation of what is different into the familiar, the stamping of their own image on the world by the colonists. The passage celebrates the work of human minds and hands and there is no sense of any other authority. The place itself, it seems, is merely a means to an end and the settlers are free to transform it in their own image.

It is becoming increasingly clear, however, that questions about the nature of reality cannot be ignored. Nor can questions of right and wrong. Injustice and cruelty, in the past as well as in the present, clearly have social consequences. The 'winners', the successful and powerful do not have a monopoly of wisdom. Indeed their very success may lock them into positions that are ultimately unsustainable. Those who were defeated, the Aboriginal dead, for example, and all those others whose lives went unvalued and unreported may have a meaning yet to be realised. Their memory may remind us that the present order of things does not represent the last word on human possibility. Meaning, as J. B. Metz remarks, 'is not a category that is only reserved for the conquerors'.[13] It is also becoming clear that freedom and justice degenerate 'wherever those who suffer are treated more or less as a cliché and degraded to a faceless mass'.[14]

Even in the nineteenth century there were those who understood this. An English visitor, Constance Gordon-Cumming, for example, deplored what she called the 'ruthless policy of [the] extermination' of Aboriginal people in Queensland according to which whole tribes have been shot down for daring to trespass on lands taken from them without any sort of right'. She rejected the view that 'the extinction of the Australian black' was not, as its advocates declared, 'a law of nature' but 'an illustration of the might that makes right'.[15]

A sense of the sacredness of every person is surely the guarantee of the 'right relationships' which are the basis of any civilised society, and the growing coarseness, insensitivity, and xenophobia evident in Australian society today underline this point. A multicultural society especially needs an authority beyond the self, some 'absolute heterogeneity that unsettles all the assurances of the same in which we comfortably ensconce ourselves'.[16] Otherwise the individual becomes merely part of what Simone Weil calls the 'social machine', a machine for 'breaking hearts and crushing spirits...[and] manufacturing irresponsibility, stupidity, corruption, slackness and, above all, dizziness'.[17]

The totalitarian implications are clear. Consider, for example, the slogan of those opposed to Aboriginal Land Rights, 'One Land, One Law, One Culture'—a slogan which echoes Hitler's 'One Land, One Law, One People.' Looking more widely, the fortress mentality underlying the government's treatment of asylum seekers and their supporters reflects a similar fear of difference and support for the Prime Minister's determination to build a society which is 'unapologetically and unashamedly Australian'—according to his monolithic definition.

Nevertheless another tradition runs through our culture which questions the assumptions of imperial history and the myth of 'progress'—at least as defined in material terms. It is concerned with those excluded from or damaged by this history, the 'losers' rather than the 'winners', those who are poor, ill, disadvantaged or different. This is the tradition of 'a fair go'. At the moment, it is true, it seems to be in abeyance, especially in public life. But, unfashionable as it may seem, it is still alive. Not long before he retired, the World Bank's James Wolfensohn, himself an Australian, for instance, noted that in a recent survey 55 per cent of the population supported aid for developing nations not for pragmatic reasons but 'because it is the moral thing to do.'

The premises of this tradition are not formally religious—indeed it is often suspicious of institutional religion. But it rests on a sense of the absolute dignity of every person, regardless of wealth, position or power. For many this also includes a reverence for the land. Joseph Furphy, for instance believed that there was a 'latent meaning' in it which it is our task to interpret 'faithfully and lovingly'.[18] In similar vein, Marcus Clarke felt a power in the land before which the 'trim utilitarian civilization which bred him shrinks into insignificance'.[19] In this tradition the settlers face a task which is imaginative, spiritual even, as well as economic, what Mircea Eliade describes as 'the transformation of chaos into cosmos'.[20] It thus looks beyond history to accept the 'vast augustness' of existence but also accepts the limits of human intention, power and knowledge when confronted with 'the icy laws of outer fact'.[21] This means respecting rather than denying or trying to conquer the strangeness of this place. To accept this strangeness may also open up the possibility Mircea Eliade canvassed when he wrote that we may have reached a point at which, in order to survive, humanity may need to desist 'from any further "making" of history in the sense in which we have made it from the beginnings of the first empires' and learn to respect cosmic reality and its authority.[22]

This may seem romantic. But it makes sense in the light of contemporary science which speaks increasingly and with increasing respect of what is unseen. To quote William James once more, this involves a 'sense of the whole residual cosmos as an everlasting presence, intimate or alien, terrible or amusing, lovable or odious',[23] a sense of the sacred. Far from being romantic, however, this puts us in tune with what is actually the case, our bodily situation—as, arguably, our present culture, resting as it does on 'the exaltation of signs based on the denial of the reality of things',[24] is not.

As James points out, however, the 'method of averting one's attention from evil and living simply in the light of the good is splendid as long as it will work...[But] the evil facts which it refuses positively to account for are a genuine portion of reality'. Indeed, as he says and as I have been arguing, they may be the 'best key to life's significance, and possibly the only openers of our eyes to the deepest levels of truth'.[25] It is all very well for politicians to promise to make us all feel 'relaxed and comfortable' but to ignore the other side of our story is no way to create a civilised and durable, much less a multicultural society.

To conclude then. I have been arguing that the discovery/recovery of a sense of the sacred may well be the crucial task facing us as a people. It is also, I suggest, the way to create a genuinely multicultural society. If that is so, those we have excluded in the past may become a key resource. This may be especially the case with Aboriginal Australians. Ken Gelder and Jane Jacobs make a similar suggestion when they write that Aboriginal Australians may have a key role to play in any attempt to recast our sense of ourselves.[26]

This is not only because their story casts a different light on our history but also because, as they put it, Aboriginal culture's sense of the sacred may be 'integral to what we might (or should) "become"'. Indeed in their view it is 'precisely because Aboriginal sacredness appears so out-of-step with modernity that it is able to be identified as the very thing modernity needs'.[27] History is not the final arbiter. Nor does it encompass the full range of reality. We need to question our culture's belief in its self-sufficiency. Without a sense of the value of every person and of the natural world on which we depend 'right relationships' will not develop. Equally, 'if an awareness of and reverence for...the sacred [is lacking], the paths of true healing cannot emerge'.[28] The sacred and the secular in this view are complementary. John Dunne puts it this way. A genuine sense of the sacred involves a 'passing over...a shifting of standpoint' which can open a way into the standpoint of another culture or another religion. In turn it can be followed by an equal and opposite process we might call coming back, coming back to new insights into one's culture, one's own way of life, one's own religion'.[29] That surely is the basis for a multicultural society, a society for the future.

ENDNOTES

[1] Turner, Ian (ed.) 1968, *The Australian Dream*, Melbourne, Sun Books, p. x.

[2] James, William 1957, *The Varieties Of Religious Experience*, New York, Collier, p. 51.

[3] Turner, 1968, p. x.

[4] Grattan, Michelle (ed.) 2000, *Reconciliation: Essays on Australian Reconciliation*, Melbourne, Black Inc., p. 278.

[5] Strelein, Lisa 2000, 'Dealing With Unfinished Business: A Treaty For Australia', *Public Law Review,* vol. 11, no. 4, p. 262.

[6] Kohler, Lotte and Hans Saner 1992, *Correspondence Hannah Arendt and Karl Jaspers 1926-1969,* New York, Harcourt Brace, p. 149.

[7] Susin, Luiz Carlos 2000/2, 'A Critique Of The Identity Paradigm', *Concilium,* pp. 79-80.

[8] Susin, 2000/2, p. 80

[9] Turner, 1968,p. 12.

[10] Baudrillard, Jean1990, *Revenge of the Crystal: Selected Writings on the Modern Object and its Destiny, 1968-1983,* Sydney, Pluto Press, p. 63.

[11] Wittgenstein, Ludwig 1974, *Philosophical Investigations,* Oxford, Blackwell, pp. 114, 48e.

[12] Mellick, J. D. S. 1982, *Portable Australian Authors: Henry Kingsley,* St. Lucia, Queensland University Press, pp. 202-3.

[13] Metz, Johan Baptist, 1980, *Faith in History and Society,* New York, Seabury Press, p. 114.

[14] Metz, 1980, pp. 112-3.

[15] Quoted in Sellick, R. G. 2002, *Venus In Transit: Australian Women Travellers, 1788-1930,* Fremantle, Fremantle Arts Centre Press, pp. 123-4.

[16] Caputo, John 1997, *The Prayers and Tears of Jacques Derrida: Religion Without Religion,* Bloomington and Indianapolis, Indiana University Press, p. 57.

[17] Finch, Henry Leroy 2001, *Simone Weil and the Intellect of Grace,* New York, Continuum, p. 84.

[18] Barnes, John (ed.) 1981, *Portable Australian Authors: Joseph Furphy.* St Lucia, University of Queensland Press, p. 65.

[19] Turner, 1968, p. 102.

[20] Eliade, Mircea 1974, *The Myth Of The Eternal Return: Or, Cosmos And History,* Princeton, Princeton University Press, p. 10.

[21] James, William 1979, *The Will to Believe, and Other Essays in Popular Philosophy,* Cambridge Mass., Harvard University Press, p. 17.

[22] Eliade, 1974, p. 153.

[23] James, 1957,p. 35.

[24] Baudrillard, 1990, p. 63.

[25] James, 1979, p.163.

[26] Gelder, Ken and Jane M. Jacobs 1998, *Uncanny Australia,* Melbourne, Melbourne University Press, p. xi.

[27] Gelder and Jacobs, 1998, p. 1.

[28] Wright, Stephen and Jean Saye-Adams 2000, *Sacred Space,* London, Harcourt, p. 25.

[29] Dunne, John 1978, *The Way Of All The Earth,* South Bend Indiana, University of Notre Dame Press, p. 56.

5. The paradox of Islam and the challenges of modernity

Kuranda Seyit

Islam today, it would seem, has become inflexible and intolerant towards the teachings and ideologies of the West. When in fact, its history shows that it has always been accommodating to other peoples and beliefs, especially Christianity and Judaism. Most people know something of Islam. For instance, that it is one of the three monotheisms or the Abrahamic faiths and that it has much in common with Christianity and Judaism. Yet, there is so much that we do not understand about Islam and its overall world view. Islam is centred on the notion of peace, justice and community, yet when we switch on our television sets or flick through the papers there is no peace, no justice and no community; actually there is more disunity, injustice and violence in the name of God – some would argue an Islamic God.

Is there a current crisis within Islam? Are Muslims simply lost or are there complex issues at hand which are preventing intellectual development? Has the 'sacred cow of Islam' been sacrificed or is it becoming more sacred than ever, so that it is beyond criticism? And is Islam compatible with modern Western secularism, and how does Islam negotiate the sacred?

The prophet of Islam once said, 'There is no religion in Islam'. Islam is not a recent doctrine or a new set of teachings, nor is it a new ideology. 'Islam' literally means to submit to your Creator and to surrender to the divine order that exists in the universe, or to what is referred to as *qadr* or destiny. This, in secular terms, means to submit to the natural laws and to obey the various truths that we as humans accept as just 'being'; for instance, the law of thermodynamics, the law of gravitation, the theory of relativity, molecular and quantum physics and so on. Islam accepts all these phenomena and submits to the omnipotent power that lies behind it.

For a Muslim, the core tenet of his faith is faith itself. Hence, to be a Muslim one must submit; that is, one who has surrendered to the concept of *Tawhid* or unity of being and one who has accepted *qadr*. This is like a large mirror that is held not before you or behind you but above you, so you can see not only your own image but all that was behind you and all that is ahead. It is more about what you will do and the actions that you will take than what you are bound to. A Muslim is in a state of submission to the sacred words that defines the way a Muslim lives, as the first man Adam had done, for he too was a Muslim.

Religion implies the belief and worship of a deity or deities and it is also a system or practice of a belief. Islam entwines all that it means to be human with the sacred; it is the conduit between our sacred heritage and the mundane existence upon Earth. Islam reminds us of our paradisaical origins, our place of creation, and our eventual home (to which we will return). Islam, therefore, is not simply a religion; it is nature and our common purpose and it is humankind's search for its innate understanding of the divine.

When Adam and Eve left their paradisaical abode and entered a new place, barren and rugged, the very first thing that they did was to build a shrine (in Mecca). The first place they arrived at became a place of sacredness—a sanctuary of peace and unity. Both Adam and Eve (Peace and blessing be upon them both) lived for a very long time, learning the secrets of existence and adapting to the hardships of life: the pains of childbirth, and the labours of working the fields, hunting for sustenance, and dealing with the mundane nature of existence. This tells us an important truth. It tells us that we, men and women, humankind, are here for a purpose, that this purpose is inherently linked to the sacred, and that the human mind must merge its rationality with sacredness and re-emerge as a whole, in unison with one's existence and environment. Therefore, natural laws, natural peace and universal being are a part of the religion of man. That is, religion and nature are inextricably linked to the divine order of existence.

From an Islamic viewpoint, it is natural for humans to be engaged in an awakening to the sacred presence in their own constitution. This presence may not be apparent to some at first, but will develop over time. It is a central component of Islamic theory that all humans are born with *fitra*. That is, an innate understanding of God, innocent and free from all forms of corruption. It is almost an instinctive aspiration toward transcendence. It is not until the human grows up and is indoctrinated with different ideologies and concepts that one takes a certain path or conviction of the truth as perceived by that person under the conditioning that he has been exposed to.

The prophet said, 'Every new-born child is born in a state of *fitra*, it is the parents (social influences) that make him Jew, Christian or Zoroastrian'. This is the idea of *fitra* that has aroused numerous theological commentaries, because it is so central to the Islamic concept of the sacred:

> So set thy face steadfastly to the one ever-true faith turning away from all that is false, in accordance with the natural disposition (fitra) which God has instilled into man; for not to allow any change to corrupt what God has thus created - this is the purpose of the one ever-true faith; but most people know it not.[1]

The Islam of the seventh century, which was initiated by Muhammed Ibn Abdullah, is merely a regurgitation and a conglomeration of all the preceding monotheistic teachings stemming from the same God of Christ, Moses, Abraham, Joseph, Zachariah, Job, John, David, Solomon, Noah and so forth, back to Adam. The beauty of Muhammed's teachings is that it completed the long line of revelations and confirmed the message that had so long ago been imparted to Adam to reinforce humankind's knowledge of the world and its purpose. Whereas preceding revelations came to specific communities, Muhammed's message was universal and eternal. Therefore, Islam is not the 1400 year old religion that it seems to be, it is older than Christianity, older than Judaism and even older than Hinduism or Shamanism; it is the original thought and the finality of revelation.

The revelations which make up the Qur'an were delivered by the archangel Gabriel over a period of 23 years, the first when Muhammed was 40, and the last in his sixty-third year, a few months before he died. Muhammed and the Meccans already knew much of the monotheism before their time; these were mostly taught as stemming from Abraham, and so elements of this faith were still practised. Of course, the teachings of Jesus were nominally accepted as well, and the highly ordered and morally sophisticated practices of the Jews were respected amongst the pagan Arabs. In general, the pure teachings of Abraham, Moses and Jesus had been neglected and the general code of conduct in society was relatively lawless and grossly barbaric, especially towards slaves, women and children (and also animals). Therefore Islam, as taught by the Prophet Muhammed, reiterated much of what Abraham had said in that there is no deity but Allah (the God). Idolatry was condemned and polytheism denounced by the Qur'an. But certain esoteric information that had never been recorded before under a divine writ was now entailed within the pages of the Qur'an.

Islam prescribed a number of laws that governed the way a Muslim should conduct his or her life, and it revolutionised societies forever. It taught us that men and women were equal. It put an end to infanticide and cruelty to slaves. It gave women the rights of equality, to inheritance, and to the ownership of property. It gave prisoners of war rights they had never imagined and it even gave animals and trees rights. Most important of all, it showed a pathway to peaceful co-existence and tolerance toward one's fellow human beings. Islam, as it came to be known, was a comprehensive way of life, and the *Shari'a* became a template for all Muslim societies. So to be Muslim meant to live by a certain standard that is explicated by the Qur'an and personified by the Prophet.

Islam, in this sense, is a new identity and a new society, and therefore it will have an associated and developed culture. When one takes an oath to become Muslim, he or she is surrendering to the natural laws that exist: the laws of one omnipotent Creator. All wrong-doings of the past are wiped clean and that person is re-born and re-united with their original *fitra*.

Theoretically, if a person declares himself a Muslim, he is renewing his relationship with God and allowing God to dictate the terms of his existence.

Islam is unique in that it did not create a new way of thinking or a new set of beliefs. Islam renewed humanity's relationship with the Earth and Muhammed was a reformer (guided by God) who changed the direction and state of the Arab people and affected the way people viewed the world forever.

There is no religion in Islam, as Islam and humanity are one and the same and cannot be divided into separate institutions. All human beings are in touch with the sacred, there are no barriers and no-one is excluded from access and equity.

The notion of religion as a distinctive practice is a relatively recent idea, founded in Western thought. In the sixteenth and seventeenth centuries, modern man tried to identify his relationship with God and to reinterpret faith. The new intellectuals began to think of ways of separating humans from God, and eventually from the state and from the purpose of being altogether. In Western Europe, religion was banished to the fringes as liberalism became the 'religion' of the West: secularism had begun to take root.

Paradoxically, it was under this new secularism that a new schizophrenia developed in the West. Islam was relieved of such a dichotomy and hence did not develop complex debates revolving around the place of religion in an ever-growing capitalist society. In the Islamic world, the sacred was preserved and remained a part of the public domain, albeit at the expense of political and economic progress.

This fateful dichotomy, upon which most of modernity's self-authentication hinges, owes its genesis to one of the bittersweet ironies of history. Hanna Arendt argues that its roots lie 'in the sacred nature of Roman politics' where religious and political activity could be considered almost as identical.[2] Arendt points out:

> For Romans the binding force of authority "more than advice and less than command" is closely connected to the religious force of auspices. Further, this conception of authority is similar to that of the *Sunnah* in the Islamic tradition: precedents, deeds of the ancestors and customs that grow out of them are deemed paradigmatic and binding. However, when the church succeeded in overcoming the anti-political and anti-institutional tendencies of the Christian faith and embarked upon her political career in the fifth century after Constantine the Great, she adopted the Roman distinction between power and authority.[3]

Waghid explains the process of secularisation more fully, and explains why it cannot occur in Islam:

> Secularisation is more than a process in the mind, a loss of religious belief and an acceptance of the scientific view of the world. It is an institutional arrangement and an ideational division of labour whereby the sacred is

separated from the realm of power. In the case of traditional Islamic societies where the sacred had no special retreats and the secular had no boundless freedom outside them, it went unnoticed.[4]

Manzoor further states that:

Although the Muslim state as an institution was all-pervasive and never had to contend with the challenge of the non-existent church, in terms of ideology it was a different matter all together. The state despite its absolute power never succeeded in establishing its autonomy and legitimacy and thus remained merely the coercive forearm of a political society that could have no pretence to any redemptive functions. The body politic of Islam expressed its ultimate aspirations through the sacred law, whose legitimate guardians were the *ulama* and not the sultan. In other words civil society was sovereign over state. And the ruler did not represent the body politic but merely embodied his personal rule or misrule. Or seen differently the state as the locus and seat of sovereignty did not exist.[5]

As the institutions of the Muslim community developed in the early centuries of the Islamic era, the people of knowledge or *ulama* emerged as a major grouping within Muslim societies. It is in this very noble body of scholars that the fate of Islam lay. In the thirteenth century, with the transition of power from the trustees of Islamic knowledge to the guardians of the state, the boundaries of the sacred also shifted, and in many ways the distinction was blurred. To this day the distinction is still in a state of confusion within the Islamic mindset.

Edward Shils writes that the intellectuals were responsible for 'the care of the sacred through the mastery, interpretation and exposition of sacred writings and the cultivation of the appropriate mental state or states were the first interests of the intellectuals'.[6] The importance of the *ulama* within Islamic society is reflected in a quote by the prophet namely, 'the scholars are the heirs of the prophets'. The famous fourteenth-century Muslim scholar Ibn Khaldoun, explained that this meant:

People who combine practical and theoretical knowledge of the law of religious scholars, the real heirs such as the jurists among the people of the second generation, the ancient Muslims, the four founders of the schools of law as well as those who took them as models.[7]

The *ulama* were not officially part of the Caliphate; they acted as critical intellectuals often providing powerful critiques of existing conditions. 'The ulama regarded themselves as the collective voice of the conscience of society'.[8]

Already by the thirteenth and fourteenth centuries, the lines were drawn between what might be thought of as the *ulama* bureaucrats and the *ulama* intellectuals.

For some the conviction developed that it was better to accept the decisions of earlier thinkers rather than to engage in independent, informed interpretation, while others saw such independent analysis as the continuing responsibility of appropriately learned scholars. This was the conflict over *taqlid* (imitation) and *ijtihad* (independent judgement).

Ijtihad plays an important role in understanding the development of Islamic theory and the science of interpretation. *Ijtihad* may be defined as independent reasoning and judgement used in cases when an issue is not clearly defined in the Qur'an or by the Sunnah. It is not an exact science and for many scholars a controversial course of action in the first place.

In the eleventh century, Abu Hamid al-Ghazzali (1058-1111) made a permanent impact on the way Muslims perceived their faith. He reverted to the practice of *ijitihad* and believed that he had the right to make fresh interpretations of the verses in the Qur'an and of Ahadith, previously accepted as authentic and immutable. The accepted standard practice of the time was called *taqlid* or 'to copy' or follow the interpretations made by previous scholars.

The 'gates of ijtihad' had been announced closed by the *ulama* since the middle of the tenth century. Islamic theology and jurisprudence hitherto had relied on the authority of the traditions that had been developed in the first three hundred years of Islam. The *ulama,* or intellectual class, had withdrawn inwards and their influence on the hierarchy was in decline. However, Islam could not develop without some relationship with the scholars and in the mid-nineteenth century, new forms of intellectualism were developing.

But several centuries before, there were scholars who challenged the conservatism of the time. Ibn Taymiyya (1263-1328), a great Hanbali scholar, stressed the need for all Muslims to follow the obligations of their faith. No-one was free from the obligation to encourage virtue and to condemn vice. Ibn Taymiyya claimed the right of *ijtihad* and used his independent judgement in rearticulating the general principles provided by the Qur'an and the *sunnah* (tradition). In his strong criticism of both political and communal life of his time and the way he articulated that critique he helped to define the intellectual's alternative to the stable *ulama* establishment that was emerging by the thirteenth century.

The *ulama* had developed as something different—as the people of knowledge, acting as intellectuals in Muslim societies. As officials, the *ulama* were a significant part of the state structure and the institutions of the *status quo* in the sixteenth century, at the peak of power of the Ottoman Empire.

The prophet said 'the nearer a man is to government the further he is from God'. The tension between the intellectuals and the powers comes ultimately from the constitutive orientation of the intellectuals towards the sacred. Within Islamic traditions, the critical Muslim intellectual tradition takes a *tajdid* (renewalist) rather than a romantic or scientific mode. In the Muslim world, three developments have been of special importance in the emergence of the Muslim activist intellectuals during the final decades of the twentieth century.

Firstly, as a part of the interaction with the West and the consequent westernisation and modernisation of the Muslim society, a grouping of secular intellectuals occurred. Secondly, there was a significant decline in the importance of the classically defined *ulama* among the intellectuals of Muslim societies. Thirdly, by the end of the nineteenth century a new kind of intellectual had emerged. In this new intellectual, characteristics of both the modern intellectual and the classical *ulama* were visible, at first often in an uncomfortable compromise, and then in increasingly effective synthesis.

The history of intellectuals in Muslim societies provides an important foundation for activist reforming intellectuals in the twentieth century. According to Esposito,

> After the first world war a new breed of intellectuals emerged, orientated in Western and secularist directions…Islam among the educated strata was absorbed into secular ideology…and the group that gained undisputed political ascendancy in both Egypt and the Fertile Crescent was the Muslim secularist.[9]

The best example of a secular model being successfully implemented in an Islamic society is arguably Turkey. However, by 1990 it was clear that the secular intellectuals and the political elite of which they were a part had been unable to transform their secularist and semi-secular ideologies into mass movements or to reconstruct the world view of the majorities in their societies in a more secularist way. The modernising and westernising secular intellectuals succeeded in providing the world view and visions for the political elite that had been created by the transformations of the past two centuries. Most states in the contemporary Muslim world are based on ideological foundations provided by the secular intellectuals in Muslim societies. By the 1990s, this form of secularism was being challenged by the older pure forms of secularism, even in countries like Turkey.

The failure of the old style *ulama* to provide any real alternative to the secular intellectuals in the nineteenth and early-twentieth centuries may be the single most important aspect of the rise of the contemporary Muslim activist intellectual. The failure of the secularist intellectuals to connect with the masses would give way to a modern, but not secular, alternative to both the conservative and secularist intellectuals. To a certain degree, the new intellectual's perspective peripheralised the old secular intellectuals and converted the traditional *ulama* into more activist Islamic advocates and reformers.

What modern thinkers attempted to do was to create a Muslim approach that could be both authentically Islamic and effectively modern. Esposito points out that,

> Tahtawi, a nineteenth-century Egyptian scholar who spent some time in Paris, believed it was necessary to adapt the *Shari'a* to new circumstances and that it was legitimate to do so…if the *ulama* are to interpret the *shari'a* in light of modern needs, they must understand what the modern world is.[10]

Tariq Ramadan, a contemporary writer based in Europe, talks about 'how to be at the same time fully Muslim and fully Western'.[11] Ramadan recognises that many young Muslims believe they have to make a choice between assimilating to Western culture and thus losing their own culture and isolating themselves from the mainstream culture. But he claims that there is no choice that has to be made. In *To Be a European Muslim*, he wrote,

> Whereas one might have feared a conflict of loyalties, one cannot but note that it is in fact the reverse…Loyalty to one's faith and conscience requires firm and honest loyalty to one's country: Shari'a requires honest citizenship.[12]

Other Muslims believe that *shari'a* is incompatible with modern European societies. One writer, Professor Bassam Tibi, believes that to acknowledge a meaningfully reformed Islam one must embrace the pluralistic spirit of the Western Enlightenment. He says,

> In the context of religious tolerance—and I write this as a Muslim—there can be no place in Europe for *Shari'a*…*Shari'a* is at odds with the secular identity of Europe and is diametrically opposed to secular European constitutions formulated by the people…secular democracy based on the separation of religion from politics; a universally accepted pluralism; and a mutually accepted secular tolerance. The acceptance of these values is the foundation of a civil society.[13]

But many more call for a progressive Islam that can blend in with Western secularism, and, since September 11, believe that it is crucial that Muslims assert their willingness to join the great Western tide of civil society and just liberalism.

D. Caldwell, religion producer for Beliefnet.com, has interviewed several Muslims who hold this view. One, Omid Safi, a Qur'anic scholar at Colgate University, sees Islam as a religion which holds the key to the future of humankind and through its universal brotherhood has the potential to unite the fundamental sacralisation of modern humanism and thought. Caldwell quotes Safi as saying, 'The sad fact of the matter is there are genuine voices of fanaticism in the Muslim community. How do these hateful voices function in our community? Why are we silent when they talk right next to us?'[14] According to Caldwell, Safi is frustrated by 'Muslims' lack of "active wrestling" with the faith':

> "On one hand, you have reformers who want to throw out the entire thing, and on the other hand, you have people who feel completely bound by it because one jurist said one particular thing in the 14th century", Safi said.

Mostly, average Muslims are exposed to what Safi calls 'testosterone Islam', run by men, many of them engineers and physicians, who are drawn to spare Wahhabi theology. Safi says their line of thinking goes like this: 'Islam is sick. We need to heal it. We need to do this and this and this.' Or: 'The circuit of Islam is broken. If we attach this and fix this, it will work.'[15]

A contemporary of Safi is South African progressive scholar Farid Esack. Caldwell's interview summarises Esack's views this way:

> "Muslims in general cannot live with people of another religion in a state of what I call 'coolness'".

> That is because, he says, "right now they have only two models for understanding their place in the world. The first is that of the oppressed as Muslims were in their early days in Mecca. The second is that of rulers, the way Muslims eventually lived in Medina."

> Esack says, however, "that embedded in the Qur'an is a story about a group of Muslims who lived in Abyssinia, a Christian kingdom. There they lived peacefully neither trying to convert Christians, nor being proselytized by Christians". "That's the way for Muslims to go", says Esack.[16]

These ideas are from a new breed of emerging modern intellectuals that believe that Islam can live hand-in-hand with the West. However, it appears that there are certain conditions for the merging of the ideas that will eventually happen over time. Some see it as a balance of social cohesion, and others see a transformation of Islamic thought which recognises the need for interpretation with caution and a reassessment of the relationship of Islam and the West, as had occurred in the middle centuries.

However, many of these scholars do not want to be seen as innovators (creating *Bidah*), by trying to change the inviolable and pure teachings of Islam that they believe were assembled 14 centuries ago. This is the position held by the swelling movement known as *Salafi*, which may be found in Indonesia, Afghanistan, Pakistan and Saudi Arabia, where it originated. Their strict observance of the traditions, and their reference point, beginning in the seventh century, are two major stumbling blocks to a friendship with the West.

They can do little to stop the natural inclination of Islam as a dynamic and changing phenomenon, however Islam changes almost at a constant rate and in every century. Islam has always had a strong tradition of critical thought. It has always been able to respond to the demands of a changing world, and it has, of course, been in the forefront of scientific research and discovery. After the devastating invasion of the Mongol hordes in the twelfth century, Muslims withdrew inwardly; the *Golden Age* was over, there was little scope for debate and discussion, and, hence, Islam began its slow decline.

It is incongruous from an Islamic historian's perspective, but Islam today appears to be stuck in a quagmire of ignorance, superstition and conflict. Islamic thought and philosophy seem out of place in a fast and furious twenty-first century. It would appear to be inflicted with a serious malaise. But is there something more complex behind the deceleration of what was once a flourishing empire of ideas? The neo-conservatives of America would hope that the emergence of twentieth-century Western democracy and secularism as a dominant force in the world has overshadowed Islam's revival and foreshadowed its painful demise towards a cataclysmic end. The fight to 'put the sick man of Europe out of its misery' once and for all by an injection of modern secularism, and to discard Islam on the trash heap of previous victims of 'isms' (Feudalism, Monarchism, Nazism, Fascism, Communism, Socialism and others) and failed ideologies appears to be gaining momentum.

Muhammed was, in his century, a great prophet, a statesman and above all a reformer. He, like Zoroaster, Buddha, Krishna and even (more recently) Gandhi and King, revolutionised the way people think. He defied the common law, upset the *status quo* and built a new society based on God's law: this society respected order, compassion, rationality and justice. So he found a common ground between universal Islam and humanity. We refer to it as Islam but we could easily call it the Arabian Revolution, and frame its evolution in the same context as the French revolution. The laws of Muhammed as embodied in the words of God through the *Qur'an* preceded the *Magna Carta*, the French Declaration on the Rights of Man and the United Nations Universal Declaration on Human Rights in 1948. So as a natural development of societal laws and conduct, we can see a definite pattern of reform and change. The Arab world was transformed into something it had never seen before and could not imagine; not only in material wealth, but in spiritual, scientific, technological, artistic, literary and cultural wealth. The renewal of Islam, or submission, was to reintroduce the notion of justice and freedom, equality, brotherhood and tolerance, and, most significantly, virtue and chivalry into a world that was generally recognised as seeped in ignorance and barbarism.

What we as modern universal thinkers must recognise is that Islam is a part of our traditions and played a significant role in the development of Western human thought. Therefore, there is no need to reform Islam per se, but there is a need to re-shape our approaches, and our relationships, and to treat each other with acceptance and dignity. Let me stress that re-interpreting the texts is not reforming them. The prophet said that we would need to do exactly that for every age, and to apply critical thinking with balance and reason.

Islam is intrinsically a part of the natural law and the cosmological nature of life. Muslims, although they admit to practising certain customs and traditions that were initiated by Adam and Abraham, and reiterated by Muhammed, do so out of their natural instinct or *fitra*, and follow a path that will lead them to the sacred and to eternal happiness. This is perceived as religion.

However, whatever we refer to it as, the Arabian Revolution or Islam, the ideology borne out of it, as an entity it depends on the interpretation of the sacred texts and traditions by expert scholars, and the direction of its future depends on the potential for independent interpretation or *ijtihad*.

For Islam science is sacred. Man is both a spiritual and physical entity. The path to God is through our investigation of the physicality and transcendence of the same reality. For Muslims, every act is sacred, and every passing of time is impossible without the permission of God. Yet, the challenge for Muslims is the application of their sacred foundations to the mundane physicality of this realm: the realm of existence. We are in a constant state of flux and people must continually adapt and reshape their understanding of this nature, and to look for the signs that remind us of our original nature. The merging of the two, without compromising either one, is the penultimate challenge to succeed, not only as one in a state of submission, but also as one might in a state of vice-regency. This is the responsibility that humankind has accepted.

There is no doubt that there are fundamental clashes with secularism, and to some degree with Western liberalism, although the commonalties are far more abundant. Islam, particularly in the West, can co-exist with liberal democracy, and in fact, enhance it and further enrich its very fabric. *Islam* as we know it must open the doors of *ijtihad* to be able to cope with modernity.

Let me leave you with a quote from the father of modern rational Islam, al-Ghazali,

> Yet some of the ulama (scholars) deny the possibility of love for God and say that it means nothing more than persevering in obedience, while true love of God is impossible, except metaphorically. They also deny any intimacy with Him, or passionate longing for Him, or the delight of confiding in Him, and other consequences of his love. Thus we must of necessity deal with the matter here.

Whoever loves God for other than God's sake does so from ignorance, for among those of insight there is no true beloved save God Most High, and none deserving of love save Him.[17]

ENDNOTES

[1] *The Holy Qur'an 30:30.*

[2] Arendt, Hanna 1991, Modernity and the Holocaust, cited in S. P. Manzoor, 1995, 'Desacralisng Secularism', The American Journal of Islamic Social Sciences, vol. 12, no. 4, pp. 545-59.

[3] Arendt, 1991, cited in Manzoor, 1995.

[4] Waghid, Y. 1996, 'In Search of a Boundless Ocean of New Skies: Human Creativity is a Matter of Amal, Jihad and Ijtihad', *The American Journal of Islamic Social Sciences,* vol. 13, no. 3, pp. 353-62.

[5] Manzoor, 1995.

[6] Shils, Edward 1932, *Intellectuals Encyclopaedia,* cited in J. L. Esposito and John O. Voll 2001, *Makers of Contemporary Islam,* New York, Oxford University Press.

[7] Mottahedeh, R. 1980, *Loyalty and leadership in an early Islamic society,* Princeton, Princeton University Press.

[8] Mottahedeh, 1980.

[9] Esposito and Voll, 2001.

[10] Esposito and Voll, 2001.

[11] Ramadan, T. 1999, *To be a European Muslim,* Leicester, The Islamic Foundation.

[12] Ramadan, 1999.

[13] Tibi, Bassam 2002, 'A Plea for a Reform Islam', in Susan Stern and Elisabeth Seligmann (eds), *The End of Tolerance?* London, Nicholas Brearly.

[14] Safi, cited in Caldwell, D. 2002, 'Something major is happening. Are we witnessing the beginnings of an Islamic Reformation?', <Beliefnet.com, http://www.beliefnet.com/story/92/story_9273_1.html?rnd=94>

[15] Safi, cited in Caldwell, 2002.

[16] Esack, cited Caldwell, 2002.

[17] Ghazali, *Ihya 'Ulum al-Din (Revivification of the Sciences of Religion).*

Section II. Sacrilege and the Sacred

6. Stretching the sacred

Elizabeth Burns Coleman and Kevin White

The term sacred tends to be used interchangeably with a wide variety of terms: terms like mystical, religious, divine, magical, and, most commonly, spiritual and religious. In 2002, the Humanities Research Centre at The Australian National University ran a conference entitled 'Locations of Spirituality: "Experiences" and "Writings" of the "Sacred"'. All of these topics were addressed in the papers presented at the conference. On one level this suggests that the term 'sacred' is inherently vague.

Yet there are some features the uses seem to have in common. A writer for the *Encyclopedia of Religion and Society*, Edward Bailey, has suggested that the realm of those things we might call sacred is generally recognised as possessing four characteristics:

> in experience, it is special, and even unique; in value, it is important, even all demanding; in consciousness, it is fundamental, even primordial; in communication, it is dynamic, yet ineffable…All these characteristics issue a single consequence that is easily described but is less a separate quality than an aspect or by product of all of them: It imposes "taboos", restrictions.[1]

The term 'sacred' tends to be used synonymously with 'religious', and it is not uncommon to see people using the terms interchangeably. Yet, when someone says 'this is sacred land', they may or may not be introducing a particular religious framework into a discussion. But they are implying that something normative follows from their statement. The issue that we wish to explore in this paper is the normative force of the attribution of sacred as a quality. What does it mean to say that something is sacred, and does it always have the same normative force across different usages?

The term sacred is stretched beyond 'religion', leaving traditional truths and virtues behind it, and used interchangeably with terms like 'spiritual'. A person need not recognise the authority of any religion, and may insist upon a highly individualistic claim to the truth or validity of their experience. Certain kinds of experience might be considered an experience of the 'sacred'. We might include amongst these altered states of consciousness such as ecstasy, a special way of knowing or hyper-consciousness, visions and auditions, the experience of paranormal or occult phenomena, or the experience of a connection with the earth, for example, as in 'nature mysticism'.

The term sacred is also applied secularly, in relation to such things as the State, memorials and ANZAC Day, and even property. The stretching of 'the sacred' to this application of the term sacred was made possible through the analysis of the concept within the social sciences, in particular, by Emile Durkheim. At the same time, Durkheim's analysis 'closes down' other applications of the term, such as the use of the term sacred to personal feelings and spiritual sentiments. Durkheim's concept of the sacred suggests that the use of the term has normative force only in connection with authority, and that therefore the personal use has none.

In the first part of the paper, we will consider Durkehim's analysis of the sacred, and the way this has been applied within the social sciences, and extended to secular society. The second part addresses Durkheim's idea that the sacred and profane are necessary, and opposite, categories and the normative content of the concept. Anthropologists have criticised Durkheim's analysis on the basis that the binary does not seem to operate in every society. Different metaphysical conceptions, as well as different understandings of the relationship between religion, spirituality and secular institutions and 'the sacred' have different implications for what might be considered taboo. Moreover, the duality sacred/profane does not seem to fully explain the normative content of the relationship in its common usages. In the third part, we will suggest a third way of understanding the normative content of the claim that something is sacred—and argue that the mobilization of the term sacred may involve different, and heterogeneous norms.

Durkheim and 'the sacred' in the social sciences

Before Durkheim, in the works of Tylor,[2] Mueller[3] and Fraser,[4] religion was considered as a property of the individual, as the individual's reaction to nature, or a series of delusions. Even William James did not break with this tradition. For William James the sacred and its experience is variable, dependent on the individual, and has its authority from the psychological experience of the individual. His focus is on religious feelings and impulses as related by individuals. He ignores the 'institutional branch of religion' completely focusing on 'that which lives itself out within the private breast'.[5] Alternatively, for Durkheim the sacred is specific and independent of the individual, based in communal action and ritual, evoking emotional responses of belonging and awe in the believer. He specifically criticises James for neglecting institutions and churches. The sacred is neither about feelings of brotherhood or a matter of voluntary association. It is a social imperative that affirms society and binds the individual to it. Against James, Durkheim argues that religion is not about belief in god(s) but in the distinction between the sacred and the profane. This was a very powerful analytic move on Durkheim's part and substantially shaped the sociology of religion.

Durkheim's approach was itself shaped by William Robertson Smith's *Lectures on the Religion of the Semites* [6] (1889) which argues that the sacrificial meal between god and men produces a sacral community and which Durkheim read in 1912, and Fustel Coulanges', *The Ancient City* [7] (1901) in which Coulanges argued that the religion of Ancient Rome reflects the social structure of Roman society.[8]

As always Durkheim is arguing against liberalism and pragmatism. No account of social life can be based on contractual theories, nor is a religion a set of 'truths' which hold good because they work for the individual (James' position). Rather religious beliefs provide the basis for social action and are based on the truth of society. What does religion function to do? It creates a social bond; it remakes social commitments through the 'effervescence'; it produces individuals who are versed in sacrifice and asceticism, which result in altruism and social service; and in bringing the group together around collective ritual it maintains the collective memory of the group, thereby producing continuity over generations.[9] As Durkheim puts it in *The Elementary Forms of the Religious Life*, religion is,

> the way societies become conscious of themselves and their history...The gods are no other than collective forces personified and hypostasised in material form. Ultimately, it is the society that is worshipped by the believers; the superiority of the gods over men is that of the group over its members. The early gods were the substantive objects which served as symbols to the collectivity and for this reason became representations of it.[10]

Durkheim attacks, then, individualist accounts of religious experience and provides his famous definition of religion as that 'unified system of beliefs and practices relative to sacred things, that is to say, things set apart and forbidden—beliefs and practices which unite into one single moral community called a Church all those who adhere to them'.[11] The importance of this definition is that religion is defined in terms of the sacred, not the sacred in terms of religion. This allows Durkheim to subsequently explore the non-religious aspects of the sacred in his exploration of what is going to hold a society with a weak *conscience collective* together.

Durkheim develops his argument on two fronts. On the one hand he argues that religion is a manifestation of the collective values of society. On the other, society is held together by religious beliefs. Religion is thus central to social solidarity and represents social solidarity. Durkheim's two arguments can be labelled as a 'religion to society' analysis, and as a 'society to religion' analysis.

Religion to society

Durkheim sees religion as the deep grammar of society because religion is the source of social norms; and social norms have the quality of religious obligation. Religion is the pre-contractual foundation of social solidarity. It is custom, ritual and morality that make contracts binding. As is well known, Durkheim also locates the categories of thought in religion.

Society to religion

Religion is a social fact. All societies are based on collective representations. But the religion is not just a collective representation. It is the symbol of the collective identity. It stands above any given collective representation, integrating all of them. As Pickering[12] puts Durkheim's position, the society-religion and the religion-society circuit is that the sacred is 'a fundamental element in the ordering of society' and the representation of collective ideals and beliefs.

It is important to note that Durkheim is defining religion in terms of the sacred, not the sacred in terms of religion. This moves him away from his institutional definition of religion as a church and generalises the concept of the sacred beyond religion. 'The sacred is the concept associated with the collective ideas represented through religious symbols and metaphors'. There can be no society without the sacred, since the sacred is society's idealised vision of itself. As Durkheim puts it:

> There can be no society which does not feel the need of upholding and reaffirming at regular intervals the collective sentiments and collective ideas which make its unity and its personality. Now this moral remaking cannot be achieved except by means of reunions, assemblies and meetings where individuals, being closely united to one another, reaffirm in common their common sentiments, hence come ceremonies which do not differ from regular religious ceremonies, either in their object, the results they produce or the processes employed to obtain the result.[13]

With the decline of religion, Durkheim suggests that nationalist sentiment and national ceremonies provide social cohesion. In *Professional Ethics and Civic Morals*[14] Durkheim points to 'a cult of the state' worshipped by citizens in which patriotism, 'the ideas and feelings as a whole which bind the individual to a certain state', performs the function of the sacred.

Another location of sacred, Durkheim suggests, is the 'cult of the individual'. As the division of labour becomes more complex, society invests more in each individual, resulting in the individual becoming sacred. 'Morality would no longer be morality if it had no element of religion…The respect which we have for the human being is distinguishable only very slightly from that which the faithful of all religions have for the objects they deem sacred'.[15] 'Society has consecrated the individual and made him pre-eminently worthy of respect'.[16] While Durkheim had developed this theme in *Suicide* and in *The Division of Labor in Society*, its strongest statement is to be found in his essay 'Individualism and the Intellectuals' in which he states that the:

> human person *(personne humaine)*, the definition of which is like the touchstone which distinguishes good from evil, is considered sacred in the ritual sense of the word. It partakes of the transcendent majesty that churches of all time lend to their gods; it is conceived of as being invested with that mysterious property which creates a void about sacred things, which removes them from vulgar contacts and withdraws them from common circulation. And the respect which is given comes precisely from this source. Whoever makes an attempt on a man's life, on a man's liberty, on a man's honor, inspires in us a feeling of horror analogous in every way to that which the believer experiences when he sees his idol profaned. Such an ethic is therefore not simply a hygienic discipline or a prudent economy of existence; it is a religion in which man is at once the worshipper and the god.[17]

He also says the same thing about property: Property is property only if it is respected, that is to say, held sacred.[18] This is explained by his insistence that the right of property consists in essence as 'the right to withdraw a thing from common usage', and that this feature of property is shared by 'all religious and sacred things'.[19]

What all these things that might be considered sacred have in common is that they are exclusionary. Durkheim says,

> The feature that distinguishes the sacred entities is that they are withdrawn from general circulation; they are separate and set apart. The common people cannot enjoy them. They cannot even touch them. Those who would have a kinship, as it were, with sacred things of this kind, can alone have access to them—that is, those who are sacred as they are: the priests, the great, the magistrates, especially where the latter have a sacred character'.[20]

This extension of the sacred away from institutional churches has been influential in twentieth century social theory. For Berger, following Durkheim, cognitively, the sacred orders chaos and a 'rumour of angels'[21] is present even in modern society. Callois,[22] like Durkheim, analysed religion as the deep grammar of society, even in modern societies, arguing that public space is divided into the sacred and profane. In Canberra, for example, we have Parliament, and the War Memorial, laid out as the axis of the city, with Anzac Parade linking them. Industrial suburbs, which include the brothels, are located on the outskirts of the city, as are the tips. The sacred is thus an organising factor in the way we lay out our cities. In this analysis, at the centre of modern societies is the sacred. A similar argument had been advanced by de Tocqueville in 1832, and then most influentially in the twentieth century by Bellah[23] with his concept of civil religions. Thus it is argued that modern societies are deeply religious, if secularised, and they have to recognise the power of the sacred in their own societies. Parsons has suggested, and subsequently Habermas, that the normative content of modernity is produced by 'the Hebrew morality of justice in the Old Testament and the Christian ethics of love in the New Testament'.[24] Modernity is still sacred, if not religious.

The moral force of the sacred-profane distinction Durkheim tends to equivocate between religion and sacred in his texts. The religious is defined in terms of the sacred, but he will often refer to the religious, rather than the sacred, as the source of moral rules.

The sacred may be defined as those things set apart, and identified by taboos, which set it apart from the profane. The profane, the opposite of the sacred, is not a clear concept. Durkheim never defines it although commentators have listed its characteristics as 'ordinariness', 'work', 'individual', or the 'body'.

According to Durkheim, in both modern and pre-modern life, morality can be defined by the interdictions of taboos around the sacred. 'It is impossible to imagine on the evidence,' Durkheim states, 'that morality should entirely sever its unbroken historic association with religion without ceasing to be itself'.[25] In *Professional Ethics and Civic Morals* he argues, 'Man is a moral being only because he lives within established societies. There are no morals without discipline and authority…Morals do not seem like obligations to us, that is, they do not seem like morals to us—and therefore we can have no sense of duty—unless there exists about us and above us a power which gives them sanction'.[26] What is clear in this comment is that the moral injunctions are those that preserve the sacred—and are based on a rules/duty model of morality. These rules are the sanctions or taboos around the sacred. In a sense, the taboos maintain and preserve the sacred. Durkheim goes on to acknowledge that individuals develop their own image of God and spirituality, but this cannot be a source of ethics for Durkheim. He argues that it is the authoritarian, and not the individual, conception of the sacred that is the source of ethics on the grounds that if the authority of the state is weakened, the sense of duty and therefore of ethics is also weakened, and this leads to a general anarchy and immorality.

Importantly here, individual experience or sentiment could not be considered 'sacred' on Durkheim's account, and cannot generate any moral force. As pointed out in the introduction, this is one of the most common features of the contemporary usage of the term. This is not necessarily a significant point against Durkheim's analysis, as it could be that the usage is a form of rhetoric that borrows its force from the Durkheimian juridical sense. Furthermore, to the extent that Durkheim's definition is stipulative, a way of using terms to identify and discuss a specific phenomenon, there is no reason not to exclude some uses. More pertinent objections are that the distinction does not seem to account for the morality and behaviour that Durkheim suggests it does, and that even where the distinction is found in other cultures, it does not necessarily have the features Durkheim suggests it does. This evidence points to Durkheim failing to give a definition that will achieve what he sets out to explain cross-culturally—the relationship between social structure and religion.

The sacred-profane distinction and the effects of 'effervescence'

The first objection is that it is not clear that the taboos that maintain and preserve the sacred can also generate and explain altruism and social service through 'effervescence'. Durkheim appears to be using one ethical code or structure, that is a rules/duty framework to explain the existence of virtue ethics.

On one level, Durkheim's definition of the sacred is not unlike that of the Catholic Church. What both rule out is the idea that 'sacrilege' could ever involve something other than a rule by an authority. For instance, the *New Advent Catholic Encyclopaedia* defines the sacred as a juridical category—only those things that the Church has decided are sacred are sacred, the sacred in this sense is something that has been consecrated, it is a special status. Joseph Delany writes,

> Theologians are substantially agreed in regarding as sacred that and that only which by a public rite and by Divine of ecclesiastical institution has been dedicated to the worship of God. The point is that the public authority must intervene; private initiative, no matter how ardent in devotion or praiseworthy in motive, does not suffice. Attributing a sacred character to a thing is a juridical act, and as such is a function of the governing power of the Church.[27]

This means that, according to the writers of the *New Advent*, there are a great many religious things that are not sacred. Hence they make a distinction between crimes of sacrilege, properly so called, which is the violation or injurious treatment of a sacred object, and transgressions against the virtue of religion, such as superstition, blasphemy and perjury, simony, idolatry and superstition, that might be commonly, and improperly, referred to as sacred.

While there is some similarity between Durkheim and the Catholic definition of the sacred, there are also significant differences. For one thing, Durkheim reduces all morality to a juridical morality, whereas the Catholic definition does not.

Durkheim appears straightforwardly wrong on this point, and there appear to be many moral codes that are not based in the sacred as he describes it—for example, the ethics of care, or loyalty to friends, and civic and religious virtues—that cannot be explained by reference to an authoritative source. Secondly, the *New Advent* recognises that although not crimes against the sacred, there are other moral values associated with religion, including a number of virtues.

Rules spell out a minimal action—they do not reflect aspirations. No-one is obliged to become a saint, or to live a life of devotion, even if they are expected to observe the rules of a religion, and practise, to the extent that they are able, the virtues. However, they are excused for failing to achieve virtues in a way that they are not excused for failing to observe rules. Durkheim might still argue that the virtues, such as good citizenship or devotion, are based on collective representations of the good, but he cannot argue that the ethics involved in these collective representations all depend on a rule-bound moral code.

The sacred-profane distinction is not universal

As W. S. F. Pickering[28] points out, from its earliest reception the duality of the sacred and profane in *Elementary Forms* has been seriously questioned. Even pupils loyal to Durkheim such as Marcel Granet[29] found in his empirical work on religion in China that the dualism was not marked. Evans-Pritchard,[30] in his studies of the Azande rejected it flatly, arguing that the two categories intermingled and were inseparable and did not negate each other. Most damaging though has been the work of Stanner,[31] based as it is on fieldwork with Australian Aboriginals. Remember that the basis of Durkheim's distinction between the sacred and profane is that religious thought reflects social organisation. Durkheim asserts that since no individual can be a member of two moieties that it is this radical separation that is reflected in the religious thought and the basis of the distinction between the sacred and the profane. Stanner's fieldwork shows that in fact members of different moieties do intermingle and that the moieties are not radically distinct. Groups can and do intermix while still preserving their identities and hence neither their social organisation, nor their conceptual thinking, reflects the dualism that Durkheim ascribes to them. What these objections show is that the distinction between sacred and profane that Durkheim develops does not explain all the features of societies that recognise something like a realm of the sacred, and that the concept of the sacred does not necessarily have the features that Durkheim suggests.

Part of this divergence between theory and reality can be explained by the fact that there is an equivocation in Durkheim's concept of the binary, as there is in the word 'profane' itself. The profane may simply mean 'not sacred', but it also has a meaning of being irreligious, and a misuse or abuse of the sacred, which might be termed the 'anti-sacred'. That these are different binaries can be shown logically. If, like Durkheim, you define the sacred as that which is set apart, then the profane defined as non-sacred, that is, as the every-day or ordinary, is a necessary condition for the concept. It is impossible to imagine a world in which some things are set apart, but nothing is ordinary. However, the profane as 'anti-sacred', that is, as acts against the sacred, is not a necessary condition for the concept of the sacred. While the sacred as 'set apart and preserved by taboos' requires rules to establish the sacred as a social fact, it does not require anyone to break those rules. It is possible to imagine a world in which there are things that are sacred, but that no-one ever breaks the rules. However, it is not necessary that we do define 'the sacred' as that which is set apart.

In his fieldwork, Jack Goody found that the Lo Dagaa of northern Ghana make no recognisable distinction between the natural and the supernatural. He wrote: 'But neither do the Lo Dagaa appear to have any concepts at all equivalent to the vaguer and not unrelated dichotomy between the sacred and the profane'.[32] The fact that the sacred is not universal should not surprise us, as different cultures also understand the world in different ways. The ways in which the different groups and people explain the world, and the relationship between the spiritual and natural world, will affect the usefulness of the term. If you think that God, or the spirit of the world, is immanent, you will have a world in which the entire world is endowed with spiritual importance. If you describe this idea of 'spiritual importance' as the sacred, everything will be sacred, however, the conception of the sacred you will be using will be nothing like that which Durkheim uses, because there is nothing that distinguishes it from the ordinary. However, as we will argue in the next section of this paper, this does not mean that your usage cannot have normative force, merely that the normative force of the claim will be nothing like Durkheim's sacred-profane distinction. In the next section of the paper we intend to analyse some of the common uses of the term, and the norms associated with their use.

The uses of the term 'sacred' and their normative content

So what does it mean when some-one says 'this land is sacred'? Following Wittgenstein's dictum that meaning is use, some theologians are now exploring the concept of the sacred in terms of its usage, giving up on the attempt at a definition. As we will show, adopting this approach this does not necessarily mean giving up Durkheim's analysis, but it does recognise the heterogeneity of moral sentiments, and give a fuller account of the ethical force of the use of the term.

For instance, Frederick Ferre and James Ross suggest that religious language serves a number of related functions:

- The expressive—that is, language to express and evoke certain feelings;
- The pragmatic—that is, language to modulate and facilitate behaviour;

- The performative—language that actually accomplishes certain kinds of behaviours, such as confirmation, baptism and marriage; and
- The cognitive—language that involves a commitment to certain facts about the world, as well as to a vision of life based on those facts.[33]

However, if, as has been assumed, the invocation of the term sacred always includes a normative force or taboo, then it always contains some kind of pragmatic force about the modulation of behaviour. Moreover, analysing the invocation of the term sacred is more specific than analysing 'religious language' in general. Hence, for this to address our question, what is the normative force of the use of the term 'sacred', we will need to adapt the analysis. We intend to categorise the use of the term sacred into three uses, giving up pragmatic as a separate category: these uses are expressive, aspirational, and juridical.

The expressive use of the term sacred involves people's feelings and intuitions. This might include what has been called by Antoine Vergote[34] the pre-religious experience; for example, experiences that focus our existence in the world and its meaning. This would include 'nature mysticism', the world and its existence (as in some physicists' response to the universe), the love we have for another, or the ethical quest. Vergote argues that these experiences all have in common the sense that they are 'supported and penetrated by a transcendent' but are not 'religious experiences', which he defines as the immediate presence or given-ness of the divine. We will also include in this category experiences of altered states that might be termed 'spiritual' or altered states of consciousness in general, such as out of body experiences, or a general sense of a divine presence. The expressive, for example, excludes us from commentary. It is protected from criticism by being too personal, a disclosure that does not allow a point of criticism or jest without offence. The taboo is a taboo based on the respect for persons and their feelings. Consider, for example, roadside memorials to the dead, the symbol and expression of love and remembrance. For Durkheim, such memorials could not be considered sacred—they are individual, sentimental, and do not involve a collective representation. Yet at the same time, they are left untouched by vandals. The taboos surrounding the desecration of memorials need not be, as Durkheim suggests, merely due to the representations as representations of the state or civic duties.

Aspirational uses include, on this account, in addition to a sense of presence of the divine, or a transcendent good, a commitment to a way of life. This might be akin to mystical experiences, and conversion. We are borrowing here not only from the idea of what Ferres calls a cognitive use of religious language, but from William James, who discusses conversion in terms of how a person is changed through experience: he argues that in addition to an experience of some kind, a person who undergoes spiritual conversion attains a new set of values, a way of life in the world. Similarly, the mystical experience is associated with a direct experience of the divine, and a commitment to a way of life. The important point here is not that it is an intuition of the immediacy of the divine, but that it translates itself into a way of acting in the world, hence the choice of the term aspirational—by which we mean acting on the basis of a 'truth'. The mystical appears to involve a virtue ethics, an attempt to lead a way of life, and a driven-ness to achieve it.

The third category, the juridical, includes the Durkheimian concept of the sacred as set apart, and involves the recognition of rule-based sanctions, as well as the recognition of what we have been discussing as the anti-sacred. The juridical concept is deontological, and based on a respect for authority and tradition.

In her abstract for the Locations of Spirituality conference, Diana James wrote:

> One early morning I was driving west along a familiar dirt road through sand dune and desert oak country. The sky ahead changed gradually from dark blue to pale as light seeped in. When the first spears of the sun shot the spinifex with gold, I stopped and jumped out of the car. My face turned to greet the sun, the eternal fire burning on the rim of the world between earth and sky. Then I knew the sun was the Son, the light of the world. Born of the union of mother earth and father sky. The young desert oaks stood still in reverence as new initiates, while their elders intoned a hymn played by the wind of dawn...The realm of the sacred must be entered and understood in it's own [sic] terms. The tools of rationality are clumsy and inappropriate in this non-material dimension of reality. Sacred space is alive with paradoxes, mystery and magic. Whether it be a cathedral well or a rockhole in the desert, it contains the water of life.[35]

James's comments are not deontological, and do not recognise the distinction between a cathedral as a sacred space, consecrated through the church, and a rock hole. She draws on religion, but recognises none. Nor is her experience related to some kind of virtue ethic about the relationship between land and humans and the land. Rejecting rationality, and not invoking a virtue ethics that might imply 'failure' of some kind, it also rejects criticism.

Contrast this with Michael Williams's abstract, for his paper at the same conference, 'Journeying with Respect':

> This presentation will be a ranging commentary on my life's journey—reflecting on how I came to this point. It will be my attempt to make sense of things as I see them and how they have come to be in my life. It will draw on my families [sic] stories and the way that the several generations of my family have been touched by an insistence on/of the efficacy of our old ways, our law and how respect for all these things have influenced my own life and the affairs of other things—how

things, people, places and broader have been affected by a 'taking of care' approach to responsibilities.[36]

Williams, an Aboriginal man from South East Queensland, makes reference to a juridical concept of the sacred; what is sacred is sacred by law, the law gives obligations and duties. What he says can be entered into, debated and discussed as an interpretation of law.

These people are saying different things, and the word sacred should not be interpreted as meaning the same things in these cases. It is based on a different conceptual understanding of the world, or metaphysics, and has different implications for action. One question it does raise is the issue of intolerance. Where spiritualism sees itself as being free from the constraints and dogmatism of organised religion, one claim (that based on religious law) is debatable, while the other (based on personal sensibility) is not. In conclusion, we do need to extend the term sacred to the personal, but at the same time, we need to recognise that different metaphysical conceptions of the world, and different experiences, will produce different normative implications. To understand the sacred, we need to pay closer attention to these metaphysical frameworks, and to allow a broader understanding of its normative force.

ENDNOTES

[1] Swatos, W. H. Jr. (ed.) 1998, *Encyclopaedia of Religion and Society*, Hartford Institute for Religion Research, Hartford Seminary, Walnut Creek, Altamira Press, <http://hirr.hartsem.edu/ency/Sacred.htm>

[2] Tylor, E. B. 1891, *Primitive Culture: Researches into the Development of Mythology, Philosophy, Religion, Language Art and Custom*, London, J. Murray.

[3] Muller, F. M. 1893 *Introduction to the Science of Religion*, London, Longman Green.

[4] Fraser, J. G. 1923-27, *The Golden Bough: A Study in Magic and Religion*, London, Mamillan.

[5] James, W. 1985 [1902], *The Varieties of Religious Experience*, London, Penguin.

[6] Smith. W. R. 1907, *Lectures on the Religion of the Semites*, London, A. and C. Black.

[7] De Coulanges, F. 1900, *The Ancient City*, Boston.

[8] Pickering, W. 1984, *Durkheim's Sociology of Religion*, London, Routledge and Kegan Paul, p. 47.

[9] Wach, J. 1949, *Sociology of Religion*, Chicago, University of Chicago Press.

[10] Durkheim, E. 1965 [1915], *The Elementary Forms of the Religious Life*, trans. J. W. Swain, New York, Free Press.

[11] Durkheim, 1965, p. 62.

[12] Pickering, 1984, p. 187.

[13] Durkheim, 1965, pp. 474-5.

[14] Durkheim, E. 1953, *Professional Ethics and Civic Morals*, Westport, Greenwood Press, p. 73.

[15] Durkheim, E. 1974, *Sociology and Philosophy*, New York, Free Press, p. 68.

[16] Durkheim, 1974, p. 72.

[17] Durkheim, E. 1973, 'Individualism and the Intellectuals', in R. Bellah, (ed.) *Emile Durkheim on Morality and Society*, Chicago, University of Chicago Press, p. 46.

[18] Durkheim, 1953, p. 159.

[19] Durkheim, 1953, pp. 142-3.

[20] Durkheim, 1953, p. 143.

[21] Berger, P. 1969, *A Rumour of Angels: Modern Society and the Rediscovery of the Supernatural*, New York, Doubleday.

22 Callois, R. 1939, *L'Homme et la Sacre*, Paris, Gallimard.

23 Bellah, R. 1967, 'Civil Religion in America', *Daedulus*, no. 96, pp. 1-21.

24 Habermas, J. 1999, 'A Conversation About God and the World' in J. Habermas and E. Mendieta (eds) *Reason and Religion*, Cambridge, Polity, p. 427. Parsons, T. 1999, 'Christianity and Modern Industrial Society', in B. S. Turner (ed.) *The Talcott Parsons Reader*, Oxford, Blackwell.

25 Durkheim, 1974, p. 69.

26 Durkheim, 1953, p. 73.

27 Delany, Joseph F. 2003, 'Sacrilege', *New Advent Catholic Encyclopaedia*, <http://www.newadvent.org/cathen/13321a.htm>, viewed 16 January 2006.

28 Pickering, 1984, pp. 143-9.

29 Granet, M. 1975 [1922], *The Religion of the Chinese People*, trans. M. Freedman, Oxford, Basil Blackwell.

30 Evans-Pritchard, E. 1937, *Witchcraft, Oracles and Magic Among the Azande*, Oxford, Clarendon Press.

31 Stanner, W. 1967, 'Reflections on Durkheim and Aboriginal Religion', in M. Freedman (ed.), *Social Organization: Essays Presented to Raymond Firth*, London, Frank Cass.

32 Goody, J. 1961, 'Religion and Ritual: The Definitional Problem', *British Journal of Sociology*, no. 12, pp. 142-64, quotation at p. 151.

33 See <http://members.optusnet.com.au/~gjmoses/relexp1.htm>

34 Vergote, Antoine 1995, 'Debate Concerning the Psychology of Religion', *International Journal for the Psychology of Religion*, vol. 5, pp. 119-24.

35 James, Diana 2002, 'How can we sing our own songs in a strange land?', Locations of Spirituality: 'Experiences' and 'Writings' of the Sacred, Humanities Research Centre, Old Canberra House, Australian National University, 26-27 October 2002, <http://www.anu.edu.au/hrc/conferences/conference_archive/2002/LocationsofSpirituality_abstracts.php>, viewed 16 January 2006.

36 Williams, Michael 2002, 'Journeying with Respect', Locations of Spirituality: 'Experiences' and 'Writings' of the Sacred, Humanities Research Centre, Old Canberra House, The Australian National University, 26-27 October 2002, <http://www.anu.edu.au/hrc/conferences/conference_archive/2002/LocationsofSpirituality_abstracts.php >, viewed 16 January 2006.

7. Sacralising the profane, profaning the sacred

Colin Tatz

Genocide produces anomalies. One example is the coincidence and coexistence of two diametrically opposed views of the same catastrophe. Some victims make sacred, or sacralise, their profoundly profane experience; some perpetrators, or their supporters, deliberately profane that now sacralised event.

Sacrilege and blasphemy have a common element: desecration and violation of the sacred rather than mere irreverence towards that which some people hold in high regard. Victims of genocide—Armenians and Jews, among others—venerate their dead, their 'cleansed', their relocated or removed people. Definable groups perish in the killing fields, or somehow disappear forever from populations and places. The survivors revere their kin and need to commemorate those events in order to maintain their ethnic coherence and their sanity and to preserve a modicum of truth in history. At times, however, reverence loses its restraints and the profane events themselves become sacralised.

The most malignant form of desecrating the victims is the subsequent denial of their catastrophe: the dead did not die in the fields and should not appear as 'cleansed' in the history books. Their sculpted memorials are defiled because they deny the integrity and dignity of the 'alleged' perpetrators. The worst of the world's perpetrators, Heinrich Himmler, once insisted that the essence of Nazi behaviour was their very 'decency'.[1] And today, in several Baltic states, convicted war criminals have public monuments attesting to their 'heroism'.

Sacralising the profane is not in the same league of indecency as profaning the sacred. However, it warrants attention because it tends unwittingly to confuse soothing the souls of the victims or of their families with warding off repetition of the catastrophe.

Sacralising what isn't sacred

In the 90-odd years since the onset of the Armenian genocide in Turkey, the catastrophe of 1.5 million dead has become enshrined in many ways. Monuments have been built in many Western countries. Western governments, at the national and regional levels, and city authorities, have publicly recognised that event as genocide. The twenty-fourth day of April each year is commemorated with an increasingly religious flavour and fervour. The day has become a rallying point for diaspora Armenians, at a time and a place where many congregate in large numbers for perhaps only that one day in the year. As time passes, so the

Armenian genocide is increasingly researched, examined, presented, discussed, and brought to a level of significance formerly reserved for the Holocaust. Hitler's oft-repeated rhetorical question posed in 1939—'who after all remembers the Armenians?'—has been more than counter-balanced by a near-universal recognition of this second[2] cosmic genocide of the twentieth century.

A sacral patina covers this event, as it does the Holocaust. It has become not just a focal point but the fulcrum of Armenian identity. Armenianness, as with Jewishness, coheres around the catastrophe, often relegating earlier and other more significant historical, cultural and religious endeavours and achievements into the byways of memory and overshadowing more recent experiences and achievements in which pride can be taken. Children are taught to locate their identity through these genocides. Formerly homeless, friendless and defenceless minorities, both peoples are now independent (armed) nations, seemingly born out of these genocidal events, united in a determination to prevent repetition of their earlier fates.

In this context, the Holocaust poses a more extreme case. For many, that *tremendum* has become a sacred event, metahistorical, beyond words, analysis and deconstruction. It was no accident that Elie Wiesel, the renowned Auschwitz survivor and Nobel Laureate, declared his preference for the word 'Holocaust' to identify the Judeocide. The small-h Greek word was first used by Marion Harland and J. Castell Hopkins in their late–1890s books, referring to 'this gigantic holocaust with all its attendant horrors of flame, rapine and violation'.[3] They were describing the 1894–96 Armenian genocidal massacres ordered by Turkey's Sultan Hamid II.

Wiesel's preferred capital-H word resonated with this Greek term, *holokauston*, meaning the destruction of everything by burning. He very much wanted to incorporate a notion of sacrifice—in this case, what we call the Abraham-and-Isaac model of religious explanation of the Holocaust. But even here there is an unintended and curious blasphemy. As a test of Abraham's faith, a beneficent God ordered him to bind his son Isaac for sacrifice. Abraham did not hesitate. Seeing such purity of faith, God sent an angel of mercy and substituted a ram for the slaughter. But in Auschwitz, Belzec, Sobibor, Majdanek, Chelmno, Kulmhof, and Treblinka there were only malevolent 'angels of death' and no four-legged last-minute substitutes.[4]

The Judeocide—which many now prefer to call the *Shoah* [5] (the Hebrew word for destruction)—was the world's most profane act in modern history. Six million Jews and close to 40 million non-Jews died in Hitler's war against world Jewry. After the Nazis had emulated many of the Turkish modes of murdering the Armenians, they became truly 'inventive', conceiving and putting into practice the idea of *creating death* as an end in itself. The chosen method was the industrialisation of the killing process on a gigantic scale. Thus the killing factories—for which sole purpose Belzec, Sobibor and Treblinka existed—could 'process' between 12 000 and 15 000 *stukke* (pieces) every 24 hours. They did this to 2.7 million Jews between February 1942 and November 1944.

Metahistorical? Sacred? In the first blush of discovery and dissemination there was only dumbfoundedness. Wiesel's first reaction was typical: 'the time has come for all of us to learn and to be silent'. Even as late as 1985, Wiesel would write:

> We do not know how to handle it. We did not know what to do before it occurred: we were totally disoriented while it occurred; and now after it we have acquired a unique knowledge from it that may crush us. We simply did not know what to do with such knowledge. It goes deep into the nature of man and has extraordinary implications about the relationship between man and man, man and language, man and himself, and, ultimately, man and God. We don't know: at the beginning that is the answer to it, and I am afraid at the end as well.[6]

Nonetheless, as Holocaust historian Yehuda Bauer has never tired of saying, this was a human event perpetrated by one group of human beings on another group of humans, in the middle of Europe in the middle of the twentieth century; it must therefore be explicable. To be silent is a counsel of despair. And so Bauer, and many others, researched, examined, delved, excavated (literally and metaphorically), analysed and thereby established a forensic history that meticulously re- or de-constructed what happened: where, to whom, by whom, when, and even why. Such precise and corroborated detail has had to withstand not only cross-examination in war crimes trials but also the bizarre claims of the denialists.

Yet there is a dreadful irony in all of this. At one level, there is an enormous growth in Holocaust research and writing, an increase in memoirs, memorialisation ceremonies, in marches of the living to Auschwitz, in archaeological excavations of mass graves, in trials of old men, in documentary and commercial films on genocide in general. At another level, there is the stubborn effort of many survivors to resist, even to reject, historical analyses. They see an 'answer' of sorts, some kind of prophylaxis or prevention of repetition in more memorials, bigger museums, more candle-lighting memorial ceremonies. The glass cases housing documents and memorabilia have become shrines and amulets, akin to *mezuzot*—the verses from Deuteronomy affixed in capsules on the doorposts of most Jewish homes—to both affirm faith in God and to ward off demons. But it can never be an 'answer', an antidote, a preventive measure that ensures 'Never Again!' Preserving historical truth and simultaneously preventing a recurrence of those events needs methods very different from this approach.

Had I survived a camp, no doubt I would want that hell frozen in time, preserved for the world to witness. I would not want my experience buried amidst the generalisations, or even amongst the detailed specifications, of broad historical abstractions. I would want candles, prayers, and imprecations of 'Never Again!'. And I would be sacralising both the banality and the profanity of unalloyed evil as I did so.

All genocides are human events, with human perpetrators, victims, bystanders, beneficiaries and denialists. As a genocide studies historian, not a survivor, I search for reasons for their behaviours, not psychologically, but historically, politically and legally. I try to find the microscopic black pinheads of malignancy which form the origins of genocide, the sources and resources of the ideologues, the justifications given for their decisions, their adoption of 'biological' solutions to social and political problems, the responsibility and accountability of those who give and those who carry out orders. For me, nothing in deliberate starvation, forced death marches, poisoning, drowning, shooting and gassing can ever be sacralised. There is no room, in my view, for a new secular religion which *enshrines* these events.

Several authors have dealt with the so-called 'Shoah business', notably Tim Cole, Peter Novick and Norman Finkelstein.[7] In varying degrees they abhor the packaging, selling and misuse of the Holocaust as an industry, a guilt-producer, an antidote to anti-Semitism, 'a way of shaking down Swiss banks' [!], a protection against criticism of Israel's Palestinian policies. They inveigh against the unnamed 'guardians' of the Holocaust, those who turn that event into all manner of myth and *kitsch*. But I often have trouble distinguishing whether these critics are attacking this 'shrinological' guardianship—or the very subject matter being guarded.

Blaspheming the sacred and the profane

The French classical scholar, Pierre Vidal-Naquet, labelled denialists 'the assassins of memory'. In the case of the Jews, the denialists are not always the *génocidaires;* in the case of the Armenians, however, they are.

Turkish denialism of the genocide of 1.5 million Armenians is official, riven, driven, constant, rampant, and increasing each year since the events of 1915 to 1922. It is state-funded, with special departments and units in overseas missions whose sole purpose is to dilute, counter, minimise, trivialise and relativise every reference to the events which encompassed a genocide of Armenians, Pontian Greeks and Assyrian Christians in Asia Minor.

In the face of irrefutable evidence of genocide, Turkey has created a massive industry of denialism. Its actions are spectacular, often bizarre, lacking any effort to distinguish between the serious and the silly. In the 1930s, Turkish pressure was put on the American government and on Hollywood studios not to proceed with an embryonic film based on Franz Werfel's 1932 novel, *Forty Days at Musa Dagh*, which depicted Armenian resistance. In the present era, there has been heavy lobbying of the American Congress not to find a path to the two-thirds majority needed for a resolution recognising the genocide. Successful lobbying led to the removal of any reference to genocide in the Armenian entry in the *Encyclopaedia Britannica*. Recently, there have been threats to sever diplomatic relations with France over the French declaration that there was such a genocide. In April 2001, the Turkish government somehow squeezed Shimon Peres, then Israel's foreign minister, to say in Ankara that 'Armenian allegations of genocide are meaningless'. (Not even Israel's geopolitical interests in a time of crisis can condone such a statement; at worst, he could have said nothing.)

There was a demand a few years ago to SBS television in Sydney that the station pulp its 25-year anniversary history book because it twice made passing reference to an event 'that never happened'. Then there was an extraordinary visit by His Excellency the Ambassador to my office at Macquarie University in 1987 in which he sought to have me delete the Armenian segment of my new course on 'The Politics of Genocide'.

What still motivates Turkey around the globe? We don't know, but I suggest the following:

- A suppression of guilt and shame that a warrior nation, a 'beacon of democracy' as it saw itself in 1908 (and since), slaughtered several ethnic populations. Democracies, it is said, don't commit genocide; *ergo*, Turkey couldn't and didn't do so.
- A cultural and social ethos of honour, a compelling and compulsive need to remove any blots on the national escutcheon.
- A chronic fear that admission will lead to massive claims for reparation and restitution.
- To overcome fears of social fragmentation in a society that is still very much a state in transition.
- A 'logical' belief that because the genocide was committed with impunity, so denial will also meet with neither opposition nor obloquy.
- An inner knowledge that the juggernaut denial industry has a momentum of its own and can't be stopped even if they wanted it to stop.

The work of those who contend, or who may even believe, that the Holocaust was and is, in Arthur Butz's language, 'the hoax of the twentieth century' has been analysed by, among others, Lucy Dawidowicz, Deborah Lipstadt and Pierre Vidal-Naquet. We now know a great deal about denialist writings, techniques and vehicles, and about their effectiveness or lack thereof. Apart from tolerance of that especial brand of denialism, so-called 'comparative trivialisation', propagated by Ernst Nolte (1985, 1988) and Andreas Hillgruber (1986) in

Germany, there has been no denial by the German state, East, West or re-united. The *Schuldfrage* (guilt question) remains a central issue in daily German life, especially among the young. Perversely, perhaps, there has been a great deal of denial in the very democracies where freedom of speech is sacrosanct: France, the United States, Canada, Britain and Australia. We may well ask why this has happened. I offer a number of reasons.

Denialism in the democracies

- In the early post-war years, denialism was believed to facilitate the 'coming out' of Nazis and Nazis in hiding. Only the nullification of the Holocaust could make Nazi-ness, and its derivatives, respectable or acceptable.
- Denialism strives to re-legitimise anti-Semitism as a political credo. This is only possible if anti-Semitism is sanitised of its practical apotheosis—Auschwitz. Political and nationalistic anti-Semitism, and political parties devoted thereto, prevalent across Europe before World War II, are undergoing a resurgence in today's Europe.
- Denialism aims to legitimise fascism as a worthy, organic political philosophy. This is only possible if you can divorce fascism from its associated death camp anti-Semitism. If the death camps can be successfully denied, then fascism and anti-Semitism can have nothing to be ashamed of and can, once again, be respectable.
- Denialism serves to disestablish the legitimacy of Israel if, indeed, Israel is the consequence and outcome of the Holocaust. This unfortunate and misleading Holocaust = Israel equation, strongly (and, I believe, wrongly) emphasised by former prime ministers David Ben-Gurion and Menachem Begin, is still, regrettably, pervasive throughout Israel and the Diaspora. If, therefore, the Holocaust can be denied, then so, too, can any rationalisation for the foundation and continued existence of the Jewish state.
- Denialism helps establish the legitimacy of the Palestinian cause. By turning Palestinians into the victims, Jews are accused of behaving like the very Nazis whom the Jews 'falsely' accuse of genocide. Radical Islam has now adopted all the techniques of an earlier European-Christian anti-Semitism, including Holocaust denialism.
- Denialism is used to reconcile the Soviets' notion of the centrality of their own history of millions lost and their antagonism, especially after the 1967 war, to a Jewry, an Israel or a Zion that has, since 1945, had the pre-eminent claim on having lost six million of its people. To avoid that contradiction, Soviet academicians turned the Nazis into fascists and didn't mention the centrality, in the Nazi *weltanschauung*, of anti-Semitism and the 'Final Solution'. In the end, for them, and for the ears of a world that may have been willing to listen, the only victims of fascism were communists. This phase—together with the Soviet system—has now passed, but it was, for

decades, a state-sponsored enterprise in the major academies, more vigorous, more pernicious and much more effective world-wide than the 'free-enterprise' efforts of a handful of American denialists like Elmer Barnes, Willis Carto and Arthur Butz.

- Denialism counteracts irrational fears of a breaking-up of social consensus in society, particularly when a society is in transition. To focus public attention on an alleged, ethnically identifiable fifth column of 'others' offers some grounds for a form of national unity.
- Denialism can magnify, in some instances, a particular victim community's suffering without having to have it compared with, and to be found to be on a lesser scale than, the Holocaust. Deliberate flattening, or even minimising, of the Holocaust magnifies and equalises all atrocities. In a morbid sense, if everyone commits horrors, then not only is no person or group any more guilty than any other, but all humankind has suffered equally—and Jews, therefore, have no greater claim on humanity's conscience.
- Denialism offers a form of ready expression of the hatred of Jews.
- Denialism can hurt, shafting corpses with the added indignity of claiming that there were no corpses, and can inflict on Jewish survivors the accusation, even the curse, that their nightmares are just that—very bad dreams. In the words of Vidal-Naquet: denialists 'are intent on striking a community in the thousand painful fibres that continue to link it to its own past'.[8]

Certainly these denialists know what they're doing: they learn, refine, become more 'academic', more sophisticated, more credible as alternative explainers or revealers of 'truth'; more subtle and less 'kooky' than they appeared immediately after the war. But while they remain professionally isolated within their communities, they are at the same time collectivised. In other words, as disparate as they are geographically, they have turned themselves into a coterie, a cult, a collective who now meet publicly—or who are sometimes prevented from meeting publicly, as in Lebanon in 2001.[9] They are assembled in a fortress of their choosing, as purveyors of hate and merchants of prejudice. While they may have a certain mass appeal, they are no longer viewed as discrete, independent scholars, worthy of attention or of a serious intellectual or academic hearing. They see themselves as an army of combatants, although their visibility renders them more capable of being grouped into an identifiable body, quartered, quarantined and made both ridiculous and unbelievable.

In 2000, and again in 2001, on appeal in senior British courts, the hubris of the new Crown Prince of ridicule, David Irving, 'the noted British historian, author of more than 20 books', ensured that a great many Humptys fell off the wall.[10] In July 2001, the three-judge Court of Appeal supported Justice Gray's initial ruling in the libel case of *Irving v Lipstadt & Penguin Books*. They declared that Irving was 'one of the most dangerous spokespersons for Holocaust denial...No objective, fair-minded historian would have serious cause to doubt that there were gas chambers at Auschwitz and that they were operated on a substantial scale to kill hundreds of thousands of Jews.' Justice Gray had concluded: 'Irving is anti-Semitic. His words are directed against Jews, either individually or collectively, in the sense that they are by turns hostile, critical, offensive and derisory'.[11]

Australian conundrums

These are case studies about what an Australian High Court judge once said were about faraway people in faraway places. In our different context, one seemingly benign and beneficent, we have a case of sacralising that which isn't so and a profaning of that which is.

The agitation for Aboriginal land rights in the late 1960s resulted in the Fraser Coalition government's enacting what the Australian Labor Party had begun in 1973: a statute in 1976 to enable Aborigines to claim vacant Crown land in the Northern Territory. Aided by some dubious anthropology, the mechanism for land acquisition in the *Aboriginal Land Rights (Northern Territory) Act* is peculiar, to say the least. Land was *not* to be allocated on the basis of need, as with some Indian lands in the United States. There is no argument about prior occupation, or adverse possession, or continued possession, as in the case of the Inuit in Canada and the Maori in New Zealand. Claimants have to be Aboriginal, with demonstrable patrilineal, matrilineal or ambilineal lines of inheritance; they have to have spiritual attachment to the land and must be able to demonstrate the strength of that spiritual attachment by way of ceremonial duties. What underlies this curious mechanism is the [white] belief that all Aboriginal land involves spirituality and is therefore sacred. Some land is, indeed, sacred, as we will see, but much, even most, of Aboriginal land is or was camping ground and hunting ground, land which is hardly profane but which nonetheless has no under- or over-lay of sacredness.

In 1976, the Federal Government's Land Fund Commission bought the pastoral lease of Noonkanbah Station for the Yungngora people of the Kimberleys.[12] In the diamond and oil rush of the time, over 500 mining claims, most of which were contested successfully by lawyers for the Aborigines, were lodged on that property. Amax Iron Ore Corporation held a five-year valid exploration permit to drill for oil. In 1979, they sent in a bulldozer to dig up ceremonial land near the homestead, named 'P' or 'Pea' Hill. Trustees appointed under the *Heritage Act* told the Mines Minister that to drill there 'would affect the site by contradicting past and current Aboriginal sacred beliefs'. The Minister ordered the Trustees to give their consent. Thereupon, the Aborigines locked the Noonkanbah gate and refused all entry. Several legal injunctions later, this *Dreamtime v Oil* issue became very political. The Premier, Sir Charles Court, commandeered the private company's oil drilling rig and sent the massive machine to Noonkanbah, accompanied by an enormous armed police convoy. There was a sense of outrage across Australia at this display of force, with the *National Times* calling the Premier Sir Charles Rommel. The point of this story is that Amax knew from geological experts that no oil was to be found at 'P' Hill—yet Court was intent on not only defying conservative federal Coalition notions on Aboriginal land, but also on defying and decrying any conceptions that Aborigines had a belief system worthy of respect. In an act of conscious desecration, Court drilled and of, course, no oil was found.

'Forgiving and forgetting'

In Australia, and elsewhere, there is a new catchcry: reconciliation, a call to the offended to 'forgive and forget', to 'move on'. No one is willing to discuss what victim groups must move on *from*. If the politics of remembering the feuds, the hatreds, and the differences produced cataclysmic deaths, then surely, they say, it must be replaced with an ideology of forgiving and forgetting.

There are, as I wrote elsewhere,[13] costs in this new fashion, costs to the victims, whether Armenian, Jewish or Aboriginal. It is they who must forgo the desire or deny their need for retributive justice. It is they who must eschew notions of guilt and atonement and, all too often, forgo compensation for harms done. It is they who must agree to the diminution, or even abolition, of that shared historical memory which holds victim groups together. It is they who must concur in the substitution of *their* memory by *our* memory and *their* history by *our* history. The Forrest River massacres were not massacres—or so we are told—and the places of such events are of no moment, let alone veneration. But Gallipoli—where thousands of young Australians were senselessly mown down in their thousands—is officially 'a sacred site', a shrine to our birth as a nation. The victims must connive at ignoring the importance of accountability for the crimes committed against them, and it is they who must agree to the obliteration of that responsibility. It is they who must cease reacting so hysterically against denialism, that major tributary of forgetting, which claims that there was nothing to remember in the first place. Such is the profanity of their being asked to 'move on'.

ENDNOTES

[1] Himmler to senior SS officers in Poznan, 4 October 1943: [explaining the 'Final Solution] 'To have stood fast through this and—except for cases of human weakness—to have stayed decent, that has made us hard…We do not want, in the end, because we destroyed a bacillus, to be infected by this bacillus and to die. I will never stand by and watch while even a small rotten spot develops or takes hold. Wherever it may form we will together burn it away. All in all, however, we can say that we carried out this most difficult of tasks in a spirit of love for our people. And we have suffered no harm to our inner being, our soul, our character…' in Arad, Y., Gutman Y. and A. Margolit, 1981, *Documents on the Holocaust*, Yad Vashem, Jerusalem, pp. 344–5.

[2] The first genocide of 'the century of genocide', the twentieth century, was the destruction of some 60 000 Herero people by their German colonisers in German South-West Africa (now Namibia) in 1904–05.

[3] Harland, Marion 1897, *Under the Flag of the Orient: the Thrilling Story of Armenia*, Philadelphia, Historical Publishing Company, p. 415; Castell Hopkins, J. 1896, *The Sword of Islam or Suffering Armenia*, Brantford, the Bradley-Garretson Co. Ltd. At p. 313 he talks about 'the full glare of the national holocaust upon the altar of Mahometan cruelty'.

[4] See Tatz, Colin 2003, *With Intent to Destroy: Reflecting on Genocide*, London, Verso, pp. 33-9, for discussion of Jewish religious responses to the Holocaust.

[5] Orthodox Jews in Israel tend to use the word *Churban/Hurban* for the destruction of European Jewry. Arno Mayer, 1990, in his *Why Did the Heavens not Darken?: the 'Final Solution' in History*, New York, Pantheon Books, used the word *Judeocide*—the killing of Jews—a term I prefer for its directness.

[6] Wiesel, Elie 1985, *Against Silence: the Voice and Vision of Elie Wiesel*, Irving Abrahamson (ed.), New York, Holocaust Library, 3 vols, p. 287.

[7] Cole, Tim 1999, *Selling the Holocaust: from Auschwitz to Schindler, How History is Bought, Packaged, and Sold*, New York, Routledge;Novick, Peter 2000, *The Holocaust in American Life*, New York, Houghton-Mifflin; Finkelstein, Norman 2000, *The Holocaust Industry*, London, Verso.

[8] Vidal-Naquet, Pierre 1992, *The Assassins of Memory*, New York, Columbia University Press, pp. xxiii–xxiv.

[9] In March 2001, 14 Arab intellectuals denounced the projected denialist conference scheduled to be held in Lebanon. The influential London Arab newspaper, *Al-Hayat*, editorialised that such conferences 'disgraced Lebanon'. *Ha'aretz*, English edition, 20 March 2001. However, in June 2001, such a conference was held in Jordan.

[10] Evans, Richard 2001, *Telling Lies About the Hitler: the Holocaust, History and the David Irving Trial*, London, Verso; Guttenplan, D. D. 2001, *The Holocaust on Trial*, New York, W.W. Norton.

[11] Evans, 2001, p. 236.

[12] See Tatz, Colin 1982, *Aborigines and Uranium and Other Essays*, Heinemann, pp. 90–92.

[13] Tatz, Colin 'Reflections on the Politics of Remembering and Forgetting', The First Abraham Wajnryb Memorial Lecture, Macquarie University, 1 December 1994, Centre for Comparative Genocide Studies.

8. Is that a human skull? All in the name of art!

Dianne McGowan

This chapter explores the ambiguities of Western beliefs in relation to the sacredness of the Western human body, especially in death. These ambiguities are highlighted by considering the contemporary transformation of Tibetan Buddhist ritual objects into Western art objects. Having the cross-cultural and historical specificity of concepts of and treatment of the body as sacred in death the chapter explores the de-sacralisation of the dead body in contemporary European culture, especially in the art of Gunther von Hagans.

The chapter is divided into three parts: the first introduces Tibetan Buddhist customs and objects; the second describes the historical European attitudes to human bone; and the third muses over the acceptance of Tibetan Buddhist human bone objects as art and Western notions towards the sacredness of the dead.

Tibetan Buddhist practices

Anyone who has glanced at Tibetan Buddhist *thangkas* (Tibetan paintings) or sculpture will have noticed a vanguard of ferocious multi-armed, multi-legged and multi-headed deities, very different from that of the compassionate and peaceful seated image of *Sakyamuni* Buddha. For example, *Yamantaka,* the defeater of *Yama,* 'The Lord of Death', has a corpulent human body with a buffalo head, on top of which are arranged multiple human heads. His 36 flailing arms hold weapons and symbols, while his eighteen legs trample animal and human bodies underfoot. The most visible ritual human bone object held by these ferocious deities and used in ritual practice by Tibetan Buddhists is the skull-cup, which has many levels of meaning depending on what it is filled with, who holds it, and the position in which it is held.[1]

For example, *Naro Dakini* may be displayed in a *thangka* as a manifestation of *Vajravarahi*. *Vajravarahi* is the consort of *Chakramsavara*, a deity around which the current Dalai Lama holds many initiation ceremonies. *Naro Dakini* is portrayed as pouring blood from a skull-cup into her mouth, the blood trickles from her mouth and her vagina, symbolising how she is both consuming, and is being consumed, by the feminine principle, wisdom. In the crook of her left arm sits a tantric staff. On the apex of this staff, above a half crossed thunderbolt and a vase of nectar, is impaled a fresh head, a decaying head, a skull and a thunderbolt. When held by a female, the whole staff represents the masculine principle, compassion.[2] Like all Tibetan symbolism, the imagery represents multiple levels and layers of meanings, such as the representation of the physical universe or an esoteric formula. *Thangkas,* like sculptures, serve as picture maps detailing how one can achieve enlightenment in just one lifetime.

Because the practice of Tibetan Buddhism[3] has the potential for enlightenment in one lifetime, it is therefore, desirable to have the most potent implements with which to overcome the obstacles that trap the human in the ever-turning wheel of rebirth; that is, trapped in *samsara.* [4] Consequently, there are religiously sanctioned lists citing the most powerful source to the least for each ritual human bone object.[5] In the *Naro Dakini* example, an ideal skull-cup would be from a violently murdered or executed individual or an illegitimate child, aged seven or eight years, who was born from an incestuous union. The least desirable skull is from someone who died of natural old age.[6] The skulls of a venerable lama or pious laymen were often embellished and furnished with a decorative tripod and cover and then placed on an altar as the vessel for the 'inner offerings' of animals and humans.[7]

Mortuary customs in Tibet varied according to epoch, resources, region, rank or cause of death. According to Keith Dowman, historical sources mention practices such as the mummification or cremation of high lamas and that epidemic victims were either buried or cast into the river.[8] The novel Tibetan Buddhist mortuary practice, known in English as sky burial or vulture disposal,[9] has been suggested as a response to the frozen landscape and the scarcity of wood, although high lamas continued to be cremated.[10] Robert Ekvall suggests that the transition to sky burials by Tibetans was brought about when Buddhism was introduced in the late 700s.[11] The introduction of the Buddhist doctrinal ban on killing any sentient beings, be it buffalo or bug, posed a dilemma for Tibetans. Put simply, they lived in a harsh environment where survival depended on them killing animals for clothing and food. Ekvall notes that if a Muslim butcher could not be employed, the animal was asphyxiated and the refrain, 'Oh, it is dead', was uttered before a drop of blood was shed. In the act of surviving, Tibetans accumulated de-merits against their desired release from the *samsara.* By voluntarily and generously giving up their own human body at death to other sentient beings, such as vultures and dogs, they acknowledge this debt. Further, the relatives watching the dismembering were reminded of the Buddhist principles, that body and life is impermanent.[12]

The general custom of a sky burial is that, after death the body is propped up in a seated position. A monk is employed to chant to the newly released spirit, instructing it on correct behaviour and how to make a successful journey through the transitional state of the *Bardo* to the next rebirth cycle.[13] The ritual chant normally takes three days. Once finished, the body is tied into a foetal position and carried on a relative's back to the nearest charnel grounds. Here, the head is shaved and then the butchers begin. They open up the body, take out the internal organs, disarticulate the limbs and cut the flesh into small pieces. The bones are pounded into powder and mixed with water to make *tsampa*-like balls.[14] Once finished, the vultures are summoned to accept the offering, while dogs and other small carnivorous animals clean up.[15] The cremated remains of high lamas were often pounded into fine ash, mixed with medicinal substances and then added to clay, which was then used to make small votive plaques for personal shrines.[16]

Historical European practices

This second section focuses on the prevailing historical European attitudes involving human bone.[17] It is well known that the trafficking of human bones in the name of Christianity was central to the economy of the Roman Catholic Church. Within a hundred years of Jesus' crucifixion, the bones of tortured devout followers were being recovered and handled as spiritual treasures.[18] The current Catholic Church continues to officially sanction the worshipping of relics and their associated miracles. In 1974, Pope John Paul II visited Edinburgh and presented to St Mary's cathedral the shoulder blade of St Andrew, the patron saint of Scotland.[19]

Whether it was the acts of martyrdom or transference of pagan beliefs, the bones of the saints were believed to be pregnant with 'heavenly' powers capable of performing miracles, and the subsequent miraculous happenings fulfilled these expectations. Peter Brown suggests that relics were potent because these 'immortalised' remains or personal belongings represented the *locus* in which earth and heaven had met.[20] Throughout Europe human bones were dug up, cut up, exhibited, toured, pillaged, stolen, and faked. The ownership of such treasures brought status and, more importantly, profit.[21] Chaucer's fourteenth century *Canterbury Tales* provides an insight into the business of pilgrimage. In his tale, 29 pilgrims are thrown together by their desire to visit the relics of Thomas à Becket. They were not to be disappointed. Canterbury Cathedral had glorified four sites to St Thomas, each exhibiting a bit of him.[22]

The cutting up of a relic to create fragments was common; the fact that Becket's body was in one location was unusual. A French researcher investigating old church inventories found that St Mary Magdalene must have had six bodies to accommodate all the relics purported to be of her.[23] Because the dispersion of 'bits of true' relics could not fill the demand, secondary relics, such as the clothes martyrs and saints had worn or implements used in their torture, were also venerated. The production of fakes and stealing were other ways of acquiring a relic, the possession of which bring renown and monetary rewards to a religious organisation. The transfer of St Foy's bones from the monastery at Figéac to the Conques monastery is an example of the importance of relics and the extraordinary means some would go to acquiring a relic. Historical legend relates that, in the 900s, a Conques monk spent ten years of undercover work as a Figéac monk until he was entrusted as a guardian of St Foy's bones, which he then stole, taking them to the Conques monastery and bringing a renewed vigour to the community.[24]

However, trafficking of human bones was not just a religious phenomenon. From the mid 1700s to 1832, the British medical profession was involved in wholesale 'body snatching'. It was estimated that, in the early 1800s, London anatomy schools were illegally procuring almost 800 bodies a year. London was also supplying Oxford and Edinburgh.[25] There was opposition to the nightly activities of these 'resurrection men', as they became known, especially if they dug up a body belonging to the upper classes. Nevertheless, others approved the 'getting' of bodies in the name of science. However, intentional murder for anatomy subjects finally forced the *Anatomy Act* of 1832 to be passed.[26]

The most common established mortuary practice in Europe was interment.[27] By the 1600s, burial meant buying a plot of land within an area designated for the disposal of bodies. In seventeenth century Britain, only royalty and priests were buried in clothes, the rest were wrapped in a shroud, and only the wealthy could afford a coffin.[28] The county council buried paupers as best befitted the pauper's beliefs, if known. By the 1700s, Vanessa Harding notes the great fear of dying as a pauper. Not being able to afford a proper burial was a social disgrace. The adherence to restrictive mourning customs identified and reinforced the family's social identity and standing within the community.[29] Nigel Llewellyn notes that all funeral paraphernalia had only one function, '...they were designed to display and reinforce the social distinctions of the dead'. He also notes that the mourning paraphernalia not only displayed social rank, it also created visually recognised public and private spaces in which particular outpourings of grief were acceptable.[30]

Musings

Having presented a general outline of the cultural practices of both Tibetan Buddhism and the West, this last section of the paper ventures to integrate this information into contemporary Western practices and ponder on the observable ambiguities. To start these musings I turn to museum exhibitions of Tibetan ritual objects including human remains, and how researchers approach and handle such material. There is no public outcry of sacrilege over a museum exhibition of human remains, or of how researchers, such as me, may handle them.[31] Why? If the skull were Thomas à Becket's or a close relative of mine, would I be treating their skull with the same apparent detachment I appear to be displaying to the Tibetan material? Perhaps the elevation and desire of Tibetan human bone objects as art objects ameliorates thoughts of sacrilege? Or perhaps time, cross-cultural circumstances or no personal attachment to the skeletal remains dampens the emotional input? Does 'political correctness' govern moral outrage? After all, the Tibetans carry no corresponding outrage. While I do not have answers to these questions, or the many others I could have asked, I will venture to appraise these questions in reference to the Tibetan example.

What attitude does the West have towards Tibet? Historically, Tibet has been an anomaly, Tibetans were not seen as 'noble savages' nor were they seen as cannibals, even though their religious imagery was full of partial corpses and skeletons, not to mention the human bone objects that would have been on the altar or seen in ritual dance.[32] Rather, the apparent worship of human bone paralleled the Catholic veneration of relics and the construction of reliquaries. Many early observers of Tibetan practices noted parallels with Catholicism, especially similarities in dress, ritual, ecclesiastical furnishing and the privileging of text. In 1661, the first European to reach and report on Lhasa, Father John Grueber, a Jesuit missionary, noted the strong similarities between Tibetan ritual and Catholicism. He suggested that Tibetan Buddhism must have begun as an early type of Christianity and that its development had since been corrupted by the Devil. He wrote that the Devil 'hath had the malice to transfer and usurp all the other mysteries of our faith to his own worship'.[33] Earlier, Marco Polo had suggested the work of the Devil. In the 1200s, he observed Tibetans at the Great Khan's court and he wrote that they were wise astrologers and great enchanters, who could change the weather at will. But they did this because they were in league with the Devil. The 1959 Polo translation reads, '[t]hey know more of diabolic arts and enchantments than any other men. They do what they do by the art of the Devil; but they make others believe that they do it with great holiness and by the work of God.'[34]

This ambiguous perception of the Tibetans as being either in the service of the Devil or their God, or of being either holy or enchanters, has continued, with many myths accepted into popular Western culture. For example, in 1930, the *New York Times* ran an article on an exhibition opening at the Field Museum of Natural History in Chicago, titled 'Made from Human Bones'.[35] What is interesting is that this article repeats a story first made popular in 1366, by John Mandeville: the practice of the Tibetan son drinking from his father's skull-cup in ancestor worship.[36]

While scholars and the increasing numbers of Westerners practising Tibetan Buddhism are discrediting these recurring popular myths, there is another re-contextualisation of Tibetan Buddhism apparent today. The labelling and cataloguing of Tibet's culture as art is effectively re-writing Tibetan Buddhist ritual objects as pieces to be valued for their colour, form, rarity and uniqueness; in short, for their aesthetic value. In 2003, there were three Tibetan 'art blockbuster' exhibitions circulating in the United States.[37] Each drew enthusiastic crowds wherever they went and each had a different agenda in their promotion of Tibetan art. All three exhibitions acknowledged that the objects were selected according to Western art aesthetics. The enthusiastic and generally uninitiated audience is given a de-contextualised version of Tibetan culture.

For example, an extract taken from a catalogue entry for *Naro Dakini* in the exhibition titled 'Desire and Devotion: Art from India, Nepal, and Tibet,' reads:

> In this rather loosely painted *thangka*, Naro Dakini stands on a lotus in the militant pose (*pratyālidha*), trampling two personifications of obstacles. Of red complexion, she is naked except for her ornaments and garland of severed heads. While holding a chopper with her right hand, she tilts the skull cup with the left to drink the blood. Her magic staff rests horizontally across her shoulder. Surrounded by an oval, flame-fringed aureole, she stands against the six-cornered (*shatkona*) diagram (*yantra*) of two superimposed triangles, also flame fringed. Curiously, however, the goddess, with her lotus base, is placed slightly off centre.[38]

There is no mention of the intent or purpose of her drinking the blood, rather the reader is left with exotic orientalist notions such as 'lotus', 'militant', 'red', 'naked', 'blood', 'magic', 'flame', 'goddess'. The catalogue entry goes on to emphasise the decorative elements of the *thangka*, and compares the illustrated *thangka* with similar *thangkas* previously exhibited—noting its rarity and potential link with a very important monastery in Tibet. Such textual processes alienate the objects from their religious and cultural associations by grounding them in an art history discourse and reducing their distinct cultural specificities into Western qualitative and quantitative measurements, which makes each piece comparable, a necessity for making judgments on value.

When museums exhibit Tibetan human bone they distance the cultural object from its cultural practices by deploying them in remote, sanitised, spotlighted museum cases, thereby effectively detaching a viewers' emotional or social response to something that, in another situation, may be abhorrent to the viewer. The human bone object is re-contextualised into the Western art history paradigm, not as once being part of a human body, but as something created from artistic resources, such as, paints, canvas, metal, and clay.[39] Further, these 'made' objects are valued and hence, desired because of their uniqueness, rarity, age, workmanship and aesthetic qualities. For example, the skull-cup furnished with metal furnishings and semi precious gems, or carved with tantric figures, is more highly valued than an unadorned skull-cup. It is interesting to note, that, the unadorned skull-cup appears not to be considered exhibition worthy and, if museums have collected such pieces, they will languish in ethnographic and fine art museum basements—perhaps a silent acknowledgement that an unadorned skull is just too raw for public viewing. Further, it is rare for any major auction houses to offer human bone pieces. Recently, Christie's offered 'A Ritual Bone Apron'; there was no mention that the bone was human.[40]

Another aspect to these musings is the question of Tibetan agency. Tibet is two nations: the geographical Tibet, governed by The People's Republic of China, and the virtual Tibet, dispersed across the globe, nominally coalesced under the fourteenth Dalai Lama. Both governments believe that they have the moral right to govern Tibet. The Tibetan government in-exile is enthusiastic about promoting 'things'. It is apparent that 'Tibetan Art' is a popular vehicle by which the 'Free Tibet' message can be propagated. His Holiness has personally endorsed many 'blockbuster' exhibitions by attending openings or writing the foreward for glossy catalogues. The reality is that many people are intrigued by what they think Tibet is—a mystical isle, cut from civilisation by a sea of mountains and which was brutally awoken by the invasion of China. Truth and fiction about Tibet can be difficult to separate. Donald Lopez suggests that the promotion of Tibet in popular culture has attracted many to the cause of Tibet, but it has also imprisoned the Tibetans within a stereotyped world of exoticisms.[41] The Chinese government understands the political agency of Tibetan culture and, in response to other Tibetan art blockbusters, has recently hosted an exhibition at The Bowers Museum, just outside of San Francisco. The art treasures were drawn from the ancestral home of the fourteenth Dalai Lama, the Potala. The exhibition was a huge success, even though there were continuous public demonstrations by 'Free Tibet' protesters outside the event.[42]

Tibetan art exhibits, whether endorsed by the current Dalai Lama or not, are very attractive exhibitions. Gold, gems and mica glitter. The grime of butter lamps and incense smoke is generally cleaned away, as is the cultural dross of temples destroyed and objects stolen. The human bone objects have been cleaned, dried and adorned. There is neither visible blood nor pungent odours. But there are art exhibitions which record or display items, which are not so kind on the senses or the emotions. I remember watching a video at the Art Gallery of New South Wales some years ago, where a young Japanese female artist lay down on a cold stone sky burial platform in a Tibetan cemetery. The butchers laid out chunks of raw meat still dripping with blood onto her naked white flesh. The vultures circled above, uneasy, sensing it was not the usual offering. Those more daring finally came down to help themselves. My mind and emotions raced and swirled. I was both fascinated and fearful for the girl—wanting to look away but I kept watching, horrified and enthralled, at the same time. Another exhibition, for which I have only seen images, has caused an outcry wherever it has gone. Gunther von Hagens' British exhibition of 'Body Worlds' displayed 25 corpses along with 175 body parts. In the exhibition, most of the body parts are exhibited in conventional fluid filled jars. However, the corpses are real bodies, which have been treated with a 'plastination' process.[43] Von Hagens has meticulously arranged each for maximum effect. For example, a flayed male body crouches over a chessboard, while his brain can be seen through his split skull.[44] Von Hagen's claim is that this type of 'Anatomy Art' will 'democratise' anatomy because it will educate the public about how their body looks on the inside. But what of the viewer? How do they feel? Did they have the same ambiguous feelings that I felt when I watched the sky burial installation? What if they were to find out that not all these bodies were willingly donated to Von Hagens' institute for plastination?[45] Can the contemporary Western viewer accept a 'real' person, which is now dead and skinned as an object of contemporary art? On the other hand, is the public still entranced by the Barnum-style sensationalism? Between 1997 and 2001, six million people had paid to enter the Von Hagens exhibitions; another 50 000 walk through the turnstiles every week it is open.

In writing this, I am left in turmoil, frightened to feel what I feel. I ground myself in distancing myself with a pitiful cry, that I am not involved in any of this. I have not paid and would not pay to see Von Hagens' exhibition, but I am not protesting over these types of displays. I remain silent. Perhaps I am trapped by the social and political ambiguities between appearing as a 'rational being' or as an 'emotional woman' unable to detach myself from my emotions and scientifically appraise what is before me.

I conclude by asking: Is the Western attitude to the sacredness of body checked by ambivalence towards the 'us' and 'other'? What of the bodies dug up by archaeologists and property developers? What roles do time, science, art consumption or cherished memories play in negotiating the sacredness of the dead? Has the replacement of personal religious spirituality by a rational and depersonalised science constructed deep holes of irrelevance or forgetting that have no labels such as sacredness or sacrilege?

ENDNOTES

[1] Robert Beer (1999) has a comprehensive discussion on skull-cups in *An Encyclopedia of Tibetan Symbols and Motif*, Shambala, pp. 263-67.

[2] For comparative Naro Dakini descriptions see Beer 1999. Beer has a comprehensive discussion on skull-cups in *An Encyclopedia of Tibetan Symbols and Motif*, pp. 263-7; Pal, Pratapaditya 2001, *Desire and Devotion, Art from India, Nepal and Tibet: In the John and Berthe Ford Collection*, Philip Wilson Publishers, London, pp. 274-5; Rhie, Marilyn M. and Robert A. F. Thurman, 1991, *Wisdom and Compassion*, Thames & Hudson, p. 299; Mullin, Glen H. 2003, *Female Buddhas: Women of Enlightenment in Tibetan Mystical Art*, Clear Light Publishers, Santa Fe, pp. 154-5; Sotheby's, *Indian and Southeast Asian Art*, Wednesday September 24, pp. 58-9.

[3] Tibetan Buddhism is also known as *Vajrayana* (Diamond Vehicle) Buddhism, Tantric Buddhism, Tantrayana or Esoteric Buddhism. It is a subset of *Mahayana* Buddhism, which itself broke away from the *Theravada* Buddhism in c. 200 A.D. Each form of Buddhism maintains the core beliefs of Sakyamuni Buddha, however, they follow varying practices in an effort to break from the ever-circling wheel of rebirth.

[4] The obstacles of *samsara* are greed, lust and ignorance.

[5] Beer provides a comprehensive list for the skull-cups in *An Encyclopedia of Tibetan Symbols and Motif*, pp. 263-4.

[6] Polo, Marco 1982 [1958], The Travels, Penguin, Hammondsworth, p. 110. It is interesting to note that Marco Polo (c. 1254-1324) mentions how in the Great Khan's court the Tibetan Buddhists had a peculiar custom, 'When a man is condemned to die and is put to death by the authorities, they take his body and cook and eat it. But, if anyone dies a natural death, they would never think of eating him'. Perhaps this is an early account of the desirability of particularly potent ritual objects.

[7] Beer, 1999, p. 266; illustration 265.

[8] Dowman, Keith 1997, The Sacred Life of Tibet, Thorsons, London, p. 234. See also Wylie, Turrell 1964-65, 'Mortuary Customs at Sa-Skya, Tibet', Harvard Journal of Asiatic Studies, vol. 25, pp. 229-42.

[9] The Zoroastrians of Persia practiced intact body sky burial, this tradition is carried on by the Parsi of India. Seshadri, Sudha September 2004, 'Buried in the Sky: Some Parsi Zoroastrians Are Having a Hard Time Accepting Changes to Traditional Death Rituals', Science & Theology News, <http://www.beliefnet.com/story/152/story_15243.html>, viewed 28 September 2005.

[10] Wylie, 1964-65, p. 232; Ekvall, Robert B. 1964, Religious Observances in Tibet: Patterns and Function, University of Chicago Press, Chicago, p. 234.

[11] Although Wylie argues that there is no clear evidence to support this claim, 1964-65, p. 232.

[12] Ekvall, 1964, p. 72-7.

[13] The journey through the Bardo is mapped in the Tibetan Book of the Dead. The version by Rinpoche 1987 has become the most popular.

[14] Tsampa is a Tibetan staple. It is made from pounded barley flour formed into small balls, which is usually served mixed in with tea and yak butter.

[15] Dowman, 1997, p. 234.

[16] Wylie, 1964-65, p. 239.

[17] I acknowledge that there were Protestant groups such as those mentioned in Ian Hunter's chapter in this volume, which were opposed to the idolisation of anything outside that of the Christian word and good deeds.

[18] Bentley, James 1985, Restless Bones: The Story of Relics, Constable & Co. Ltd., London, p. 37.

[19] Bentley, 1985, p. 183.

[20] Brown, Peter L. R. 1977, Relics and Social Status in the Age of Gregory of Tours, Berkshire, University of Reading, p. 4.

[21] St Thomas à Becket's bones attracted not just English attention. For example, in 1179, King Louis VII of France gave to Canterbury Cathedral 'a cup of pure gold, a huge ruby known as the Régale of France, and an annual allowance of about 1 600 gallons of wine'. Butler, John 1995, The Quest for Becket's Bones: The Mystery of the Relics of St Thomas Becket of Canterbury, Yale University Press, New Haven, p. 20. See also Bentley for an account of the profit made from ordinary pilgrims visiting Canterbury Cathedral, 1985, pp. 108-12.

[22] Bentley, 1985, pp. 108-12.

[23] Hermann-Mansard, cited in Bentley, 1985, p. 29.

[24] Geary, Patrick 1978, Furta Sacra: Thefts of Relics in the Central Middle Ages, Princeton University Press, Princeton, pp. 70-1.

[25] Anon., 1900, 'History of Modern Anatomy', <http://www.fact-index.com/h/hi/history_of_modern_anatomy.html>, viewed 28 September 2005.

[26] The Anatomy Act of 1832 provided anatomists with bodies from execution, and bodies which were not claimed within 48 hours of death, unless they had left behind a request in writing for their body not to be dissected. As workhouses reduced in number, the Inspector of Anatomy in 1920 ruled that unclaimed bodies from asylums could be used. The increasing secularisation of Western society since WWI has witnessed an increasing number of bodies being left to science, so much so, that almost all bodies dissected today for medical purposes in Great Britain have been donated. Channel 4, 'The Anatomists: The Anatomy Act', <http://www.channel4.com/science/microsites/A/anatomists/ethics1.html#act>, viewed 28 September 2005.

[27] Contemporary funereal practices can send a dearly departed into space, have a star named after them and have their ashes built into an artificial reef. See websites such as Space services inc. & eternal reefs.

[28] Neely, Paula Kripaitis 2001, '17th Century Jamestown Burials: Tell Tales of Stressful Beginnings', Press Release, <http://www.apva.org/apva/burial.pdf>, viewed 28 September 2005.

[29] By the twentieth century, the expanded middle class could prove their economic and social status by acquiescing to restrictive mourning customs, which not only prescribed specific clothing, jewelry

and hats but also restricted the bereaving family members from economic activities and social contact for up to two and a half years. Vanessa Harding in Channel 4, 'An Interview with Vanessa Harding', *The Great Plague;* Channel 4 history programme transcript, <http://www.channel4.com/history/microsites/H/history/e-h/harding.html>, viewed 28 September 2005.

[30] Llewellyn, Nigel 1991, *The Art of Death: Visual Culture in the English Death Ritual c.1500-c.1800,* Reakton in association with Victoria & Albert Museum, London, pp. 60, 85.

[31] Interestingly, I watched the exhibit space throughout the day and few conference attendees went near it, hence I was aware that the exhibit was possibly having an impact. After the conference closed a small number of attendees did speak off the record, noting their discomfort at sharing the room with human bone objects.

[32] Many British missionaries and East India Company personnel wrote about the 'Devil Dances' in Hemis, Ladakh, historically referred to as 'Little Tibet'. See Coombe, G. 1975, [1926] *A Tibetan on Tibet: being the travels and observations of Mr Paul Sherap (Dorje Zödba) of Tachienlu; with an introductory chapter on Buddhism and a concluding chapter on the Devil Dance* Kathmandu, Ratna Pustak Bhandar, pp. 179-200; Anon. 1926, 'The Realm of the Devil Dancers', *New York Times,* 25 July.

[33] Kircher, Athanasius (ed.), 1677, *China Illustrata,* apud Jacobum á Meurs, Amstelodami, p. 109. Greuber's letters were edited by Kircher.

[34] Polo, *The Travels,* p. 110.

[35] Anon., 'Made from Human Bones', *New York Times,* 19 April 1930, p. 25.

[36] Mandeville, 1964, pp. 203-4.

[37] Note all three exhibitions traveled to one or more venues within the United States. One was 'Himalayas: An Aesthetic Adventure', (The Art Institute of Chicago, 5 April to August 17, 2003). The agenda of Himalayaswas aesthetic representation only. Pal, 2001. Another was 'Circle of Bliss' (Los Angeles County Museum 5 October 2003 to 4 January 2004). The agenda was the re-introduction of Tibetan and Nepalese devotional/meditational knowledge back into objects selected for their aesthetic values. Huntington, John and Dina Bangdel, 2003, *Circle of Bliss,* Serindia Publications, Chicago. In 'Tibet: Treasures from the Roof of the World'(The Bowers Museum, 12 October 12 2003 to 12 September 2004), the agenda here was art aesthetics but it was also caught in a controversial political framework. The People's Republic of China authorised the exhibition of Tibetan treasures from the Potala Palace and in doing so claimed sole ownership and access to objects that were the current self-exiled Dalai Lama's birthright. Byrd, Vickie C., Nancy R. Johnson, and Kathie A. Hamilton, 2003, *Tibet: Treasures from the Roof of the World,* Bowers Museum of Cultural Art.

[38] Pal, 2001, pp. 274-5.

[39] In some cases, the exhibition caption accompanying the exhibit may just state 'bone' and only the reading of the catalogue explains the type of bone—human. For example, see 'Ritual Apron' in Hall, Dawn (ed.) 1997, *Tibet: Tradition & Change,* The Albuquerque Museum, Albuquerque, pp. 170-1.

[40] Christies, *Indian and Southeast Asian Art,* 25 March 2004, p. 98.

[41] Lopez, Donald Jr. 1998, *Prisoners of Shangri-La: Tibetan Buddhism and the West,* University of Chicago Press, Chicago.

[42] Amateau, Albert 'Chinese takeover of Tibet protested at art opening', *The Village,* 3 March 2005, <http://www.tibet.ca>, viewed World Tibet News (WTN) 18 September 2005. Although this article, published in *The Village,* was written when the Bowers Museum exhibition arrived at the Rubin Museum of Art in New York City, it does present a good summary of the arguments used by both the protester and the collector.

[43] Stuart Jefferies, 'The naked and the dead', *The Guardian,* 19 March 2002, <http://education.guardian.co.uk/higher/arts/story/0,,670045,00.html>, viewed 28 September 2002. 'Plastination' is a process developed by Von Hagens by which the body is preserved by replacing water in the cells with plastic materials. It takes about 1500 hours work and costs up to A$50 000. The result is an odourless and durable realistic-looking corpse.

[44] I could not include in the body of the text the fact that Von Hagens also included in his British exhibition a bisected cadaver of an eight-months pregnant woman with her womb opened to reveal the foetus. O'Rorke, Imogen 'Skinless wonders…', *The Observer,* 20 May 2001, <http://observer.guardian.co.uk/review/story/0,,493200,00.html> viewed 28 September 2005; Jefferies, 'The naked and the dead'.

[45] O'Rorke, 'Skinless wonders…'. Because of Cyrillic characters identified on a flayed skin in the Berlin exhibition, it was discovered that 56 Siberian peasants and mental patients from Novosibirsk were in Von Hagens institute collection; they had not been donated.

9. The bourgeois sacred: Unveiling the 'secular society'

Liam Dee

Debates over Globalisation and The War on Terror often accept that shifting agglomeration called The West as the bastion of secularism. Whether this is a progressive force of freedom and enlightenment or a profane, cold sweatshop machine, this secularism is established against an exotic Other of primal passionate faith or feudal, superstitious zealotry, depending on your position. My talk aims to examine this image of the West and to propose that the arationality associated with the sacred is not a feudal left-over, or even just a tolerated 'personal choice'. In fact I hope to show that the sacred is an integral component of the institutions of modern power and especially that core of capitalist secularism: the commodity relationship.

To begin, it is worth looking critically at one of the key moments regaled by boosters of the Western Tradition. The supposed birth of science and philosophy in sixth century BCE Greek Asia Minor, shedding the chrysalis of mythos like some enlightenment butterfly, is itself somewhat of a myth. Though this period did indeed see the introduction of a sceptical materialism, identifiable to the modern scientific method,[1] it was 'contaminated' by the Homeric mythopoeic life-world that still predominated, 'Thales, the father of materialism, still conceived of the principle of life, movement and dynamism in terms of the gods'.[2] Nor was such a mix simply early teething problems. The seventeenth century, designated in Europe as the 'scientific revolution', saw foundational figures like Kepler, Descartes and Newton as interested in astrology, the Bible and the occult as they were in astronomy, mathematics and physics; indeed often combining these interests.[3] If contemporary scientists rarely combine *séance* with their science, Erik Davis, in his book *Techgnosis* shows that this syncretism continues to exist in a manner no less forceful for its sublimation.[4] Noting that the term 'electricity' was coined by a seventeenth century magus and chemist, Davis sees an 'electromagnetic imaginary' that renders this 'invisible force' in our information technology world. The mythos of cyberculture entreats a gnostic transcendence of ethereal data over 'old economy' matter. Though sublimated, this mix of mysticism and materialism is generally acknowledged by the coexistence of religion and the modern state.

Whether or not Weber's thesis of a foundational Protestant Ethic to the 'Spirit of Capitalism' is valid[5] the entwinement of religion and bourgeois governance continues to remain, such as to make any notion of archaic detritus problematic to say the least. This is, after all, the age of *Pax Americanus* where the seat of imperial power cannot, by unwritten law, be held by a professed atheist and the tenets of Christian Puritanism impact on imperial policy (such as the withdrawal of family-planning aid). Even within the laid-back secularism of Australia, the elements of shadow theocracy lurk, as adduced in David Marr's *The High Price of Heaven* by the influential role of conservative church leaders in social policy issues like censorship, drugs and education.[6] Given the aridity of secular parliamentary politics, where cynicism is a basically accepted, if not necessarily celebrated, fact, it is hardly surprising that religion should remain so predominant. In fact one could rightly ask, given the alacrity with which religion is accepted, to what degree the bourgeois political-economic apparatus is distinctly 'rational' at all.

Of course, if the history of science is entangled in the mystical, it should not surprise us that any definitive description of rationality is vexed to say the least. If deconstructionist critiques have problematised the foundations of mind/body duality, and even the objectivity of scientific methodology, I will at least claim that such understandings of objective reason represent an unprecedented *effort* at closure of signification. It is this effort to achieve closure that marks modern rationality. The construction of bourgeois society has seen the systematisation of almost every aspect of social life to an analogue of scientific closure such that that which fails the test, signification that is incomplete, can be policed more effectively as 'irrational'. However, such rigour cannot expunge signification in excess, that which overflows closure: the extra-ordinary, the arational (in case it needs to be reiterated, the same behaviour can be classified as either irrational, like madness, or arational, like eccentricity, depending on the overall system of rationality). Modern administration has thus been forced to call upon the traditional gatekeeper of the mystical: the sacred; that which allows the inevitable heterogenous surplus of hope, passion and faith to flow, though within defined channels. It is the guarantor but also the guard of the amorphous border zone between the rational and arational. How is the sacred able to fulfil both of these potentially contradictory roles?

To understand the 'dynamic boundedness' of the sacred we need to move beyond the oscillation between the non-rational as merely illusional and the non-rational as transcendentally real. It is here Wolfgang Fritz Haug's notion of the 'technocracy of sensuousness' is extremely useful, as much for its flaws as its conceptual attributes. For Haug, the social harnessing of the arational is the control of appearance.[7] The embodied grounding of structures of domination becomes an elaborate conjuring trick where reality is disguised by a mystical aura that justifies hierarchical accumulation. This surface abstraction is totally malleable, being detached from logico-empirical constraints and can thus similarly detach, 'sensuousness and sense from an object and...[make] them available separately'.[8] The semblance is a shadow of 'real' sensuality that displaces and channels desires and emotions to form a technocracy of sensuousness.

Yet, though Haug is right to show the way rational systematisation mediates sensuality, he pushes this mediation until it becomes almost determination. On what basis is a desire declared real or false without collapsing arationality into rationality? Yet by retaining the sense of mediation, we can avoid such a subsumption without weakening the notion of a technocracy of sensuousness. There are no administrative protocols for ecstatic joy or hope; but does that mean such effects exist beyond social relations? To the extent our feelings are social, they are mediated by power, as theorists like Foucault have shown in the intimate nature of discipline within institutions like schools, prisons and hospitals. But to maintain a lasting mediation—a technocracy of sensuousness—this discipline needs to be balanced with a genuine concession to the arational.

Nietzsche, in noting the constructed nature of 'reality', also implied that we habitually 'forget' this artifice to get through our lives (we can stop in the middle of traffic and deconstruct the concept of 'on-coming truck' or immediately respond to it as a given and live).[9] To feel as real as this truck, any technocracy of sensuousness must certainly impose a ubiquitous form and a taken-for-granted status. But to ensure this form is 'forgotten' as a manipulated artifice, it is imperative that it develop through a degree of contested openness and discontinuity. Combined, this provides a sense of authentic belonging, reassuring 'common sense' and a touch of the ecstatic unfathomable to feed our desire for transcendence. Contrary to the Poststructuralist consensus that such discontinuity is inherently subversive, the fact that the mystical continues to exist within reproducing systems of power raises the possibility that the arational may have an important role in these systems. Certainly, this can never be a direct correlation, as the arational remains dangerous and unstable (as any morality tale about dabbling in the occult will tell you). Technocracies of sensuousness thus function like casinos, which must provide a real chance of transcending the rational norms of earning money to stay in business, with the consequent threat of the casino going broke. The calculated risk embodied in sacred mysticism, that transcendent ecstatic visions will be so demanded as to transcend the political *status quo*, is also what reinforces legitimated power. The sacred as a technocracy of sensuousness aims to bring a sense of closure to the affective world of the mystical, not by denying its arationality but by mediating it with laws open to the *possibility* of transcendence.

Thus, religions like Christianity have never closed the loop with the dictates of earthly power. I must make a brief digression here to say that I find the distinction between 'religion-as-institution' and 'religiosity'/'spirituality' to be very problematic. Such a dichotomy implies a clear separation between a politically compromised sense of religion, which can be conceded in the face of overwhelming evidence of such a 'compromise', and a transcendent, individual spirituality beyond such tarnished 'organisation', thus salvaging some pure sense of religion (which is then used by the powerful, such as the current American government, when they refer to 'faith-based initiatives' rather than 'religion'). Not only does such a conceptualisation play fast and loose with the social mediation of *all* spiritual beliefs (such as the New Age, which, dressed in the mysterious rags of plundered exotic beliefs and without credibility-draining institutions, also contains a self-help philosophy of American capitalist 'can-do')[10] but it even overstates the complicity of religion-as-institution with systems of mortal power and rigid orthodoxy. For these religions, like Christianity, multiple interpretations continue to slew off from the core, despite the reactionary efforts of fundamentalists. Yet, rather than imploding the core, this heterogenous *différance* has maintained the passionate commitment, the trans-historical 'reality', of Christianity, even as it has been superseded as the locus of the Western technocracy of sensuousness.

The emergent European bourgeoisie of the eighteenth century were keen to establish their hegemony on soil as distinct from feudal absolutism as possible, which meant trying to foster a distinctly modern sacred. Such a concept was found in the resuscitation of an ancient Greek term, *'aisthesis'*. Though used by Platonists to describe shallow sense-perception, *aisthesis* had an alternative usage amongst ancient materialist philosophers that equated it to the breadth of 'consciousness', both sensual and cerebral.[11] After nearly two millennia of semantic ostracism under Christian idealism, the term was reintroduced into the modern lexicon as 'aesthetics' (initially *'aestheticus'*) by the eighteenth-century German rationalist Baumgarten to describe the enigmatic human senses. However modern rationality based its identity against the whimsical, subjective world of the sensory, how could the latter be corralled by rational methods? Baumgarten acknowledged the difficulty of this enterprise, eventually succumbing to the ambiguity created between 'reason' and 'sense-perception' in his promotion of an 'aesthetic knowledge', which he saw as more effective than abstract reason in many ways.[12] Kant, a few decades later, tried valiantly to protect Enlightenment rationality from such aesthetic erosion by mapping epistemological boundaries rather than content, thus ostensibly keeping the tools of rational conceptualism clean from perceptual affective flux. But without a proper interstitial agent between reason and aesthetics, Kant's boundaries proved porous, as he himself implicitly admitted in the *Critique of Judgement*.[13] It was after Kant that such an agent was found to preserve the sacred mysteries of imaginative, sensual, free-willing aesthetic subjectivity within the scientific-industrial complex. Thus was Art born amidst the Industrial Revolution.

New bourgeois movements like Romanticism had no time for the theoretical niceties of Kant and took the formal similarities between Artistic and aesthetic beauty as reason to bind the two and thus to ensure 'an excess of individual, subjective autonomy in which to locate bourgeois identity'.[14] Here then was a sanctioned form of 'arationality', the inevitable and celebrated residue of rationalism. Just as divinity embodied absolutism, and all its contradictions, in a sacred, 'arational' form in Western Christianity, so Art was embodied as the sacred, arational form of bourgeois values and subjectivity. The arational energy of the aesthetic was bound to Art the way the amorphous energy of Christian mysticism was bound to institutional icons and rituals.

Yet the exclusivity of Art, replicating the exclusivity of Christian learning amongst the educated medieval clergy,[15] has increased the impetus for a broader bourgeois technocracy of sensuousness. To this end the locus of the modern sacred is being gradually moved from Art to the very germ of capitalist rationality: the commodity. 'A commodity appears, at first sight, a very trivial thing, and easily understood. Its analysis shows that it is, in reality, a very queer thing, abounding in metaphysical subtleties and theological niceties'.[16] If Christianity's sacred excess is felt in the hope of salvation and Art's in the irreducibility of subjective expression, then the commodity's is the liberation of desire. This capitalist excess is the Romanticist dream of liberated subjectivity free from stuffy social convention, eternal horizons to adventure towards and whatever we want when we want it. The sacred catch, to make sure this fantasy does not fly free of rational closure, is that this liberated desire is only meant to be enacted within the commodity relationship. If we all decided to enact our desires beyond commodities, capitalism would crumble. The sacred thus balances the arational dreams of the liberated subject with the very rational demands of profit valorisation.

To this end, the aesthetic, initially quarantined within the Art work, has been paroled as the design of commodities and advertising style have taken precedence over more logocentric marketing (framed as appeals to reason). Corporations spend inordinate sums of money on advertisements high in style and low on product information (unless you consider 'Coke adds life' or 'Just Do It' product information). They also fight tooth and nail to protect their ephemeral brand icons, which, as Naomi Klein has documented in *No Logo*, have become powerful markers of status and self.[17] If that sounds conspiratorial you should note that the CEO of advertising company Saatchi & Saatchi has just written a widely marketed book called *Lovemarks*, which demands that businesses create long-term emotional relationships with consumers by infusing their brands with mystery, sensuality, and intimacy.[18] But it is in the very design of everyday lifestyle products that the inscrutable aesthetic is most effective, becoming more and more like Art where form does not follow function. Or, are we to believe that the animistically organic smooth curves of iMacs and mobile phones make them faster and more efficient?

However, before we glibly declare consumerism the 'new religion', we need to remember that religion derives from *'religio'* referring to social bonds,[19] something the alienating individualism of consumer culture retards. As well, the push to 'spiritualise' commodities is rather young (thus lacking the authenticity of duration), not to mention the overt association commodity exchange must hold with rationalism; the opposite problem of religion, which must maintain its association with the spiritual and remain furtive about relations with earthly power. Yet, any cynicism this generates is also evidence of the open discontinuity of commodity aesthetics that many have taken as evidence of genuine egalitarian authenticity. All these ironic digs at advertising (which advertisers engage in as well), if framed without substantial alternative visions, simply promote more interest in the commodity and diminish its manipulative aura. It thus seems dynamically negotiated even as it reaches omnipresence, dictated by an oligarchy of near unaccountable marketing and sales executives.

Even if the gamble of playing to ironic engagement fails, there remain older technocracies of sensuousness like religion, Art and patriotism, whose survival as 'tradition' implies legitimacy, regardless of how much this relates to top-down manipulation. These 'traditional' forms function to soak up ecstatic, transcendent yearning and keep disillusionment in check. The much applauded 'tolerance' of the West is less a function of bourgeois generosity than a necessary aid to the sacralisation of capitalism. The aforementioned coexistence between religion and capitalism is as much to do with how much this religion makes itself 'tolerable' as anything else. This is either through directly augmenting overt commodity values like individualism (*à la* Protestantism) and property rights, or upholding latent values like respect for authority (this does not have to be explicit doctrine, even the implicitly hierarchical nature of monotheistic worship is enough, not to mention the gender politics of God as a He), which are vital for the commodity relationship but which must be formally disavowed. The bare minimum for tolerance is to not directly contradict the commodity with 'extremist' morality against greed, usury and free markets. Such is the tacit understanding of 'moderate Islam', loudly preached by the Coalition of the Willing lest anyone mistake their War on Terror as a War on the Sacred.

Indeed far from signalling absolute profanity, consumer societies are in fact overwhelming us with the sacred. That this regulation of the mystical cannot be reduced to mere political interest is hardly grounds for apolitical acquittal, especially as it is the irreducible arational element of the sacred that entices passionate identity with abstractions that maintain priestly or profiteering elites. The underlying premise of negotiating the sacred is that its arational form, the passionate faith it evokes, problematises the critical scrutiny that we accept for political rationalism. But if the presence of arationality was to foreclose critique then there would be none, for the arational is as much a part of our social mediation as the rational. Rather than merely accepting the sacred as, for better or for worse, the only way to access the mystical and passionate, perhaps we can begin pondering the removal of the sacred gatekeeper to be replaced by arational agents that open the social resources of imaginative ecstasy and transcendent yearning to more immanent, democratic forms.

ENDNOTES

1 Koestler, A. 1964, *The Sleepwalkers: A History of Man's Changing Vision of the Universe*, Harmondsworth, Penguin, p. 22.

2 Novack, G. 1965, *The Origins of Materialism*, New York, Pathfinder Press, p. 174.

3 Popkin, R. H. 1999, 'Introduction', J. E. Force and R. H. Popkin (eds), *Newton and Religion: Context, Nature, and Influence*, Dordrecht, Kluwer Academic Publishers, pp. xi-xii.

4 Davis, E. 1999, *Techgnosis: Myth, Magic and Mysticism in the Age of Information*, London, Serpent's Tale.

5 Turner, B. S. 1983, *Religion and Social Theory: A Materialist Perspective*, London, Heinemann Educational Books, p. 112.

6 Marr, D. 1999, *The High Price of Heaven*, St Leonards, Allen and Unwin.

7 Haug, W. F. 1987, *Commodity Aesthetics, Ideology and Culture*, New York, International General, p. 113.

8 Haug, 1987, p. 115.

9 Nietzsche, F. 1979, 'On Truth and Lies in a Nonmoral Sense', D. Breazeale (trans. & ed.), *Philosophy and Truth: Selections from Nietzsche's Notebooks of the Early 1870s*, Atlantic Highlands, Humanities Press, pp. 79-91.

10 Carlson, P. 'UFOs? When Penguins Fly! Sedona Exposes Those Amazing Extraterrestrials', *The Washington Post*, 10 November 1998, p. B02.

11 Modrak, D. M. 1981, 'An Aristotelian Theory of Consciousness?' *Ancient Philosophy*, vol. 1, no. 2, pp. 160-70.

12 Eagleton, T. 1990, *The Ideology of the Aesthetic*, Oxford, Basil Blackwell, p. 15; Welsch, W. 1997, *Undoing Aesthetics*, A. Inkpin (trans.), London, SAGE Publications, p. 40.

13 Kant, I. 1987 [1790], *Critique of Judgement*, W. S. Pluhar (trans.), Indianapolis, Hackett Publishing Company, pp. 89, 162.

14 Cazeaux, C. 2000, 'Introduction', C. Cazeaux, (ed.), *The Continental Aesthetics Reader*, London, Routledge, p. xv.

15 Bloch, M. 1989, *Feudal Society: Volume I, The Growth of Ties of Dependence*, Manyon, L. A. (trans.), London, Routledge, p. 82.

16 Marx, K. 1967 [1867], *Capital: A Critique of Political Economy, vol. 1 The Process of Capitalist Production*, S. Moore and E. Aveling (trans.), New York, International Publishers, p. 71.

17 Klein, N. 2001, *No Logo*, London, Harper Collins.

18 Roberts, K. 2004, *Lovemarks: The Future Beyond Brands*, New York, Power House Books.

19 Turner, 1983, p. 8.

Section III. The State, Religion and Tolerance

10. Sacrilege: From public crime to personal offence

Ian Hunter

In this chapter I will be looking at sacrilege in the context of Western European religion and politics in the early modern period. I will be adopting an historical-anthropological approach, with a view to making this discussion of sacrilege comparable with those of people working in other religious and cultural settings. Moreover, there is an important sense in which the societies of early modern Western Europe were themselves multicultural, not just because most contained diverse ethnic 'nations', but more importantly because they contained mutually hostile religious communities. In fact, 'religious cleansing' in early modern Europe provided the prototype for later acts of ethnic cleansing, and the methods by which states attempted to deal with religious conflict led to forms of government still in place today.[1] This is the context in which I will address my particular theme: how sacrilege was transformed from public crime into personal offence.

Whether sacrilege is possible, and the form in which it takes place, depends upon the disposition of the sacred, of which sacrilege is the violation. And the disposition of the sacred itself varies with the beliefs, doctrines and practices that characterise particular religious cultures. In Western European Christianity, the sacred is understood in terms of the earthly presence of a transcendent divinity.[2] It is the mediation of this divinity in the world by special persons, places, and things that makes them sacred, and that makes other persons, places and things profane. In this setting, sacrilege occurs when sacred persons, places or things are misused, abused or violated - in short, profaned. Sacrilege thus occurs at the boundary of the sacred and the profane—in transcendent salvational religions like Christianity a particular sharp and fraught boundary—and represents an improper crossing of the boundary itself. Where the boundary also marks the borders of a community—as in the circle of Eucharistic communicants—then sacrilege threatens the community itself (threatens its communication with the divinity) and can result in violent expulsion.[3] The extent to which the transcendent divinity is manifest in earthly things, and the forms in which this occurs, differ radically between different Christian confessions. Those stressing God's transcendent and supra-human character minimise the forms in which the divinity can be represented or manifested, and may indeed treat such forms—icons, rituals, shrines, priests—as themselves sacrilegious. Those versions of Christianity teaching the mediated presence of God in the world typically treat such icons, rituals, shrines and priests as sacred, and view their more puritan or iconoclastic rivals as sacrilegious. But to keep this all in perspective, we need to observe that not all disciplines of life operate the distinction between sacred and profane that gives rise to sacrilege. In non-transcendental arts of living—such as ancient Stoicism and Epicureanism—we find no equivalent category of the sacred, and avoiding sacrilege is treated as a matter of politeness towards those who worship the gods.[4]

Throughout the medieval and early modern period, however, European Christianity was more than just a spiritual locus. It was a formidable earthly force. It exercised direct political and juridical power through an archipelago of armed prince-bishops, the diocesan structure being in fact the footprints left by Christian warriors as they made their way across Europe, stamping out 'paganism' in the early middle ages.[5] And it exercised indirect power through secular princes, who enforced the law of the most powerful prince-bishop—the bishop of Rome—as part of their exercise of lordship.[6] Under these circumstances, where there was no clear distinction between the religious and political community or between the Christian and the citizen, sacrilege was both a spiritual transgression and a juridical felony, attracting severe criminal punishment.

We can suggest then that sacrilege emerged as sin and crime in Western Europe as the result of a particular set of cultural and political circumstances: broadly, those of a transcendent sacralising religion exercising overwhelming political and juridical powers, both through its own authority and that of the secular prince or emperor. When these circumstances changed—when in the sixteenth century Western Christendom split into a diversity of churches and then gradually lost its capacity to exercise direct juridical and political power—then sacrilege too was radically transformed. This transformation of sacrilege, which can be characterised as a shift from public crime to personal offence, is what I want to sketch today, in the briefest of terms.

Sacrilege and sacramental violence

We can begin by quickly indicating how sacrilege—together with the closely associated religious crimes of heresy, blasphemy and witchcraft—took shape in the ecclesial and juridical institutions of late-medieval European Christendom. There are two broad factors to take into account. In the first place, as the obverse of the sacred, sacrilege was a powerful and authentic expression of core Christian sacramental practices, finding expression in both popular devotion and elite theological speculation. A common focus was provided by those earthly things held to be bearers of the transcendent divinity—the church and within the church the Eucharistic host—which, as the most sacred and beneficial of things, were also the most vulnerable to profanation and degradation. Thus, in many parts of late-medieval Europe, as the magical source of God's blessing on the community, the host was paraded through the village and fields in early spring to ensure a good harvest.[7] Concomitantly, the allegation of sacrilegious profanation of the host was the routine way of triggering murderous Christian pogroms against local Jewish communities, non-believers from outside the circle of communicants whose polluting presence threatened communication with God.[8]

Second, if sacrilege was deeply rooted in sacramental religious practice, then during the thirteenth and fourteenth centuries it underwent a major elaboration and codification in canon law, where it was linked to heresy, blasphemy and witchcraft. This was the time at which the university canonists of Northern Italy developed a common legal process for dealing with this array of crimes; a process that could be initiated by denunciation, deployed oaths of veridiction, permitted the regulated use of torture to obtain evidence, denied appeal, and could result in the death sentence.[9] The extension of canon and Roman law across Western Europe during this period resulted in a centralised system of legal authority, permitting the papacy to exert religious and civil jurisdiction via local clerical and secular authorities.[10] Sacrilege thus came to be prosecuted in a much more systematic manner and, because of its linkage to heresy, blasphemy and witchcraft, participated in a cross-referring nexus of religious criminality. Heretics were thus routinely denounced as sacrilegious, their guilt being proved by the fact that they performed mock masses, feasted on Eucharistic wafers, broke crucifixes, declared Jesus to be a fraud, and so on. And those on trial for sacrilege were routinely denounced as heretics, their profane acts being indicative of their secret adherence to erroneous and ungodly beliefs.

The presence of the criminal sin of sacrilege in early modern Europe was thus symptomatic of a tightly woven and far-flung matrix of sacramental practices, juridical procedures, and authority structures, anchored ecclesiastically in the papacy and politically in the Holy Roman Empire. Despite the relative civil autonomy of the Northern Italian city states, elsewhere in Europe this matrix resulted in a virtual super-imposition of the sacramental community on the civil community. Threats to the sacramental community resulting from sacrilege, heresy and blasphemy, once proved by the ecclesiastical courts, were subject to the harshest of punishments by the civil authorities. Conversely, threats to civil authority were themselves treated as analogous to sacrilege against the sacred person of the prince, who was God's viceroy on earth.[11] It is this very superimposition of the sacramental and civil communities, however, that explains the intensity and uncontrollability of the religious-political conflicts that followed from the splitting of the church at the beginning of the sixteenth century. For once the heresy that would become the Protestant church had escaped the juridical and political machinery designed to contain such outbreaks, Protestant princes immediately used this machinery to defend their religion against the Roman church.

Given that faith communities were demarcated by the border between the sacred and the profane—between true believers and the heretical monsters—the civil conflicts that erupted across Europe assumed a specifically religious intensity, as those one sought to exterminate were not just political enemies but polluting threats to the sacramental community and its capacity to communicate with God.[12] Further, this sacramental violence was made all the more difficult to control by the fact that the new religion differed from the old, both in its construction of the sacred and therefore in its sense of sacrilege. The Calvinists in particular stressed the transcendence and inscrutability of God, rejecting the notion of real presence in the Eucharist, and regarding other forms of Catholic immanentism—rituals, processions, pilgrimages, relics—as sacrilegious idolatry, making sacrilege itself into a flashpoint for sacramental violence. In June 1528, for example, the first act of Calvinist iconoclasm in Paris—the vandalising of an image of the Virgin   was answered by an act of Catholic ritual cleansing, as all parishes and the university organised processions to atone for this sacrilege.[13] Ritual burnings, disembowelments, and massacres were soon to follow as France descended in a series of religious civil wars in which both sides viewed the extermination of the other as necessary for cleansing a spiritual pollution and restoring the purity of the sacramental community.

At the same time, however, the very ferocity of this violence, which threatened the survival of the state itself, led Bodin and the *politiques* to make the first attempts to separate religious and political community, by developing a secular conception of sovereignty. We can see this in the terms with which the Chancellor Michel de L'Hôpital addressed a peace colloquium during the first war of religion in 1562:

> It is not a question of establishing the faith, but of regulating the state. It is possible to be a citizen without being a Christian. You do not cease to be a subject of the King when you separate from the Church. We can live in peace with those who do not observe the same ceremonies.[14]

In fact Chancellor L'Hôpital's words proved to be in vain in the French context, as France would eventually solve the problem of religious conflict by suppressing then eliminating the French Calvinists or Huguenots. Nonetheless, they pointed forward to a profound change—the uncoupling of political governance from Christian spirituality—which would radically transform the character of the sacred and of sacrilege.

The spiritualising of religion and the desacralising of law and politics

During the seventeenth century all of the major European powers were faced with the same set of problems: how to achieve religious peace and how to establish stable rule in territories containing bitterly divided religious communities. The measures that evolved to meet these problems—religious toleration being just the tip of the iceberg—would alter the disposition of the sacred and lead to the sidelining of sacrilege (together with heresy and blasphemy) within an increasingly autonomous civil domain. Unfortunately for the historian, these developments differed significantly both within the German Empire and among the other sovereign territorial states, so that there is no typical case. In order to keep my exposition manageable, I will thus focus on developments in the German states—Brandenburg-Prussia in particular—making do with just a few comparative remarks on Britain and France, acknowledging upfront the element of historical bias thus introduced.

The developments that saw the institution of religious peace within the German Empire were piecemeal, protracted, and never fully successful. Nonetheless, we can detect a pattern of development in the century that separated the Religious Peace of Augsburg of 1555 and the more permanent Peace of Westphalia in 1648, which brought an end to the Thirty Years War by declaring that henceforth all three main confessions—Catholicism, Lutheranism and Calvinism—would be recognised and tolerated under imperial law. In his account of this complex process, the German historian of church law, Martin Heckel, points to a number of key elements: the relegation of theology in favour of European public law as the key discourse in the peace negotiations; the gradual acceptance of the permanence of heresy by leading figures, even if the churches would have none of this; and, most important of all, the dropping of religious truth as a criterion for peace in the great treaties, and its replacement by a quite different kind of norm for legitimacy: namely, the attainment of social peace.[15] In making social peace the prime duty of the sovereign (as opposed to defending the faith or enforcing religious law as God's earthly viceroy) these developments led to a profound secularisation of the political domain. Yet, as Heckel has argued, this was not a secularisation driven by some all-embracing secularist philosophy (in the manner of the French *philosophes*), but one carried forward by many anonymous jurists and statesmen who remained devoted Christians.[16] Far from attempting to expunge Christianity, their prime objective was to secure the survival of their own confessions in the face of wholesale religious slaughter. Yet they gradually accepted that for this to happen it would be necessary to separate the church's pursuit of salvation from the state's aim of worldly security.

In the case of post-Westphalian Brandenburg-Prussia, this led to a profound dual transformation of the religious and political landscape. On the one hand, there was remarkable desacralisation of politics, as jurisconsults and political philosophers attached to the court began to reconstruct the objectives of the state in quasi-Hobbesian terms; that is, in terms of maintaining external and internal security while eschewing all higher level religious and moral aims. On the other hand, there was a no less remarkable spiritualisation of religion, as the Pietists aided by important lay theologians attempted to undermine the whole idea of religious orthodoxy—that is, the idea that salvation was tied to a particular set of theological doctrines and sacramental practices—arguing instead that salvation came rather from a purely personal inner relation to God.

The manner in which this dual desacralisation of politics and spiritualisation of religion transformed the prior construction of sacrilege, heresy, and witchcraft can be seen in the writings of Christian Thomasius, professor of law at the University of Halle in the late seventeenth century, lay theologian, and jurisconsult to the Brandenburg-Prussian court. In his works attacking the legal prosecution of heresy, witchcraft and sacrilege, Thomasius argued along two convergent paths. First, in keeping with his spiritualist theology, he argued that there was no true visible church; that the true church was invisible, known by no outward doctrinal or liturgical signs, and that its members were permanently scattered across the globe. This detachment of salvation from the church removed the theological grounds of heresy and sacrilege by (in effect) denying that God was mediated by specific sacred doctrines or by sacred rituals in holy places.[17] Second, in keeping with the quasi-Hobbesian conception of politics which he had learned from his mentor Samuel Pufendorf, Thomasius argued that the state had no religious objectives and must be restricted to the ends of maintaining domestic peace and external security.[18] For this reason there should be no laws against sacrilege, heresy and witchcraft as such, unless the actions associated with them gave rise to violence or civil disorder, in which case they would be punished for that reason, and not because they profaned the community of the faithful.[19] Unlike his more famous contemporary, John Locke, Thomasius did not base his arguments for toleration on the philosophical notion of natural rights, but on the dual imperatives to spiritualise religion and desacralise the state, whose overarching goal was not personal liberty but the stable governance of multi-confessional societies.

Thomasius thus marks the moment at which, after a century and a half of religious war, the web of canon laws which had tied the political to the religious community began to be unpicked, allowing the persona of the citizen to be differentiated from that of the Christian; although even in Western Europe this moment was neither epochal nor universal. In late-seventeenth century England, religious peace was achieved in a quite different way: not by dismantling the confessional state, but by rebuilding it in a more stable, less persecutory form. This was achieved in accordance with two broad strategies. First, the Anglican church that was to be established as the state religion, was purged of enough

Anglo-Catholic theology to bring back on board moderate dissenters, providing a stable religious middle ground. Second, using a combination of test acts and toleration acts, non-conforming Protestants and Catholics were excluded from office-holding in the Anglican state, while permitted freedom of private worship. While this set of strategies proved no less successful in securing religious peace than those used in Brandenburg-Prussia, its effect on the laws pertaining to heresy, witchcraft, sacrilege and blasphemy was far less dramatic and uniform. While heresy and witchcraft laws were repealed during the eighteenth century, blasphemy remained a common law crime as a means of protecting the state religion, leading it to form a new juridical series with sedition and obscenity. And it was in this form, as one of a trio of libels—obscene, seditious and blasphemous—that sacrilege maintained a kind of half-life into the modern period of English common law.

Concluding remarks

Let me conclude by offering a few tentative remarks on how the history I have sketched might bear on current issues, including some of those raised at this conference. I have stressed that the European religious settlements of the late seventeenth century took no single form, and were we to look at France whose settlement had to wait another century, that would only add a third quite different model to those of Germany and England. Nonetheless, despite this, it still makes sense to talk of a broad European-wide movement in which the religious crimes of heresy, sacrilege and blasphemy would lose their status as public crimes. They underwent a sea change, such that the boundary between the sacred and the profane no longer marks the perimeter of the political community but only that of particular religious communities, or sometimes simply particular religious sensibilities.

The historical account offered of this complex of developments should lead us to be sceptical of two modern philosophical and theological attitudes towards the transformations in question. First, it should lead us to question the accounts of toleration given by philosophical liberalism, which seek to ground toleration in the recovery of universal reason and universal subjective rights. As I have already indicated, in Brandenburg-Prussia, Thomasius's arguments for toleration and against heresy, witchcraft and sacrilege laws were grounded not in universal reason and subjective rights, but in an intensely spiritualist theology and a quasi-Hobbesian politics oriented to the desacralisation of the state. Second, for the same reasons, though, we should also be sceptical of philosophical-communitarian accounts of these developments which portray them in terms of the loss of identity-affirming community membership, the emergence of atomised rights-bearing individuals, and a privatisation of religion that would rob political life of depth and meaning. It is true that the undoing of heresy, sacrilege and blasphemy laws gradually allowed for the uncoupling of the religious and political communities, but this multiplied rather than diminished the number of communities to which individuals might belong, or the number of personae they might cultivate. Moreover, while it is also true that religion was privatised in the sense of eventually being removed from the coercive apparatus of the state, the threshold of the 'public' that was established—namely, the likelihood of causing civil violence—was high enough to allow for a wide variety of religious institutions and activities to flourish in the civil arena. In fact, the more the state came to approximate a detranscendentalised security envelope, the more it became possible for religious communities to pursue intensely transcendental forms of religious cultivation inside this envelope, without having to fear reprisals from neighbouring communities to whom their version of the sacred might appear sacrilegious.

As a result of the broad developments we have discussed, in those Western European-based jurisdictions where sacrilege and blasphemy laws remained on the books, they lost their sacral character. As these laws evolved in the modern period, it was no longer the violation of persons, things and places inhabited by a transcendent divinity that defined the crime, but something else altogether: the giving of offence in a manner that might lead to civil disorder or violence. Thomasius had already reconstructed the laws pertaining to heresy, blasphemy and witchcraft in this way during the 1690s, in order to prevent their use as weapons of mutual persecution by those who disagreed about the way in which the Christian God inhabited the world. And this broadly is the history of blasphemy law presumed by the New South Wales Law Reform Commission in its Blasphemy Report of 1994; for the Commissioners argue that the key element of the law—that of offensiveness likely to cause civil disturbance—obviates the need for a special law on blasphemy, as this element is well covered by other public-order and anti-discrimination laws.[20] I would suggest that this kind of recommendation is indicative not of a state of affairs in which society has lost touch with the sacred; rather, it is indicative of one in which the sacred exists only at the level of society—that is, at the level of voluntary religious associations—having been purged from the coercive apparatus of the state as a result of the early modern religious settlements.

ENDNOTES

[1] Wokler, R. 2000, 'Multiculturalism and Ethnic Cleansing in the Enlightenment', in P. G. Ole and R. Porter (eds), *Toleration in Enlightenment Europe*, Cambridge, Cambridge University Press; Seidler, M. J. 2002, 'Pufendorf and the Politics of Recognition', in I. Hunter and D. Saunders (eds), *Natural Law and Civil Sovereignty: Moral Right and State Authority in Early Modern Political Thought*, Basingstoke, Palgrave, pp. 235-51.

[2] Brown, P. 1982, 'Society and the Supernatural: A Medieval Change', in P. Brown (ed.), *Society and the Holy in Late Antiquity*, Berkeley, University of Californian Press, pp. 302-32.

[3] Schilling, H. 1989, 'Sündenzucht und frühneuzeitliche Sozialdisziplinierung: Die calvinistische, presbyteriale Kirchenzucht', in Emden vom 16. bis 19. Jahrhundert, in G. Schmidt (ed.), *Stände und Gesellschaft im Alten Reich*, Stuttgart, Franz Steiner Verlag, pp. 265-302.

[4] Brown, P. 1995, *Authority and the Sacred: Aspects of the Christianisation of the Roman World*, Cambridge, Cambridge University Press, pp. 34-5.

[5] Bartlett R. 1993, *The Making of Europe: Conquest, Colonisation and Cultural Change 950-1350*, Princeton, Princeton University Press, pp. 5-23.

[6] Padoa-Schioppa, A. 1997, 'Hierarchy and Jurisdiction: Models in Medieval Canon Law', in A. Padoa-Schioppa (ed.), *Legislation and Justice*, Oxford, Oxford University Press, pp. 1-15.

[7] Baur, J. 1992, 'Lutherische Christologie', H. C. Rublack (ed.), *Die lutherische Konfessionalisierung in Deutschland*, Gütersloh, Gern Mohn, pp. 83-124.

[8] Nirenberg, D. 1996, *Communities of Violence: Persecution of Minorities in the Middle Ages*, Princeton NJ., Princeton University Press.

[9] Trusen, W. 1992, 'Rechtliche Grundlagen des Häresiebegriffs und des Ketzerverfahrens', S. S. Menchi (ed.), *Ketzerverfolgung im 16. und frühen 17. Jahrhundert*, Wiesbaden, Otto Harrassowitz, pp. 1-20.

[10] Padoa-Schioppa, 1997.

[11] Kantorowicz, E. 1957, *The King's Two Bodies: A Study in Medieval Political Theology*, Princeton, N. J., Princeton University Press.

[12] Crouzet, D. 1990, *Les Guerriers de Dieu. La violence au temps des troubles de religion*. Seysell, Champ Vallon.

[13] Ramsey, A. W. 1999, *Liturgy, Politics, and Salvation: The Catholic League in Paris and the Nature of Catholic Reform, 1540-1630*, Rochester NY, University of Rochester Press, p. 8.

[14] L'Hôpital, M. de. 1824-5, *Oeuvres Completes de Michel de L'Hôpital*, I, 425.

[15] Heckel, M. 1989, 'Zur Historiographie des Westfälischen Friedens', in K. Schlaich (ed.), *Martin Heckel Gesammelte Schriften: Staat, Kirche, Recht, Geschichte*, Tübingen, J. C. B. Mohr. I, pp. 484-500; Heckel, M. 1992, 'Religionsbann und landesherrliches Kirchenregiment', in H. C. Rublack (ed.), *Die lutherische Konfessionalisierung in Deutschland*, Gütersloh, Gerd Mohn, pp. 130-62.

[16] Heckel, M. 1984, 'Das Säkularisierungsproblem in der Entwicklung des deutschen Staatskirchenrechts', G. Dilcher and I. Staff (eds), *Christentum und modernes Recht. Beiträge zum Problem der Säkularisation*. Frankfurt a. M., Suhrkamp, pp. 35-95.

[17] Thomasius, C. 1705, 'Ob Ketzerei ein straffbares Verbrechen sei? (An haeresis sit crimen)', C. Thomasius (ed.), *Auserlesene deutsche Schriften, Erster Teil*, Halle, Renger, pp. 210-307.

[18] Thomasius, C. 1701, *Dreyfache Rettung des Rechts Evangelischer Fürsten in Kirchen-Sachen*, Frankfurt; Thomasius, C. 1705, 'Vom Recht evangelischer Fürsten in Mitteldingen oder Kirchenzeremonien' (*De jure principis circa adiaphora*, 1695), in C. Thomasius (ed.), *Auserlesene deutsche Schriften Erster Teil*, Halle, Renger, 1, pp. 76-209.

[19] Thomasius, C. 1701, *De crimine magiae / Von dem Verbrechen der Zauber- und Hexerey*, Halle, Renger.

[20] New South Wales Law Reform Commission, 1994, *Blasphemy Report 74*, Sydney.

11. Expressions of religiosity and blasphemy in modern societies

Riaz Hassan

Until recently a widely held view in sociology was that the conditions of modernity inevitably lead to the secularisation of society. It was further argued that in a secular society, religion becomes increasingly a private concern of the individual and thus loses much of its public relevance and influence. The conditions of modernity were seen as conducive to promoting religious pluralism in which people were voluntary adherents to a plurality of religions, none of which could claim a position of hegemony in society. These and similar views appeared in the works of a number of prominent scholars including Talcott Parsons,[1] Thomas Luckmann,[2] Peter Berger[3] and Robert Bellah.[4]

The secularisation thesis was predicated on the nature of modernity and its sociological consequences. The core attribute of modern society was its institutional differentiation and functional rationalisation. Functionally differentiated societal institutions specialise around specific kinds of actions, for instance, polity, economy, law, science, education, art, health, religion and the family. These institutions not only performed specialised functions, but they were also relatively autonomous. In other words they developed their own norms to evaluate performance and were largely free from the interference of other societal institutions in carrying out their specialised tasks. Under these conditions, religious institutions also occupied a specialised functional domain which dealt purely with religious matters such as the sacred, religious beliefs, rituals and morality.

Secularisation was thus a consequence of the institutional differentiation and relative independence of various institutional spheres from religious norms, values and justifications. A logical and necessary outcome of this process is that religion not only retreats from the many public aspects of social life but it also comes under pressure to develop a specialised institutional sphere of its own. These conditions encourage the privatisation of religion. While religion can still direct the lives of individuals and subgroups, it becomes essentially a private concern of the individual. As a result, institutional religion cannot compete in the new structural environment and, therefore, weakens, leaving the religious tasks of constructing and guaranteeing holistic meaning systems primarily with the individual and a multitude of voluntary organisations.[5] In short, institutional differentiation in modern societies leads to secularisation by restricting the influence of religious norms and values on other institutional spheres.

As mentioned above, in modern societies religious institutions also come under pressure to develop their own specialised functions and public role in society. Until recently this question was not adequately addressed in sociological theory because it was assumed that religion would continue to weaken in modern society and would eventually lose its public influence and social relevance. However, the continuous strength of religion in modern societies like the United States, Australia and other European societies, as well as newly modernising societies like India, the Philippines, Singapore, Brazil, Mexico and in Muslim societies, has raised important questions about the validity of the conventional explanation of the status and role of religion in modern societies. Religion is proving to be resilient not only in terms of the number of adherents and the degree of their involvement in religious organisations but also in terms of its public influence.[6]

To better understand this phenomenon we turn to the work of Niklas Luhmann. Luhmann agrees that the central feature of modern society is its institutional differentiation and functional specialisation. The specialised institutions operate as relatively autonomous functional instrumentalities. However, Luhmann argues that while the functional autonomy is real, it is conditioned by the fact that the other institutions are also operating in the same milieu. This leads him to explore the difference between how an institution relates to the society and to other institutional systems. He uses the terms 'function' and 'performance' to explore this. The term 'function' refers to religious communication and actions such as worship, devotion, salvation, morality and spirituality. Function, in other words, is the communication involving the sacred and the aspects that the religious institutions claim for themselves, as the basis of their autonomy in modern society.

Religious performance, by contrast, occurs when religion is 'applied' to problems such as economic poverty, political oppression, human rights abuse, domestic violence, environmental degradation, racism, etc., generated in the domains of other institutional systems but not solved or addressed there or elsewhere.[7] Performance thus is concerned purely with the profane. It is through the performance relations that religion establishes its importance for the profane aspects of life and in the process reinforces the autonomy of religious action. There is a tension between the two, which is accentuated in certain strata of modern societies, but function and performance are in fact inseparable and mutually reinforcing. In Australia and elsewhere in the Christian West, for example, churches have been historically involved in education, social welfare and health care and the same type of involvement is present in Muslim societies from Indonesia to Morocco and Nigeria.

For Luhmann, the functional problem of religion in the modern world is in fact a performance problem. As mentioned earlier, increasing pressure towards secularisation and privatisation of religion under conditions of modernity tend to place religion in a position of disadvantage. The solution to this problem lies in finding effective religious applications, and not in more religious commitment and practice.[8] The main reason is that religion, as an institution concerned purely with its functional role of promoting the sacred as an all encompassing reality, runs counter to the specialised and instrumental pattern of the other dominant institutional systems. The functional role of religion in the past involved religious performance through moral codes that were used to explain the existence of social problems as consequences of sin and other contraventions of religious codes. Under these conditions, religious codes favoured morality as a privileged form of social regulation. This is precisely what is undermined by social structural conditions of modern society. The decline in the central regulatory role of morality is the principal cause of the functional problems, including the decline in the public influence of religion in modern society.

Religion and blasphemy

What are the implications of these developments in the role of religion in modern society for the acts of blasphemy? I will examine this question after a brief overview of the concept of blasphemy. The word blasphemy is derived from a Greek term meaning 'speaking evil'. In the Judeo-Christian tradition it refers to all acts of verbal offences against sacred values. A seventeenth-century Scottish jurist described it as 'treason against God'. In Catholic theology it is defined as 'any word of malediction, reproach, of contumely pronounced against God', and is regarded as a sin. Blasphemy exists to prevent challenge to the notions of the sacred in organised religion. Its existence is a litmus test of the standards a society feels it must enforce to preserve its religious beliefs and morality and to prevent mockery of its gods. It constitutes an intolerable affront to the sacred, the priestly class, the deeply held beliefs of the believers and the basic values a community shares. Its commission invariably evoked severe punishment. In Judeo-Christian-Islamic traditions, its commission is/was punishable by death. Denying the existence of God or reviling God is also recognised as an offence under common law.

From the seventeenth century onwards, blasphemy increasingly became a secular crime in England and that tradition was also followed in the United States. The state began to supplant the church as the agency mainly responsible for instigating and conducting prosecutions. The connection between religious dissent and political subversion and the belief that a nation's religious unity augmented its peace and strength accounted in part for the rising dominance of the state in policing serious crimes against religion. But in the post Enlightenment age, blasphemy prosecutions began to decline.

There have been no prosecutions in the United States since 1969, and the last successful blasphemy prosecution in England was in 1977. There has been no prosecution in the state of Massachusetts in the United States since the 1920s, but in 1977, the State legislature refused to repeal its three hundred year old act against blasphemy. In general, in the Anglo-American world, the conditions of modernity have made the legal prosecutions against blasphemy not only rare but also obsolete. People seem to have learned that Christianity is capable of surviving without penal sanctions and that God can avenge its own honour. The sentiments against blasphemy in the religious segments of the populations, however, continue to persist.[9]

In Islam there is no exact equivalent of the Christian notion of blasphemy, but offering insult to God (Allah), to the prophet Muhammed, or any part of the divine revelation constitutes a crime under Islamic religious law. From the perspective of Islamic law acts of blasphemy can be defined as any verbal expression that gives grounds for suspicion of apostasy. Blasphemy also overlaps with infidelity (*kufr*), which is the deliberate rejection of Allah/God and revelation. In this sense expressing religious opinions at variance with standard Islamic views could easily be looked upon as blasphemous.[10]

The Salman Rushdie affair in 1988,[11] Nasr Hamed Abu Zeid affair in Egypt in 1994,[12] and Hashem Aghajari Affair in Iran in 2003,[13] signify that religious sanctions against blasphemy and apostasy have a powerful presence in contemporary Muslim countries and can have real legal and personal consequences for the accused persons. As my knowledge about the existence of formal blasphemy laws is limited to Pakistan I will use Pakistan as a case study to highlight the situation in Muslim countries in which such laws may also exist. During the Islamisation campaign of the late Pakistani President Zia-ul Haq several new sections relating to religious offences were added to the Pakistan Penal Code. In 1980, section 298-A was introduced which made the use of derogatory remarks in respect of persons revered in Islam an offence, punishable with up to three years imprisonment.

In 1986, this was further narrowed down, by inserting an offence specifically directed at the person of the Prophet. Defiling the name of the Prophet Muhammed was declared a criminal offence, which under section 295-C was punishable with death or life imprisonment. According to section 295-C:

> Use of derogatory remarks, etc., in respect of the Holy Prophet: whoever by words, either spoken or written, or by visible representations, or by any imputation, innuendo, or insinuation, directly or indirectly, defiles the sacred name of the Holy Prophet (peace be upon him), shall be punished with death, or imprisonment for life, and shall also be liable to fine.

In October 1990, the federal Shariat Court (The Islamic Court) ruled that 'the penalty for contempt of the Holy Prophet…is death and nothing else', and directed the Government of Pakistan to effect the necessary legal changes. As the Government did not appeal this decision the death penalty is thus the mandatory punishment for blasphemy in Pakistan.

Since their introduction the new laws relating to religious offences against Islam, including section 295-C, have been extensively abused to harass members of the religious minorities such as Christians and Ahmadis as well as members of the Sunni majority. According to Amnesty International, hundreds of people have been charged under these sections. In all cases these charges have been arbitrarily brought, founded on malicious accusations, primarily as a measure to intimidate and punish members of minority religious communities or non-conforming Muslims. There are reports that suggest that factors such as personal enmity, professional envy, economic rivalry and political reasons play a significant role in these prosecutions. A common feature of accusations of blasphemy in Pakistan is the manner in which they are uncritically accepted by the prosecuting authorities who themselves may face intimidation and threats should they fail to accept them.[14]

Amnesty International has also reported that Pakistani authorities have introduced administrative measures to prevent abuse of Section 295-C blasphemy law. These measures appear to have been more successful in the case of Pakistani Christians but not in the case of Muslim minority sects such as the Ahmadis. The administrative measures do not alter the legal position of blasphemy law in Pakistan. While the death penalties have been imposed under section 295-C, all have been quashed on appeal to the higher courts. However, at least four persons who were acquitted on appeal have so far died at the hand of armed attackers alleged to be religious extremists.

Recently, I also had a personal encounter with Pakistan's blasphemy law. In 2000, I submitted the manuscript of my book, *Faithlines: Muslim Conceptions of Islam and Society*, which has been accepted by Oxford University Press in Pakistan for publication. When the page proofs of the book arrived I noticed that the letters PBUH (peace be upon him) were inserted in parentheses every time the name of Muhammed appeared in the manuscript. I did not think that it was an appropriate thing to do in an academic book and contacted my editor at the Oxford University Press in Karachi, Pakistan, to convey my opinion. She responded promptly and without any hesitation by saying that the protocol pertaining to the use of PBUH after Muhammed's name was 'the in-house policy of the Press'. She then went on to say that it was all right for authors who were safely overseas but it was they (the Press and its staff) who had to face the wrath of the people who felt that such omissions were offensive. I had no choice but to accept the Press's policy although I did not think then and I still think that it was not an appropriate thing to do in an academic book.

Attitudes towards blasphemy in Muslim countries and Australia

So far, I have focused on the impact of modernity on religious institutions and on the concept of blasphemy in Judeo-Christian-Islamic traditions. I have briefly examined the nature and position of blasphemy laws in the Anglo-American world and used Pakistan as a case study to highlight the situation in Pakistan and other Muslim countries where blasphemy laws may also exist. In this section I would like to report findings from a survey on the attitudes of respondents towards blasphemy in Australia and seven Muslim countries.

Between 1996 and 2002 I carried out surveys of Muslim religiosity in seven Muslim countries namely, Indonesia, Malaysia, Pakistan, Iran, Egypt, Kazakhstan and Turkey. In these surveys over 6300 Muslim respondents were interviewed about their religiosity and social attitudes.[15] In 1999–2000, I also carried out a survey of Muslim and Christian religiosity in Australia.[16] These surveys included a question about attitudes towards blasphemy. More specifically, the respondents were asked:

> Suppose a person publicly admitted that he/she did not believe in Allah/God, would you agree or disagree that the following actions should be taken.

1. A book he/ she wrote should be removed from the library;
2. He/she should be fired from a job in government;
3. He/she should not be allowed to teach in a university/school;
4. He/she should be tried for heresy;
5. He/she should not be allowed to preach his beliefs;
6. He/ she should not be allowed to hold public office.

The survey findings are reported in Table 1.

Table 11.1. Suppose a person publicly admitted that he/she did not believe in Allah, would you agree or disagree that the following actions should be taken against him/her (per cent agreeing with the statement)

	Turkey (n = 527)	Iran (n = 536)	Malaysia (n = 801)	Egypt (n = 573)	Pakistan (n = 1185)	Indonesia (n = 1472)	Kazakhstan (n = 978)	Australian Muslims (n = 82)	Australian Christians (n = 88)
A book he/she wrote should be removed from the library	37	53	85	91	69	64	19	56	4
He/she should be fired from a job in the government	31	43	60	69	50	67	17	44	-
He/she should not be allowed to teach in a university/school	40	51	73	90	67	79	21	49	6
He/she should be tried for heresy	23	54	84	78	65	50	22	41	1
He/she should not be allowed to preach his beliefs to others	51	45	91	94	79	88	24	54	20
He/she should not be allowed to hold public office	43	45	79	85	63	58	18	50	30

Source: Unpublished Survey Data

The empirical evidence shows that there were significant variations in attitudes towards blasphemy among Muslims in different countries. In general, attitudes towards blasphemy were weakest in Kazakhstan, followed by Turkey. The attitudes were strongest in Egypt, Pakistan and Malaysia. The Australian Muslims displayed moderate attitudes but the Australian Christians have very weak attitudes towards blasphemy. These attitudes were classified into three categories using the following methodology. For each item if more than 60 per cent of respondents in a country agreed with the statement that country was classified as 'high'; if the agreement rate was between 40 and 60 per cent, the country was classified as 'medium' and if the agreement rate was below 40 per cent the country was classified as 'low'. This classification was applied to Australian Muslims and Christians as well. A further procedure was performed to classify countries as having 'strong', 'moderate' and 'weak' attitudes towards blasphemy. If four to six statements had been classified as 'high' in a country it was regarded as having 'strong' blasphemous attitudes, if a country had scored 'medium' for four to six statements it was classified as 'moderate' and if the score for four to six statements was low the country was classified as having 'weak' blasphemous attitudes. The result obtained from the application of this procedure showed that Turkey and Kazakhstan had 'weak', Iran had 'moderate' and Egypt, Pakistan, Indonesia and Malaysia had 'strong' blasphemous attitudes. The Australian Muslims had 'moderate' and the Australian Christians had 'weak' attitudes towards blasphemy.

Blasphemous attitudes and religiosity

Blasphemy exists wherever there is organised religion. It is a powerful and effective check on actions deemed by the believers as undermining the core beliefs pertaining to the sacred. Does this mean that the intensity of blasphemous attitudes is related to the level of religiosity? Religiosity refers to the degree of religious commitment or piety. Different measures of religiosity are widely used in sociological analysis to ascertain the intensity of religious commitment. One of the most widely used approaches to measure religiosity has been proposed by Stark and Glock[17] and Glock.[18] Their approach conceptualises religiosity as a multidimensional phenomenon consisting of five dimensions namely, ideological, ritualistic, intellectual, experiential and consequential. In my study of Muslim religiosity I used a modified version of this approach with very useful results.[19] These dimensions were also found to be significantly inter-correlated.

In order not to overload this paper with statistics I will use the values of only one dimension of religiosity here. This dimension in my study was labelled as Ideological. It corresponds to Stark and Glock's intellectual dimension and refers to the fundamental beliefs to which a religious person is expected and often required to adhere. For the purposes of this paper this dimension is clearly relevant since it refers to the knowledge of core religious beliefs a person must hold as a believer. The belief structures can be divided into warranting, purposive and implementing beliefs. The first type of beliefs warrant the existence of the divine and defines its character; the second type of beliefs explain the divine purpose and define the believers' role with regard to that purpose and the third type provide the grounds for the ethical strictures of religion.[20]

It should be obvious that this dimension of religiosity has a direct bearing on whether or not certain acts are blasphemous. With this in mind I will use the findings of my religiosity survey pertaining to the ideological dimension to ascertain if the level of religiosity is related to the strength of blasphemous attitudes. The results reported in Table 2 show that the level of religiosity is strongly associated with the strength of blasphemous attitudes.

Religion, modernity and blasphemy

In the first part of this paper I have reviewed the theoretical expositions in sociology about the relationship between modernity and religion. To reiterate the main argument: according to sociological theory, conditions of modernity lead to increasing secularisation and privatisation of religion. Consequently religion gradually loses its relevance and public influence in modern society. I have outlined the dynamics of this process in some detail in the introductory section. I have also argued that in his theoretical work Luhmann has offered a more nuanced and useful analysis of the role of religion in modern societies. If we follow the widely held view that under conditions of modernity religion loses its relevance and public influence then it can be argued that attitudes towards blasphemy in modern society are likely to be weak. This is a difficult issue to explore without an appropriately executed sociological study. In the absence of such a study, is there any evidence that can be used to examine this issue? I will attempt to do this by using the Human Development Index (HDI). The HDI is a composite index published in the UNDP Human Development Report annually. It measures the quality of physical, human and social capital in modern societies using a number of indicators. While this is not an ideal or flawless index, it is a useful measure that is now widely used in social analysis and to rank modern societies in terms of the quality of human life in them. The HDI values extracted from the 2002 Human Development Report for the countries included in this paper are included in Table 2 as well.

Table 11.2. Blasphemous Attitudes, Religiosity, and Human Development in Selected Countries

Country	Blasphemous Attitudes[i]	Religiosity[ii]	Modernity/ Human Development Index[iii]
Turkey	Weak	57	.734
Kazakhstan	Weak	4	.765
Iran	Moderate	59	.719
Egypt	Strong	89	.648
Pakistan	Strong	96	.499
Indonesia	Strong	83	.682
Malaysia	Strong	88	.790
Australia			.939
Muslims	Moderate	87	-
Christians	Weak	41	-

[i] Blasphemous Attitude index was constructed from my unpublished survey data, see text for explanation for the methodology used.
[ii] Religiosity refers to the knowledge of core beliefs a Muslim is required to hold and in the case of Christians adherence to the core beliefs of Christianity. The numbers refer to percentage 'orthodox'. The data for Egypt, Pakistan, Indonesia and Kazakhstan is from Hassan (2003), and for Turkey, Iran and Malaysia from unpublished survey data. Data for Australian Muslims and Christians is from Hassan (2002). For methodology used to obtain the values, see Hassan (2003).
[iii] Human Development Index is from the UNDP (2002).

With the exception of Malaysia the general trend appears to be that countries with lower HDI tend to have high levels of religiosity and strong blasphemous attitudes. This trend appears to support the argument that if we accept HDI as a proxy measure for modernity then the trend reported in Table 2 would support the sociological hypothesis about the relationship between modernity and religion.

Discussion and implications

The findings reported in Table 2 and discussed above identify two possible trends about the relationship between religiosity and modernity. The first trend indicated by all countries except Malaysia is that the HDI is negatively related to the intensity of religiosity. This trend is consistent with the relationship posited by the sociological theories of Parson, Berger and others as discussed in the introductory section of this paper. The second trend characterises Malaysia where the level of modernity is positively related to the intensity of religiosity. One plausible reason for this may be that Malaysia's demography is different from other countries. About 60 per cent of Malaysia's population consists of the Muslim Malays and the rest of them are non-Muslims, mostly of Chinese origin. The Chinese are also economically much more prosperous compared with the Malays. This economic disparity may be a factor in producing the higher HDI score for Malaysia.

Another plausible explanation for this second trend may be that ethnic diversity and economic disparities between the Malays and non-Malays in Malaysia may be a significant factor in this relationship. Malays, unlike other ethnic groups, use Islam as the defining feature of their ethnic identity. One consequence of that may be a greater level of religious consciousness among them which is reflected in their higher religiosity. These are offered only as plausible explanations and more focused research is required to satisfactorily explain the Malaysian situation.

The relationship between religiosity and blasphemous attitudes is positive and consistent with sociological theory. But here again there is the interesting case of Iran, which warrants a brief commentary. Iran is an Islamic Republic and it is the only country among the Muslim countries examined in this paper in which religion performs an overarching function in the affairs of the state and society. Under such circumstances one may have expected that both the level of religiosity and the intensity of blasphemous attitudes would be stronger than indicated by the data in Table 2. A possible explanation of this unexpected finding may be that the institutional configurations play a critical role in shaping the public influences of religious institutions and patterns of personal religiosity.

As I have argued elsewhere, there are institutional configurations in which religion is fused with the state, and public trust in religious institutions tends to decline which may also influence the expressions of religiosity at the individual level.[21] In other words, the existence of an Islamic state, as is the case in Iran, can have a depressing impact on religiosity at the individual level. The converse may also be true. The existence of a secular state in which religion and state occupy separate and distinct spaces may produce a high level of personal religiosity. This may happen when the religious institutions act as a mobiliser of resistance against the state that is authoritarian and lacks political legitimacy. In other words, as suggested by Luhmann, when religion plays a strong applied role in a modern society its public influence increases, which may also produce a higher level of personal religious commitment at the individual level.[22]

There is another sociological implication of the strong relationship between the level of religiosity and blasphemy in a Muslim society. According to Gellner, in Muslim society strong religiosity is conducive to reinforcing Islamic communalism rather than civil society.[23] This view is highly contested among scholars of Islam and Muslim society. For example Lewis, Pipes, and Huntington hold similar views to Gellner.[24] But other scholars, like Ibrahim, Kamali, Norris and Inglehart, and Hefner, strongly contest the view that Islam and civil society are incompatible.[25]

As suggested by Gellner, if the core of civil society is the idea of institutional and ideological pluralism that prevents the central institutions of the state from establishing monopoly over power and truth in society, then it can be argued that religious traditionalism (as reflected by strong religiosity) can act as an impediment to the functioning of a robust civil society.[26] One can argue that persecutions of religious minorities for blasphemy and other deviations from traditional religious beliefs are indicative of a relatively weak civil society in Pakistan. Similarly, in Iran the enforcement of laws relating to women's dress code as well as pressure to conform to a particular reading of the sacred texts is also an infringement of civil liberty and human rights.

It can also be argued that if an important condition for the existence of civil society is that there should be an independent public sphere which is relatively autonomous of the state and whose legitimacy is normatively protected then the historical as well as contemporary variants of Muslim societies display elements of these conditions. The most visible representation of this is the position of the *ulama* (Islamic scholars and teachers) and their access to the *mambers* (pulpit) to influence public opinion on a wide variety of issues; this influence is universally acknowledged. The importance of *mambers* in propagating and legitimising political ideas, de-legitimising others, and mobilising support is part of Islamic history. In recent history the fortunes of, and survival of, political leaders have been strongly influenced by the activities of the *ulama* through *mambers* in Pakistan, Indonesia, Palestine, Malaysia, Lebanon, and Algeria and is now evident in the developments taking place in the American-British occupied Iraq.

The *ulama* can also influence the state policies through their access to the market (bazaar). It can, therefore, be argued that elements of religious ideology in Islam can also underpin the existence of an independent and strong civil society of a particular type. It is through these mechanisms that in Iran, notwithstanding the theocratic nature of the state and conservatism of the ruling Islamic party, there have been remarkable developments which have opened up space for political activism from professional bodies, women's organisations and from the reformist elements from within the Shiite Islamic clergy and the ruling party. Similar developments have taken place in Indonesia in the post-Suharto era.

To conclude, in this paper I have argued that conditions of modernity play a significant role in shaping the role of religion in modern society. It is conducive to increasing secularisation as well as revitalising the role of religion. Using empirical evidence I have explored the relationship between modernity, religiosity and blasphemy in several Muslim countries and in Australia. The paper has also explored the sociological implications of prevailing religious traditionalism in Muslim countries and in particular its implications for the functioning of a robust civil society.[27]

ENDNOTES

[1] Parsons, T. 1960, 'Some Comments on the Pattern of Religious Organization in the United States', *Structure and Process in Modern Societies*, New York, Free Press, pp. 385-421.

[2] Luckmann, T. 1967, *The Invisible Religion: The Problem of religion in Modern Society*, New York, Macmillan.

[3] Berger, P. 1967, *The Sacred Canopy: Elements of a Sociological Theory of Religion*, Garden City, Doubleday.

[4] Bellah, R. 1970, 'Religious Evolution', *Beyond Belief: Essays on Religion in a Post-Traditional Society*, New York, Harper & Row.

[5] Meyer, P. 1997, *Religion and Globalization*, London, Sage Publications; Berger, P. and T. Luckmann 1966, *The Social Construction of Reality: A Sociological Treatise in the Sociology of Knowledge*, Garden City, Doubleday.

[6] Beyer P. 1997, *Religion and Globalization*, London, Sage; Bellah, R. et al. 1985, *Habits of the Heart: Individualism and Commitment in American Life*, New York, Harper & Row.

[7] Luhmann, N. 1982, *The Differentiation of Society*, Holmes, Stephen and Larmore, Charles (trans.), New York, Columbia University Press, pp. 238-42; Beyer, 1997, pp. 70-81.

[8] Beyer, 1997.

[9] Levy, L. 1987, 'Blasphemy', in M. Eliade, (ed.), *The Encyclopaedia of Religion*, New York, Macmillan Publishing House.

[10] Ernst, C. 1987, 'Islamic Concept', in M. Eliade, (ed.), *The Encyclopaedia of Religion*, New York, Macmillan Publishing House; Adams, C. 1995, 'Kufr', John L. Esposito, (ed.), *The Oxford Encyclopedia of the Modern Islamic World*, New York, Oxford University Press.

[11] Salman Rushdie's novel *Satanic Versions* gave a fictional account of a prophet who was misled by the devil to include verses denying the unity of God. The account was similar to the issue of the Satanic Verses of Prophet Muhammed. It offended Muslims around the world and in 1989, a *fatwa* was issued by the supreme religious leader of Iran Ayatollah Ruhollah Khomeini that his novel was blasphemous and called upon Muslims to kill him. As a result he went into hiding to avoid being killed. In 1998, the Iranian President, Mohammad Khatami, distanced the government from his *fatwa*, but the Iranian ayatollahs maintain that the *fatwa* is irrevocable.

[12] Dr Nasr Hamed Abu Zeid was an Associate Professor of Arabic Studies at the Cairo University. His problems began when he applied for promotion to the post of professorship and submitted two examples of his research, *Imam Al-Shafei* and *A Critique of Religious Discourse*, to an examining Committee. One of the members of the committee rejected his application and accused him of rejecting fundamental tenets of Islam. In 1995 a Cairo Appeals Court ruled that his writings included opinions that made him an apostate and annulled his marriage. The verdict was based on *hisba*, a doctrine that entitles any Muslim to take legal action against anyone or anything he considers to be harmful to Islam. The appeals followed. A court in 1995 dismissed the case against him but that decision was reversed by a Superior Court. The University decided to promote him and provided him with armed protection. But for many militant Islamists, the court decision was tantamount to a death sentence. Abu Zeid's life was under grave threat. In July 1995, he and his wife went into exile and he now teaches at Leiden University in the Netherlands.

[13] Dr Hashem Aghajari is a history Professor in one of the Iranian universities. He is a disabled veteran of the 1980-88 Iraq-Iran war. He is an active member of the reformist Organization of the Mujahideen-e-Enqelab-e Eslami (The Mujahideen of the Islamic Revolution). In a speech in August 2002, Aghajari

called for a religious renewal of Shiite Islam and declared that Muslims were not 'monkeys' and 'should not blindly follow' religious leaders. For these pronouncements he was declared by the clergy an apostate and sentenced to death by an Iranian court for blasphemy and apostasy. The decision caused a big uproar in Iran and led to large student demonstrations. The Supreme religious leader Ayatollah Khamenei ordered a judicial review and his death sentence was quashed by Iran's Supreme Court and sent back to the lower court for retrial. After the retrial the Court verdict upheld the original verdict in April 2004, and Aghajari is now held in a Tehran prison waiting for the appeal process to conclude. The Iranian President has condemned the sentencing of Aghajari.

[14] Amnesty International, Report on Pakistan (ASA 33/10/96), London <www.thepersecu-tion.org/ai/amnst196.html>, 1996.

[15] For some of the main findings from phase one of the study see Hassan, R. 2003, *Faithlines: Muslim Conceptions of Islam and Society*, Karachi, Oxford University Press.

[16] Details of this are reported in Hassan, R. 2002, 'On Being Religious: A Study of Christian and Muslim Piety in Australia', *Australian Religion Studies Review*, vol. 15, no. 1, pp. 87-114.

[17] Stark, R. and C. Glock, 1968, *American Piety and the Nature of Religious Commitment*, Berkeley, University of California Press.

[18] Glock, C. 1962, 'On the Study of Religious Commitment', *Religious Education, Research Supplement*, vol. 57, no. 4, pp. S98-S110.

[19] Hassan, 2003.

[20] Stark and Glock, 1968.

[21] Hassan, 2002; and Hassan, 2003.

[22] See Hassan, 2003; Beyer, 1997.

[23] Gellner, E. 1994, *Conditions of Liberty: Civil Society and its Rivals*, Penguin Books.

[24] Lewis, B. 1993, *Islam and the West*, New York, Oxford University Press; Pipes, D. 2002, *Militant Islam Reaches America*, New York, Norton; Huntington, S. 1993, 'The Clash of Civilization', *Foreign Affairs*, vol. 72, no. 3, pp. 22-49.

[25] Norris, P. and R. Inglehart 2003, 'Islamic Culture and Democracy: Testing the 'Clash of Civilzation' Thesis', *Comparative Sociology*, vol. 1, no. 3-4, pp. 235-63; Ibrahim, S. 1996, *Egypt, Islam and Democracy*, Cairo, AUC Press; Kamali, M. 2001, 'Civil Society and Islam: A Sociological Perspective', *European Journal of Sociology*, vol. 42, vol. 3, pp. 459-82; Hefner, R. 2000, *Civil Islam: Muslims and Democratisation in Indonesia*, Princeton, Princeton University Press.

[26] Gellner, 1994.

[27] This paper is part of a research project funded by a grant from the Australian Research Council. I am also indebted to Kate Hoffmann, Julie Henderson and Jessica Sutherland for their research assistance.

12. Negotiating the sacred in law: Regulation of gifts motivated by religious faith

Pauline Ridge

Many people would be surprised to learn that they do not have unlimited power to give away their property as they choose. In fact, legal restrictions on gift giving operate upon gifts that take effect during the donor's lifetime (*inter vivos* gifts) as well as upon gifts that operate only upon the donor's death (testamentary gifts). Some of these constraints are readily comprehensible; for example, it makes sense that the law would seek to protect donors against improper exploitation by would-be donees. Other legal constraints upon gift giving, however, are more difficult to explain. Why is it, for example, the financial needs of the donor's family may take precedence over the autonomy of the donor in relation to testamentary gifts?

This paper considers legal constraints on gift giving in relation to gifts motivated by strong religious beliefs. Such gifts are not unusual. They encompass gifts to those who share the donor's religious convictions (gifts to one's faith community or a spiritual leader or mentor, for example) as well as gifts to others *because of* the donor's religious convictions (a gift to a charitable organisation or a will that is drawn up consistently with religious laws of succession, for example). What constraints are imposed by the law upon such gifts and, specifically, how does the law negotiate the 'sacred' in this process? The topic is an important one both for the light it may shed upon the limits of gift-giving autonomy in general, as well as for its specific relevance in a multicultural society such as Australia in which a diversity of religious faiths are practised. I have discussed such questions in more detail elsewhere; my aim in this chapter is to provide non-lawyers with an overview of the legal regulation of gifts motivated by religious faith.[1]

Paradoxically, these questions arise against a backdrop of purported non-intervention in religion by the law. It is often said that judges do *not* adjudicate upon questions of religious faith. So, for example, Gray J of the English Queens Bench recently refused to allow a defamation action to proceed as it would require him to decide a matter of doctrinal dispute (whether the claimant was a validly consecrated bishop or not).[2] Similarly, Australian courts have refused to adjudicate on the doctrinal disputes concerning ordination of women within the Anglican Church.[3] Although sometimes explained as due to the complexity of religious doctrine, in fact the refusal is public policy based: courts should not engage in a *qualitative* assessment of religious doctrine.[4]

Murphy J, of the High Court of Australia, in deciding whether or not the Church of Scientology constituted a 'religion' for taxation exemption purposes explained it thus:

> Religious discrimination by officials or by courts is unacceptable in a free society. The truth or falsity of religions is not the business of officials or the courts. If each purported religion had to show that its doctrines were true, then all might fail.[5]

The courts will only decide disputes occurring in a religious context if they raise legal questions not dependent upon a qualitative assessment of religious doctrine. Thus, property disputes arising out of church schism can be determined because the court simply applies the principles of property law.[6] The courts will even decide whether a set of beliefs and practices of a group constitutes a religion.[7] In doing so the court does not make a qualitative assessment of the purported religion except to the extent that parody or sham religions are not accepted.[8]

How, then, does this 'hands off' approach to matters of religious belief translate to the legal regulation of gift giving? Presumably legal regulation of gifts motivated by religious beliefs is possible because the motivations are seen as peripheral to the legal issue of the validity of the gift. The courts are not asked to directly evaluate the donor's motivations and the legal principles that apply to religiously motivated gifts are the same as those that apply to all gifts. What is interesting is that in fact, the law *does* confront the religious faith of the donor ('the sacred') and pass judgment upon it in regulating gifts motivated by religious faith. This is done both directly—through protection from exploitation of religious belief and by prioritising other demands upon the donor's property—and indirectly, through the use of objective standards in the relevant legal doctrines.

Before considering these points in detail, it may be helpful to briefly describe the relevant law. Inter vivos gifts and testamentary gifts are largely regulated by separate bodies of judge-made law. The doctrines that regulate inter vivos gifts come mainly from Equity (the body of law initially developed by the Court of Chancery in England). The two equitable doctrines most relevant to gifts motivated by strong religious faith are equitable undue influence and unconscionable dealings. Testamentary gifts fall into the law of succession (a mixture of probate law, Equity and legislation). The most relevant doctrines are probate undue influence and the suspicious circumstances doctrine.

It is also possible to create a trust of the donor's property for the benefit of whatever person (or, possibly, purposes) the donor chooses rather than make an outright gift of the property. The principles of trust law (which are also part of Equity) operate equally upon inter vivos and testamentary gifts. Finally, gift giving is also subject to legislative regulation. The legislation most pertinent to this discussion is family provision legislation which exists under different names in all Australian jurisdictions and only applies to testamentary gifts.[9]

Whichever source of law is used to regulate gift giving, the gift must be a significant one relative to the donor's overall assets. For pragmatic reasons a gift will not be disputed in the courts (a costly process) unless it is sufficiently large to cause pain/outrage to the person(s) who otherwise expected to benefit; and legally, the relevant doctrines tend not to be activated by small gifts. With this background in mind then, how does the law negotiate the sacred in its regulation of gifts motivated by strong religious beliefs?

Direct consideration of the donor's religious motivations

Protection from exploitation

The first way in which the law directly confronts the religious motivations of a donor is by protecting donors from exploitation of those motivations. The legal doctrine most relevant to inter vivos gifts in this context is equitable undue influence. Equitable undue influence is concerned with gifts arising out of a relationship of influence or potential influence. The doctrine developed in the late eighteenth century and some of the leading cases concern religiously motivated gifts. A presumption that 'undue' influence has been exercised over the donor arises upon evidence that:

- a gift was made to a donor's spiritual 'leader'; and,
- the gift is 'so large as not to be reasonably accounted for on the ground of friendship, relationship, charity, or other ordinary motives on which ordinary men act…[10]

Alternatively, in place of the first requirement, a relationship of influence can be proved by evidence of the particular relationship, in which case the presumption is similarly activated once the second requirement is also proved. Once a presumption of undue influence arises (either automatically or because a relationship of influence is proved) then the gift is overturned unless the donee rebuts the presumption by evidence that no advantage was taken of the donor who in fact exercised a fully informed, free and independent judgment.[11] Whether the donor received independent advice regarding the gift is relevant to rebuttal of the presumption.

There is strong rhetoric in the equitable undue influence cases concerning the danger of spiritual influence. Spiritual influence was said to be 'the most dangerous and the most powerful' of all influences upon a donor or a party to a contract.[12] The following statement by counsel arguing a case at the beginning of the nineteenth century, whilst no doubt calculated to sway the court, nonetheless encapsulates the concerns of lawyers at the time:

What is the authority of a guardian, or even parental authority, what are the means of influence by severity or indulgence in such a relation, compared with the power of religious impressions under the ascendancy of a spiritual adviser; with such an engine to work upon the passions; to excite superstitious fears of pious hopes; to inspire, as the object may be best promoted, despair or confidence; to alarm the conscience by the horrors of eternal misery, or support the drooping spirits by unfolding the prospect of eternal happiness: that good or evil, which is never to end? What are all other means to these?[13]

Unsurprisingly, there is a string of English cases throughout the nineteenth and early twentieth centuries in which gifts motivated by strong religious beliefs, and generally involving fringe religious groups, were set aside.[14]

Importantly, equitable undue influence affects not only gifts that are the product of clear and deliberate exploitation of influence but also gifts where there is only the possibility of exploitation and where all parties have acted in good faith. The leading case of *Allcard v Skinner*, decided in 1887, illustrates this point. A novice Anglican nun (Miss Allcard) gave all her assets to the Head of her Order (her mother superior) as required by the rules of the Order. The property was used for charitable purposes of the Order. The English Court of Appeal stressed that all parties had acted with complete propriety; nonetheless the presumption of undue influence that arose automatically due to the relationship of Miss Allcard and her mother superior was not rebutted. Crucially, Miss Allcard had not received independent advice before making the gifts and could not be shown to have exercised a fully informed and free judgment, free of the influence of her mother superior. Thus, the doctrine is concerned with the potential for undue influence to be exercised and will err on the side of caution; gifts will be set aside if it cannot be conclusively proved that the donor acted free from undue influence.

Equitable undue influence continues to be applied today across a spectrum of religious faiths.[15] There have been five reported Australian cases since 1986 (all involving female donors). The donees have included a Baptist pastor, the leaders of a Hare Krishna community and the leader of a breakaway sect from the Church Universal and Triumphant.[16] It is not necessary that the donee be formally recognised as a spiritual 'leader'; a recent Queensland case acknowledged the possibility of a bible study group leader being in a position of spiritual influence.[17]

I will return to the second requirement of equitable undue influence (that the gift is 'so large as not to be reasonably accounted for on the ground of friendship, relationship, charity, or other ordinary motives on which ordinary men act') below; however, it is also worth noting that this requirement limits the doctrine's utility regarding 'repeat offenders'. In other words, it is possible that a spiritual leader or mentor may abuse his or her position of influence with respect to *many* donors but in relation to relatively small gifts which do not activate the presumption. Equitable undue influence is concerned not so much with the regulation of spiritual leaders/mentors as such, as with undoing particular gifts; thus there is still the need for vigilance and appropriate self-regulation by religious groups. Codes of conduct for Christian churches are growing in popularity (partly because of a growing awareness of sexual abuse within churches) and these may include provisions regarding receipt of financial benefits.[18]

The related equitable doctrine of unconscionable dealings also may apply to inter vivos gifts motivated by strong religious beliefs. While equitable undue influence considers the relationship between donor and donee, unconscionable dealings looks more to the circumstances of the particular gift. If a donor suffers from a 'special disadvantage' relative to a donee, and if the donee knows or ought to know of that disadvantage it may be unconscionable for the donee to accept the gift. 'Special disadvantage' traditionally included conditions such as drunkenness, ill health, lack of education and poverty. The court considers whether there is a special disadvantage by comparing the relative abilities and conditions of the two parties to the gift. Strong religious faith—especially in the first flush of a religious conversion—may be characterised as a 'special disadvantage'; that is, a person of strong religious convictions may be considered so vulnerable to exploitation that it is unconscionable for the donee to accept the gift knowing these facts. In this instance, the implication is that although the donor acted with autonomy the donee should not have benefited from their spiritual fervour without ensuring that they received independent advice. There are no decided cases in which unconscionable dealings has been applied to religious enthusiasm; however, this can be explained by the fact that the doctrine is not often applied by the English courts and is relatively recent in its Australian usage.

Interestingly, the law is not so concerned with the danger of exploitation of religious faith in relation to testamentary gifts. Two doctrines that protect against exploitation in relation to testamentary gifts motivated by strong religious faith are probate undue influence and the suspicious circumstances doctrine. Unlike *equitable* undue influence which is concerned with the potential for abuse of influence, *probate* undue influence requires proof that the donor was actually coerced into making a gift that did not represent their intention and desire at all.[19] Thus, in a case where the residuary beneficiary of a will (a Roman Catholic priest) was chaplain and confessor to the testator, a challenge to the gift on the basis of probate undue influence failed because there was no evidence of coercion:

> No amount of persuasion or advice, whether founded on feelings of regard or religious sentiment, would avail, according to the existing law,

to set aside this will, so long as the free volition of the testatrix to accept or reject that advice was not invaded.[20]

Because of this the doctrine of probate undue influence is notoriously difficult to establish.

The suspicious circumstances doctrine may be more helpful in overturning a testamentary gift motivated by religious faith. One requirement for a valid will is that the testator knew and approved of the will's contents. If there are suspicious circumstances surrounding the making of the will, then the propounder of the will must prove knowledge and approval affirmatively. There is no limit on what may constitute a suspicious circumstance; one example is where the sole or major beneficiary assisted in the preparation of the will.[21] So, for example, in *In the Will of Thomas Walsh* the testator's priest drew up the will in the testator's last days and while he was seriously ill.[22] The whole of the estate went to projects associated with the priest. A'Beckett J found that the circumstances surrounding preparation and execution of the will cast doubt on the testator's knowledge and approval of the will's contents and he therefore refused probate.

Why is the law concerned about exploitation of religious faith in relation to inter vivos gifts but not to the same extent in relation to testamentary gifts? Elsewhere I have suggested that it is because the donor of a testamentary gift is, by definition, not impoverished by the gift and thus, there is no immediate and direct 'victim' of the gift: but that this is unsatisfactory because those who otherwise would benefit from the donor's bounty are also affected.[23] More cogent reasons are that the succession doctrines developed during the mid to late nineteenth century when quite blatant lobbying of testators was socially acceptable, the difficulty of proving the circumstances of a will long after it was made and when the disaffected parties may not even have been present, and the different jurisdictional origins of the applicable law. It may be that equitable undue influence (which at present does not apply to testamentary gifts) will influence the development of the law of succession in the future.

Priority given to competing values

A second way in which the law directly confronts the sacred when regulating gifts occurs when other values are given priority over the autonomous expression of the donor's religious faith. The clearest example of this is in relation to testamentary gifts where the law recognises a societal norm that the financial needs of one's dependents must be catered for before one acts benevolently towards others. A distinction is drawn between a right of inheritance by the donor's family (which is not recognised) and a right to provision for financial needs (which is recognised). Two cases illustrate the point. The first case, *The Trustees of Church Property of the Diocese of Newcastle v Ebbeck*, is authority that a donor may impose religiously motivated conditions upon a gift. That is, no one, other than the testator (and, presumably, the testator's creditors) has any *right* to the testator's property. In the words of Windeyer J of the High Court of Australia:

> [A testator] may, if he wishes, provide that his property shall go only to persons of a particular religion. He may stipulate that a prospective beneficiary will be disqualified unless he renounce a particular faith...Furthermore, a testator may disqualify from participation as a beneficiary anyone who should marry a spouse of a particular religion, or not marry a spouse of a particular religion.[24]

This is a strong endorsement of the autonomy of a religiously motivated donor and confirms my comments in the introduction regarding the hands-off approach of law to religious faith; however, the second case, *Wenn v Howard*, shows that such autonomy must give way to the financial needs of a testator's dependents.[25] In that case a testator deliberately excluded some of his children from his will because (it was said) they did not practise the Catholic faith. It was held by the court that this would not disentitle them to provision from the estate if financial need was established; in other words, there was no right to inheritance but there was a right to family provision and the latter overrode the autonomy of the religiously motivated testator.

Although the details of family provision legislation (also known as 'testator's family maintenance') vary between jurisdictions, such legislation generally provides that testamentary gifts (and even gifts made shortly before the donor's death) can be overridden to the extent that the financial needs of the donor's immediate family and dependents have not been provided for. The Court may order that provision be made out of the deceased donor's estate for the 'maintenance, education or advancement in life' of a family member or dependent.[26] To the extent that religiously motivated gifts may be overridden by court ordered family provision the law is prioritising the financial needs of the donor's family over the autonomous expression of the donor's religious faith. In some jurisdictions the court has power to determine which gifts under the will should bear the burden of a family provision order and this may further disadvantage religiously motivated gifts.

Protection from exploitation and legislative acknowledgement of the right of family members to financial provision from a deceased donor's estate are two ways in which the legal regulation of gifts directly confronts the donor's religious faith; but there are more subtle ways in which the law negotiates the sacred and this is by use of objective standards.

Indirect consideration of the donor's religious faith through the application of objective standards

The legal regulation of gift giving is premised upon objective standards of behaviour that encapsulate societal norms. In the second part of this chapter I will suggest that the law negotiates the sacred in an indirect and possibly discriminatory way through the application of objective standards. Donors motivated by strong religious faith are likely to fall outside societal norms embedded in the relevant legal doctrines and are disadvantaged by an unthinking application of such norms in the law. This happens in two ways. First, donors of strong religious faith are less likely to meet objective standards based upon societal norms. Secondly, the content of such standards, whilst appearing neutral, may reflect the dominant religious values of the time at which the standard was set or may be given content by a judge's own religious acculturation. These points are now discussed more fully.

Objective standards in legal doctrines and their application to donors of strong religious faith

Objective standards are not unusual in the law. The standard of the 'reasonable person' in the law of negligence is probably the most well known: whether a person is negligent is determined by comparing that person's conduct with how a reasonable person would have behaved in the same circumstances. Similarly, in legal doctrines regulating gift giving, the conduct of the donor of a gift is often measured against an objective standard of conduct. We have seen one objective standard already: the second requirement of equitable undue influence is that the gift is 'so large as not to be reasonably accounted for on the ground of friendship, relationship, charity, or other ordinary motives on which ordinary men act'.[27] Provided that a relationship of influence is found, the gift is measured against a societal norm of the 'ordinary motives of ordinary men'. Similarly, the case law that has interpreted family provision legislation requires that the donor of a testamentary gift has acted as a 'wise and just testator' 'determined by community standards of what is right and appropriate' in providing for his or her family and dependents.[28] This also is an objective standard encapsulating a societal norm of the ideal testator. If the court finds that the donor did not meet this objective standard then it may order that family provision be paid by the donor's estate, to the diminution of the testamentary gifts that were in fact made by the donor.

The difficulty for donors motivated by strong religious faith is that their conduct may well be outside such normative standards; indeed, such donors may *pride* themselves on acting against such norms. A hypothetical (but not unrealistic) example is that of a Christian who chooses to give away all his or her property as an act of faith in God. Indeed, the equitable undue influence case of *Allcard v Skinner* involved a similar scenario. Thus, a gift motivated by strong religious beliefs, particularly if those beliefs are outside the mainstream of religious beliefs in Australia, is likely to be more vulnerable to challenge on this ground. Professor Bradney has demonstrated in relation to English law that the application of objective standards in law generally is problematic for persons of strong religious conviction (whom Bradney calls 'obdurate believers').[29]

Despite the difficulties that objective standards may cause for donors of strong religious faith, can it be argued that the application of objective standards in law is in fact a good thing? Surely one of the functions of law is to regulate behaviour so that it complies with societal norms? Furthermore, it could be said that the law is simply prioritising other values over the religious autonomy of the donor: protection from potential exploitation and recognition of the financial needs of the donor's family, for example. In other words, a compromise is being made. This may be so; nonetheless, it is important to be *aware of* the consequences of the discriminatory impact of objective standards upon gifts motivated by strong religious beliefs. First, such gifts are more vulnerable to challenge and thus security of receipt on the part of donees is correspondingly diminished. Secondly, in many instances it is not the donor who later seeks to overturn the gift, but the donor's family who would otherwise have stood to benefit. Thus, any discriminatory impact of objective standards that makes the relevant doctrines easier to comply with in relation to religiously motivated gifts may be exploited by persons other than the donor and this makes it important that such doctrines are scrutinised and critically evaluated. To give just one example, being aware that objective standards may impact unfairly on religiously motivated donors is relevant in considering how easily the presumption of equitable undue influence should arise. If the presumption is activated too readily then it is too easy to overturn an autonomous gift; if the presumption is too difficult to raise then there is a danger that gifts tainted by exploitative behaviour will stand.

The content of objective standards

Another danger with objective standards in their application to donors of strong religious faith concerns the content of such standards. The content of objective standards such as the 'ordinary motives of ordinary men' and 'the wise and just testator as determined by community standards of what is right and appropriate' is likely to reflect the dominant religious and cultural values of the society.[30] This compounds the problems of a donor from a minority religious group who has strong religious beliefs. Not only are they unlikely to meet an objective standard based upon social norms, they are even less likely to meet a standard based on moderate Judeo-Christian or even secular world views (if we accept that these are the most likely influences upon the content of Australian legal standards).[31] The problem is compounded because of our legal system's doctrine of precedent whereby judges must follow the decisions of higher courts; there may be a time lag in relation to the content of objective standards so that they do not keep apace with changes in societal norms. Thus, even though Australia is indisputably a multicultural society, this fact may take longer to infiltrate the content of objective standards in the law. Furthermore, judges may (consciously or unconsciously) rely upon their own religious acculturation in determining whether objective standards are met. For example, recently an Australian judge (apparently at the suggestion of legal counsel) applied Jesus' parable of the Forgiving Father in order to decide whether a testator had met the wise and just testator standard in family provision law.[32] Thus, minority religious groups and/or religious groups new to Australia are disadvantaged if the content and application of objective standards in doctrines regulating gift giving encapsulate a moderate Judeo-Christian world view and all religious groups may be disadvantaged by objective standards that encapsulate a secular world view.

Conclusion

This brief review of the law concerning gifts motivated by strong religious beliefs shows that notwithstanding the professed reluctance of the courts to engage in a qualitative assessment of religious belief, the law does consider the donor's beliefs both directly and indirectly. Direct intervention in gift giving is justified on the basis of protection from exploitation: there is a strong concern regarding the power of spiritual influence with respect to inter vivos gifts motivated by religious faith but such concern lessens if the gift is testamentary. In addition, through family provision legislation, the religious motivations of a donor of testamentary gifts will be overridden if he or she has not provided for the financial needs of family members and dependents. Indirect engagement with a donor's religious beliefs occurs through the use of objective standards in the law. Objective standards based upon societal norms of gift giving are more difficult for 'obdurate believers' to comply with; furthermore, the content of such standards may embed a society's dominant religious values to the detriment of minority religions; the content of standards is also influenced by judicial religious acculturation.

What then, if anything, should be done about the law's negotiation of the sacred in this area? First, it is important simply to be aware of the issues outlined in this chapter so that the relevant case law and legislation can be evaluated in an informed manner, and so that reform may be advocated where necessary. It is impossible for the legal regulation of religiously motivated gifts to be entirely neutral in its treatment of the religious beliefs of the donor. Indeed, we may not want complete neutrality. Rather it is a matter of self awareness on the part of those who make and apply the law. It is important to consider competing values such as freedom of religion, autonomy of gift giving and expectations of close family and dependents of the donor for example, rather than to unthinkingly impose standards of acceptable gift giving that look value neutral but in fact discriminate against minority religious groups. The question of judicial acculturation is troublesome but also can be minimised by self awareness and education.

Two recent occurrences provide some encouragement that the Australian legal system and Australian law are on the right path in negotiating the sacred. The first concerns judicial discrimination against a minority religious group's beliefs. The NSW Court of Appeal recently overturned a finding of negligence in part because the lower court had improperly considered and criticised the defendants' religious motivations.[33] Mason P, speaking for the court in a strongly worded judgment, made it clear that judges are expected to overcome religious acculturation:

> In the eye of the law it may not be unreasonable to hold categorically divergent opinions about certain matters of faith, morality or even good taste.

The second example concerns the law of charitable trusts. Historically, a bias against Roman Catholicism was apparent in the content and application of the legal requirements for a valid charitable trust.[34] One such requirement was that the trust have a demonstrable 'public benefit'.[35] Because of this the English courts refused to recognise trusts for the purposes of closed (predominantly Catholic) religious orders. It was said that a religious order which did not interact at all with the public could not be providing a public benefit through its activities and therefore a trust for the purposes of such an order would be invalid.[36] Not surprisingly, the Irish High Court decided differently, and strongly endorsed the value of such religious activities within Ireland holding that, '[M]en's notions of public benefit will vary with the outlook of their age'.[37] The position in Australian law may have been clarified by the recent enactment of the *Extension of Charitable Purpose Act 2004* (Cth). This Act provides that for the purposes of Commonwealth legislation an institution has a purpose with a public benefit if it is 'a closed or contemplative religious order that regularly undertakes prayerful intervention at the request of members of the public'.[38] While the legislative change only applies when Commonwealth legislation is in issue, undoubtedly it will affect the case law requirement of public benefit as well.

These two recent examples are encouraging as they show that it is possible to challenge judicial bias based upon religious acculturation, and that through political action there is the opportunity for those interested in the interaction of law and religious belief to take part in law reform. Religious institutions also have an important role in regulating and educating their members about such matters.

ENDNOTES

1 Ridge, Pauline 2003, 'The Equitable Doctrine of Undue Influence Considered in the Context of Spiritual Influence and Religious Faith', *University of New South Wales Law Journal,* no. 26; 2003, 'Legal and Ethical Matters Relevant to the Receipt of Financial Benefits by Ministers of Religion and Churches', *Griffith Law Review,* no. 12; 2004, pp. 91-113. 'Testamentary Gifts Motivated by Religious Faith and Family Provision Legislation', Paper presented at the Centre for Cross-Cultural Research, *Negotiating the Sacred* conference, The Australian National University, Canberra, 31 May 2004.

2 *Blake v Associated Newspapers Ltd* [2003] EWHC 1960 (Unreported, Gray J, 31 July 2003) [21]. See also, Hill, Mark 2001, 'Judicial Approaches to Religious Disputes' in Richard O'Dair and Andrew Lewis (eds), 2001, *Law and Religion,*Oxford, Oxford University Press,p. 409.

3 *Scandrett v Dowling* (1992) 27 NSWLR 483.

4 Ogilvie, M. H. 1992, 'Church Property Disputes: Some Organizing Principles', *University of Toronto Law Journal,* no. 42, pp. 377, 392-393. Ogilvie criticises the Canadian courts for abdicating their role.

5 *Church of the New Faith v Commissioner for Pay Roll Tax (Vic)* (1983) 154 CLR 120, 150.

6 *Attorney-General for New South Wales v Grant* (1976) 135 CLR 587.

7 *Church of the New Faith v Commissioner for Pay Roll Tax (Vic)* (1983) 154 CLR 120.

8 *Church of the New Faith v Commissioner for Pay Roll Tax (Vic)* (1983) 154 CLR 171 (Wilson and Deane JJ, citing *United States v Kuch* (1968) 288 F Supp 439).

9 For example, *Family Provision Act 1982* (NSW).

10 *Allcard v Skinner* (1887) LR 36 Ch D 145, 185 (Lindley LJ).

11 *Johnson v Buttress* (1936) 56 CLR 113.

12 *Allcard v Skinner* (1887) LR 36 Ch D 145, 183 (Lindley LJ).

13 *Huguenin v Baseley* (1807) 14 Ves Jr 273, 288; 33 ER 526, 532 (Sir Samuel Romilly, during argument). These concerns were reiterated recently in *Quek v Beggs* (1990) 5 BPR [97405].

14 See, for example, *Nottidge v Prince* (1860) 2 Giff 246; 66 ER 103, *Lyon v Home* (1868) LR 6 Eq 655; *Morley v Loughnan* [1893] 1 Ch 763; *Chennells v Bruce* (1939) 55 TLR 422.

15 See, Ridge, Pauline 2003, 'The Equitable Doctrine of Undue Influence Considered in the Context of Spiritual Influence and Religious Faith' *University of New South Wales Law Journal,* no. 26, 66.

16 *Quek v Beggs* (1990) 5 BPR [97405]; *Hartigan v International Society for Krishna Consciousness Inc* [2002] NSWSC 810 (Unreported, Bryson J, 6 September 2002); *McCulloch v Fern* [2001] NSWSC 406 (Unreported, Palmer J, 28 May 2001). See also, Ridge, Pauline 2002, '*McCulloch v Fern*', *Journal of Contract Law,* no. 18, 138.

17 *Illuzzi v Christian Outreach Centre* (1997) Q ConvR pp. 54-490.

18 For example, Uniting Church in Australia, *Code of Ethics and Ministry Practice,* section 5.

19 For example, *Hall v Hall* (1868) LR 1 P & D 481; *Winter v Crichton* (1991) 23 NSWLR 116.

20 *Parfitt v Lawless* (1872) LR 2 P & D 462, 474 (Lord Penzance).

21 *Barry v Butlin* [1838] 2 Moo 480; 12 ER 1089; *Tyrrell v Painton* [1894] P 151; *Nock v Austin* (1918) 25 CLR 519.

22 (1892) 18 VLR 739.

23 Ridge, Pauline 2004, 'Equitable Undue Influence and Wills', *Law Quarterly Review,* no. 120, 617.

24 (1960) 104 CLR 394, 414.

25 [1967] VR 91.

26 *Family Provision Act 1982* (NSW) section 7. See generally, Pauline Ridge, 'Testamentary Gifts Motivated by Religious Faith and Family Provision Legislation' (forthcoming article).

27 *Allcard v Skinner* (1887) LR 36 Ch D 145, 185 (Lindley LJ).

28 *Bosch v Perpetual Trustee Co* [1938] AC 463; *Permanent Trustee Co Ltd v Fraser* (1995) 36 NSWLR 24.

29 Bradney, Anthony 2000, 'Faced by Faith' in Peter Oliver, Douglas Scott Sionadh and Victor Tadros (eds), *Faith in Law: Essays in Legal Theory,* Oxford, Hart Publishing, p. 89.

30 See in relation to tort law, Calabresi, Guido 1985, *Ideals, Beliefs, Attitudes and the Law,* Syracuse, N.Y., Syracuse University Press.

31 See generally, Mason, Keith 1990, *Constancy and Change: Moral and Religious Values in the Australian Legal System,* Sydney, Federation Press.

[32] *Hackett v Public Trustee* (Unreported, ACT Supreme Court, Higgins J, 2 May 1997).

[33] *The Local Spiritual Assembly of the Baha'is of Parramatta Ltd v Haghighat* (2004) Aust Torts Reports 81-729.

[34] See Ricketts, C. E. F. 1990, 'An Anti-Roman Catholic Bias in the Law of Charity?' *The Conveyancer and Property Lawyer*, no. 34, pp. 34-44.

[35] *Gilmour v Coats* [1949] AC 426. See generally, Ford and Lee, 1983.

[36] *Gilmour v Coats* [1949] AC 426. See generally, Ford and Lee, 1983.

[37] *Maguire v Attorney General* [1943] IR 238, 244 (Gavan Duffy J).

[38] Section 5(1)(b).

13. Negotiating a religious identity in modern Japan: The Christian experience

Colin Noble

On the morning of 24 February, 1989, in freezing rain, a cavalcade of officers in military uniform accompanied the funeral cortege of the Shôwa Emperor (Hirohito) through the streets of Tokyo to the site of his funeral in Shinjuku Gyoen. The funeral was conducted in two parts—the first a brief religious ceremony performed by the emperor's family as a private rite of the imperial house, and the second an ostensibly non-religious one paid for by the Japanese government and attended by about 10 000 invited guests, including numerous world leaders and representatives of foreign governments. The two ceremonies were differentiated by the presence of a curtain drawn to separate the secular space of the second ceremony from the religious inner sanctum of the first. This physical separation was a begrudging acknowledgement by the government of the notional separation of state and religion in the Japanese constitution drafted in 1946 during the Allied Occupation.[1]

Had the Japanese government had its way, the ceremonies would not have been divided. In the period following the emperor's death on 7 January, government spokesmen had repeatedly argued that performance of the two ceremonies in the same place and time was not in fact a breach of the constitution. The argument met with stiff opposition from a number of sources. Among these were numerous Christian voices. The stipulations in Article 20 of the constitution that 'the State and its organs shall refrain from…religious activity' and in Article 89 that 'no public money or other property shall be expended or appropriated for the use … of any religious institution or association' remained a point of controversy in the ensuing 22 months until the completion of the rites of succession of the new emperor.[2]

One scholar's suggestion that the controversy was 'largely orchestrated by Christians'[3] credits Christians with more influence than is their due, but is nevertheless helpful because it draws attention to two elements critical to this chapter. The first is the ineffectiveness of the Christian voice: despite the opposition, the two-part funeral ceremony still went ahead in one place, and was paid for with state funds, as were the subsequent succession rites of the following year. The second is that the ineffectiveness of the Christian-led opposition contrasts markedly with the influence Christians had in Japanese national politics earlier in the twentieth century. The Christian voice had not always been so devoid of political influence as it appeared in 1989–90.

The chapter follows the lead of sociologist John Clammer in asserting that the study of 'ethnically and linguistically entirely Japanese' minorities such as the Christian community 'throws considerable light on the mechanisms through which social exclusion is accomplished in Japanese culture and minority status is established and maintained.[4] The point of departure from Clammer, though, is that the question addressed here is the path to political, rather than social, exclusions. Why has Christian political influence in Japan waxed and waned, but on the whole waned, over the course of the twentieth century? As the evidence presented below shows, the first third of the century was a period in which Christian influence was accepted as part of the national social and political fabric, to the point that Christian opposition to government legislative initiatives directed specifically at control of religions proved effective in preventing those initiatives from being implemented. This was not the case, however, in 1989. It is also clear from the evidence that the Christian community has throughout the second half of the century maintained a confrontational approach to the state despite changes in social and political circumstances over time.

The argument of this chapter is that this sustained confrontation has been an outcome of the attempt by Christians to negotiate a place for Christianity within Japanese society. Protestant Christian leaders were representatives of a newcomer on the religious scene in late nineteenth century Japan. They used confrontation with the state over legal definitions of religious behaviour as an avenue through which to carve out a political and social identity for the new religion. The legacy of the early years of Christianity in modern Japan remained at the end of the twentieth century as Christians continued to assert their right to be involved in negotiating the sacred. It is arguable that the decline in political influence has resulted, paradoxically, from this insistence on confrontation as the route to establishing a political identity within Japanese society.

The post-war experience

Two questions arise from the approach taken by Christians to the state in 1989–90. The first is why they chose such a confrontational approach. It is possible to argue for opposition to the state from biblical texts, but confrontation with the state is not an integral part of mainstream Christian thought.[5] Nevertheless, the suggestion that Christians orchestrated the controversy of 1989–90 is understandable given the events of the late 1980s. It was clear from before the emperor died that Christians were not pulling any punches in the debate. In the last years of the Shōwa era, and particularly after the emperor's first major illness was announced in 1986, Christians broke social taboo in no uncertain terms by publishing numerous works which addressed the issue of an appropriate Christian response to the emperor's impending death. In 1988 alone, for example, the following titles appeared from Christian publishing houses: *Imperial Successions and Us*; *Imperial Funeral Rites*; *Thinking About X-Day [the day the emperor dies] Now*; *In Preparation for the Succession of the Emperor: What Should the Church Do?* and *From the Decision in the 'Nakaya Case' to the Succession of the Emperor*.[6]

The second question is why Christians opted to frame their critique of government involvement specifically in terms of the constitution. In answering questions about post-war Japan such as this, there is a temptation to seek answers only in the post-war period. And indeed, there are a number of features of post-war Japan which, in comparison with the pre-war period, made the job of challenging the state and the imperial system easier in 1989–90 than it had ever been. Among these must be counted several which will merely be mentioned in passing here in the interests of looking at more interesting features in depth. Freedom of religion was unconditionally guaranteed in the 1946 constitution (at least in terms of the letter of the law, although arguably not in its interpretation), whereas Article 28 of the previous 1889 constitution provided for only conditional freedom of religion.[7] 1989 marked the death of a controversial emperor, and the end of an era of controversy and qualified national success, in contrast to 1912 for example, which saw the death of a revered emperor and the end of an unparalleled positive period of Japanese history. By 1989 a Japanese Christian theology had emerged which was characterised by independence from foreign influence and reflective of its own history, in contrast to the early twentieth century, at which time the dominant theology was influenced strongly by social evolutionary theory and liberal interpretation of doctrine. Of more interest, though, are three other instrumental influences on the behaviour of Japanese Christians in the last years of the twentieth century: the structure and standing of the post-war legal system; the experience of public debate and confrontation with authority built up by Christians since the 1950s; and the issue of war guilt.

The legal system

Clearly without the post-war constitution's guarantee of freedom of religion, as well as of thought and conscience, of assembly and association, and of expression,[8] things would have been different. The post-war church was free to criticise without fear of being shut down on the grounds that it was being either unlawful or disorderly, and Christians were also no longer open to the accusation on constitutional grounds that by questioning the actions of the emperor or the government they were neglecting their obligations as citizens. However, this alone cannot account for the church's vociferous opposition to the government's behaviour at the end of the 1980s, or for the fact that Christians have chosen to use the courts as a means of confronting the state in the second half of the twentieth century.

In addition to the constitutional changes, there were also several changes after the war in the structure and social standing of the legal system that made it easier for Christians to pursue legal action than had previously been the case. A basic change to the Civil Code had been the introduction of adversarial procedures in which the onus was on plaintiffs to present their arguments forcefully, rather than on the judge to delve into the facts of the matter. Linked to this was the 1962 Administrative Litigation Procedure Law, which established three categories of administrative litigation, opening the way for 'protest litigation' (kôkoku soshô)[9] as an avenue for action against the state. In particular, the law facilitated legal challenges to the constitutionality of state acts. The viability of constitutional review, argues Kyoto University's Taniguchi Yasuhei,

> has brought about one major social change, a society has been developing in which the constitutionality of legislation and other State acts can be freely discussed before a court of law....one thing cannot be disputed: the new institution of administrative litigation has brought about a society in which an act of the administration can be attacked by the persons affected.[10]

Citizens have been able to take the state to lower courts over acts of the state they believe to be illegal, such as the use of public funds on religious activities.

In addition, the legal system has achieved a certain level of respectability in the eyes of the public that it did not have prior to the war. Taniguchi argues that in fact it was not until the late 1950s, when steps were taken to attract more capable people into the legal system, that more respect was accorded legal process and its outcomes. It was thus just as the legal system was achieving widespread respectability that Christians were first beginning to engage with the state through the courts.

Moreover, in addition to increased freedom of legal action and the respectability afforded such action, the likelihood of Christians tackling the Japanese government was arguably increased by the removal of two psychological barriers that stand in the way of litigants in Japan.[11] Taniguchi argues that one psychological barrier to litigation is lowered when a grievance is shared by many people, and when the grievance can be directed at an impersonal body, such as a government department, rather than an individual, thus minimising the implication of direct confrontation. The introduction of protest litigation has allowed for the depersonalisation of the state, while the category of people's litigation has allowed for the initiation of legal proceedings on behalf of a group rather than just an individual. In summary, then, well before 1989, using the courts as a forum for resolving disputes had become both a respectable and an accessible avenue of political action.

The rising respect accorded legal process was somewhat seductive to those seeking to justify their position through the courts. A positive outcome of a legal action would vindicate the position taken, require that the relevant action of the state be redressed, and lend credibility in the eyes of the wider public to the plaintiff's stance. Alternatively, though, a dismissal of the claims made would, in addition to establishing the basis on which the state could argue the legality of similar actions in the future, add weight to general public perception that the plaintiff had been out of step with accepted cultural norms in taking the state to task in the first place.

Experience opposing the state

It was against this backdrop that Christians built up a history of opposing the state in public debate over points of law and constitution in the decades preceding the death of the Shôwa Emperor.[12] The most well-known legal battle, and the one which was to be adduced most frequently by the government in the debate of 1989–90, was the court case regarding the payment by Tsu City council of money to a Shinto priest for performing a Shinto ground breaking ceremony on the construction site of the City gymnasium in 1965. One key aspect of the Supreme Court decision in the Tsu City case was the introduction into the debate over the separation of state and religion of the term shakai tsûnen, which might be translated as 'social consensus'. The argument of the two-thirds majority of the panel of judges who upheld the constitutionality of the expenditure in their 1977 decision was that,

> in considering whether or not a particular act constitutes 'religious activity' [the term used in Article 20 of the constitution]...we must judge objectively in accordance with the social consensus.[13]

The concept of 'social consensus' re-surfaced in the government's justification of its interpretation of the constitution in the debate over the nature and funding of the 1989–90 succession rites.[14]

The fact that the nature of 'social consensus' is not adequately defined partly accounts for the vigour with which the church debated the constitutional issue in 1989–90. The introduction into the debate of the notion of 'social consensus' in the Tsu City case was conducive to Christians' involvement in the later debate of 1989–90, because it gave them a particular issue on which they could legitimately challenge the prerogative of the state to pronounce judgment on religious behaviour. Paradoxically, although the focus on the concept of social consensus did liberate Christians to challenge the state, it also resulted in that challenge conforming to the mould of legal debate.

The question of 'social consensus' is also raised by anthropologist and missionary Robert Ramseyer in his discussion of yet another legal precedent on which

Japanese Christians flexed their muscles prior to the succession debate.[15] He argues that in Japan individuals have come to accept myths about their society, some of which have been perpetuated in relation to the church-state issue. One instance of this was the most celebrated test case about freedom of religion, the Nakaya Case. The case was brought against the Self Defence Force, as an organ of the state, by the Christian widow of an officer who objected to her non-Christian husband's enshrinement as a war hero in the local Shinto shrine for the war dead. In this case the Supreme Court ultimately ruled in 1988 against the widow. The majority of the bench who voted for the ruling commented on the difference between Christians and Japanese, either inadvertently overlooking, or deliberately ignoring, the reality that the person on whom they passed judgment was both.[16] The popular perception that being Christian and being Japanese were incompatible had now been given a legal stamp of approval by the Supreme Court. The newfound respect accorded legal institutions meant that the impact of decisions such as this was to sway public opinion generally, not just within the legal fraternity.

Both the Tsu and Nakaya cases came after the initial instance of clear confrontation between Christians and the government in post-war Japan. In 1955 the ruling Liberal Democratic Party (LDP) moved to establish a Constitutional Review Committee. This resulted in 1957 in a proposal to legislate for February 11th to be declared National Foundation Day (*Kenkoku kinenbi*). In response, the United Church of Christ's Tokyo District Social Issues Committee raised a petition of protest containing 6000 signatures, and in 1962 the National Synod of the Church issued a counter declaration naming the date 'Defence of Religious Freedom Day', an appellation clearly hinging on the constitutional guarantee.

Roughly coincidental with this, a movement began directed at amending the status of Yasukuni Shrine, the central Shinto shrine in which war dead, including some convicted at the Tokyo war crimes trials, are enshrined. The intent of the movement was to have Yasukuni declared a non-religious entity, and thus make it eligible for government funding. An opposition movement also emerged, in 1959. The Yasukuni Shrine debate was to become the third major long-running and important debate over the separation of state and religion in which Christians, as well as other groups, developed their rationale and technique for the confrontation of 1989–90.

One of the noticeable features of the opposition to attempts to pass bills relating to Yasukuni Shrine was the cooperation between Christian and other groups. Opposition parties in parliament led the voices of protest when the first such bill was introduced in June 1969, while the Christian anti-Yasukuni movement held sit-ins, hunger strikes and rallies. By the end of the following month, 3.7 million signatures were on a petition against the nationalisation of the shrine.[17]

Christians worked alongside other dissident groups in opposing the bill, which was eventually laid to rest in 1974 after being presented to parliament five times. In July 1969 the National Christian Council, the All Japan Association of Buddhists and the Religious Federation of Japan, representing mainly new religions, issued a joint statement in response to the statement by Yasukuni officials that they would renounce their religious status immediately were the bill passed. By 1973, when the bill had been presented in parliament four more times, the opposition movement had embraced several Sect Shinto groups (i.e. those who dissociated themselves from the legally non-religious State Shinto) and newer Buddhist offshoots such as Rissho Koseikai.[18] A key point, to which we return shortly, is that the ecumenical nature of the cooperation was reminiscent of the situation over 40 years earlier, when Christians opposing state legislative initiatives had been joined in the battle by other religious groups.

But let us return now to the issue of the 1989–90 succession rites. We can trace a line from the Supreme Court split decision to uphold the constitutionality of the payment by Tsu City of money to a Shinto priest, through the Yasukuni shrine nationalisation debate and the Nakaya case, to the debate in question. As noted above, the 'social consensus' legal precedent set in the Tsu case was used by the government, which argued that there was a consensus that the ceremonial procedures should take place in line with 'the traditions of the imperial household' (kôshitsu dentô). Awareness of the concept of social consensus enabled church leaders to engage in debate, as typified by United Church of Christ leader Tomura Masahiro, who points out that what effectively happened was that 'social consensus' (shakai tsûnen) became elevated to 'state consensus' (kokka tsûnen).[19] In essence, however, the Supreme Court had already decreed the definition of social consensus. The accepted understanding was that Shinto ground breaking ceremonies were not religious, and that Christians and Japanese were different. Thus, Tomura's insistence that there is a qualitative difference between a ground breaking ceremony and an imperial succession carried little weight. Arguing this particular point is an example of the way in which the church's political involvement was shaped, to its detriment, by its prior experience.

The point to note here is that the momentum begun in the 1950s carried over into the following decades. Although the battle over the Yasukuni Shrine bills, unlike the Tsu City and Nakaya cases, was fought in the national assembly rather than the courts, it really provided the psychological groundwork, as well as some political and legal experience, for later court cases. A movement called Christians for Defence of the Constitution[20] was begun in 1962 in the wake of the renewal of the US-Japan Security Treaty. Its members 'were active in the Nakaya case, the litigation against the constitutionality of the Tsu City groundbreaking ceremony, and the opposition to the official visits by cabinet and members of parliament to Yasukuni Shrine...and became the driving force in the opposition to unconstitutional national policies.'[21]   The fact that, particularly on the Yasukuni issue, Christian opposition was echoed by many sectors of society lent to Christians the sense that they did not stand alone in their opposition to state acts, and that the government could be tackled without undue concern about direct personal confrontation with any individual representing the government.

Guilt

A third critical component in the post-war Christian experience is the impact of the ongoing process of reflection by Japanese Christians on the role they played in complying with the militarist regime of the 1930s and 1940s. Immediately after the war, widely respected Christian leader Kagawa Toyohiko called for repentance,[22] but the first significant institutional admission of guilt was the *Confession of Responsibility During World War Two* issued in 1967 by the United Church of Christ in Japan, the remaining core of the combined Protestant church compelled into existence by the Religious Organisations Law of 1939. This was but the first of what has since become a torrent of such statements, a torrent which has included more recently an apology from Japanese Christians to the people of Asia (1990), a Japan Evangelical Association apology for supporting Japan's invasion of Asian countries (1995), and even an apology from the Holiness group of churches (1995), which might well be justified if they felt they had nothing for which to apologise, since they stood out during the war years for their opposition to the state and consequent persecution at the hands of the government.

The fact that the issue of war guilt was not formally addressed by the largest denomination in Japan until 1967, a full generation after the end of the war, is a key to understanding the relationship between church and state in the later post-war years. Why was there such a delay? In general, the Japanese church in the immediate post-war period was viewed extremely positively by non-Christians. The acceptability of Christianity was sustained by a combination of factors which could be summed up in terms of Christians having shared two significant experiences with all other Japanese: suffering under repression in the 1930s and 1940s, and the struggle for reconstruction after the war. 'The positive public image of the church at the end of the war had the effect of numbing the church to its wartime responsibilities. In a sense the church indulged itself in the limelight and capitalised on the opportunity. Of course, one could understand the church's desire to evangelise. However, the lack of reflection and repentance'[23] left unanswered the question of the appropriate relationship between church and state. And that was the question which still faced the Japanese church at the end of the 1980s.

A trans-war perspective

The fact that there were significant elements in the Christian experience in post-war Japan which were absent before the war seems to suggest that the late twentieth century church-state confrontation is explicable as a purely post-war phenomenon. However, investigation of the pre-war period reveals that the confrontation of the late twentieth century exhibited an essential continuity with the Christian experience of particularly the 1920s and 1930s.

Early background

Scholars of various disciplines and writers exhibiting a range of objectives for writing seem united in their understanding that by the time Protestant Christianity arrived in 1859 there was a well established practice in Japan of religion being used by the state to further its own purposes, and that this was generally not considered remarkable. Such a situation presents a clear contrast with the insistence on separation of state and religion in the United States, the cradle of much of the Christianity that reached Japan in the nineteenth century. Nevertheless, Japan's first modern constitution, promulgated in 1889, included a stipulation of religious freedom, albeit with restrictions. Article 28 of that constitution stated that the freedom of religion of Japanese citizens was conditional upon it being 'limited to the extent that it does not hinder law and order, and does not oppose the duties of citizens.' This was the bedrock legal principle on which the government's treatment of religions rested until 1945. As the government's definition of law and order, and its idea of the duties of citizens, became more and more restrictive, so too did its treatment of religious groups.

According to the Japanese government's own analysis, 1899 marked a turning point in its treatment of Christianity. From the removal of the prohibition of Christianity on 2 June 1873 until 1899, the government approach had been to give tacit permission for Christianity to expand, even though it had no official status as a religion.[24] December 1899 saw the first attempt to introduce legislation specifically pertaining to religious organisations.[25] The government expected resistance to the bill. To lay the groundwork, several months before the bill was put to parliament, it issued a combination of sub-legislative regulations, which it insisted were required to enable it to bring Christianity adequately under the umbrella of Japanese law and offer Christianity the same legal protections enjoyed by Buddhism and Shinto shrines.[26] The aggregate effect of these initiatives of 1899 was to hold out to the Christian community the carrot of equality with other religions in Japan, in return for the right to use the stick of legislation to keep Christianity, and Christian schools in particular, in line with government preferences. The Christian reaction was to accept the carrot, but resist the use of the stick. At a later point in time, hunger for the carrot would fuel acceptance of the stick, but at this point the result was strident opposition to the bill put to parliament in December of 1899. In contrast to the futility of the Christian voice 90 years later, that opposition was ultimately successful.

1900–26

The picture that emerges from early twentieth century events is of a Christianity which has had a long held ambition fulfilled. Evidence abounds of the Christian desire for acceptance by mainstream Japanese society from at least as early as the 1870s. Notwithstanding the defeat of the 1899 bill, the other ordinances enacted in 1899 essentially meant that Christianity had now been granted official equality with other religions, and it used its newly acquired status to resist attempts by the state to control it. The successful defeat of the 1899 bill was early evidence that Christians now had significant social and political influence.

At least on the surface, Christianity was given tacit support from government sources in the early years of the new century. When the Tokyo venue for the Eighth International Sunday Schools Convention was destroyed by fire in 1908, for example, business leaders and the government contributed to restoration costs, and more interestingly, so did the imperial household. In 1909, when the Protestant Christian churches held a week long conference in Kanda, a central suburb of Tokyo, to celebrate fifty years of Protestant missions in Japan, they received congratulatory letters from the Prime Minister, the Minister of Education, the governor of Tokyo Prefecture, and the Mayor of Tokyo. Christianity's political status seemed in some ways on a par with Buddhism and Shinto, with representatives of all three being asked for input into government decision making processes. In 1912 the Home Ministry invited all three to what came to be known as the Three Religions Conference, at which the Minister sought their opinions on the best means for promoting the morals of the people. Christians were included again in discussions with the Prime Minister about the best way to instil enthusiasm in people after World War One in 1919, and about how to improve the thinking of the nation in 1924. It is clear that in the second and third decades of the twentieth century, the Christian church was well accepted within the power structures of Japan, even though individual Christians may have felt singled out for criticism of their stance on certain issues.[27]

The responses of the church to the 1912 Meiji-Taishô and 1926 Taishô-Shôwa successions further indicate the extent to which Christianity had become entwined in the power structures of the time. Dohi and Tomura record in detail the initial reactions of the churches to the news from the then Imperial Household Ministry in July 1912 that the Meiji emperor was seriously ill.[28] The Alliance of Christian Churches of Japan (ACCJ), the umbrella Christian organisation of the time, immediately sent two representatives, including essentially conservative evangelical Kozaki Hiromichi (1856–1928), to the ministry to pay respects. It also issued a call for all churches in the Tokyo area to hold meetings to pray for the emperor's recovery, and these were followed by larger combined gatherings of churches, with all centers reporting 'good attendances, given that it is summer'.[29] The non-Japanese Episcopalian Bishop of North Tokyo drew heavily on the Church of England Prayer Book prayers for the occasion of a death in the royal family to pen a special prayer which gave thanks for the blessings of the years of the emperor's reign before asking that 'prayers of loyalty' for the emperor's recovery be heard.[30]

In short, the reaction of institutionalised Christianity was indistinguishable from that of the rest of society. In fact, so enamoured were the churches with the emperor, that they requested the government to allow Christian representatives to attend the emperor's funeral in September 1912. That the church was seen as acceptable by the government of the day is attested by the fact that not only were 150 Christian representatives permitted to participate in the large ceremony in Hibiya Park, but seven were included in the much smaller group within the temporarily constructed funeral building. Even Uchimura Kanzô (1861–1930), the outspoken leader of the non-church movement and object of censure for his refusal to bow to the 1890 Imperial Rescript on Education which demanded loyalty to the emperor, expressed his sadness at the passing of the emperor by suggesting that this was the type of situation referred to by Old Testament prophet Joel's prophetic description of the day when 'The sun and the moon are darkened, and the stars withdraw their shining' (Joel 3:15).[31]

When the Taishô emperor died in 1926, he happened to do so on 25 December. One would expect that the fact that the death occurred on such an important day in the Christian year would have produced unavoidable conflict with Christian activities. However, if anything the churches in 1926–28 altered their own agendas to support the imperial institution and the government's actions to an even greater extent than they did in 1912–14. Christian representatives were again sent to the palace to inquire after the emperor's health in the days leading up to his death, and Christians again attended the emperor's funeral, although on this occasion their request to attend the smaller private ceremony was denied. The church went beyond its level of support in 1912–14 by issuing a statement, at the October 1928 Conference of the Christian Churches, which congratulated the Shôwa emperor on his ascension to the throne.[32]

1927–29

By the end of the 1920s, then, it appears that the church in Japan had moved 180 degrees from its 1899 opposition to the state's attempt to legislate for control over religious organisations. The state had supported the church, and the church was reciprocating by overtly identifying with the state. The events of 1927–29, however, mark a second turning point after 1899 in the relationship between Christians and the state.

In 1927 the Wakatsuki government attempted again to pass a Religions bill, and yet again was unsuccessful. Opposition came from Christians as well as other religious groups. In fact, to judge by the headlines in editorials of the major newspapers, the opposition did not appear to be limited to religious groups.[33] The situation in 1927 was more complicated than that of 1899. In June 1926 the government had decreed the establishment of the Religious Structures Investigative Committee. The Committee was charged with drafting a Religions bill, which it duly did, and the bill was submitted to the January 1927 session of parliament. Members of major religions, including Christianity, were included among the 40 members of the Committee. In that sense, the situation had changed little from the Three Religions Conference of 1912. Christians were still among the privileged few religious groups given a role in shaping government policy.

1927, though, sees the beginning of the souring of state-Christian relations. And it is only after the relationship sours that the mood of legislation also begins to display an ominous tone as far as Christians are concerned. The government's fundamental position was that the 1927 bill was redressing an enduring oversight on their part. Here was Christianity, recognised as a religious group other than Shinto and Buddhism for almost 30 years since Ordinance 41 of 1899, yet unlike those two, it was not protected adequately by legislation pertaining to religions.

The government argued on a number of grounds that Christians ought to embrace the bill. The lack of legal certainty for Christianity was a problem; all 56 branches of Buddhism and 13 schools of Shinto had agreed to treat Christianity as equals; and any attempt to differ in the treatment of Christianity was morally reprehensible. The government rebuttal of suggestions that Christianity be treated differently is worth quoting at length not only because of the content, but because the savagely sarcastic tone of the response indicates just how far the government had moved in the 15 years since it deemed Christianity worthy of a seat at the policy planning table.

> Surprisingly, in response to the Religious Bodies Law, the basis of which is equality of the three religions of Shinto, Buddhism and Christianity, arguments have emerged, albeit an extremely small number, that Christianity ought to be segregated and excluded....The second [of three arguments] is the movement among a number of Christians which in general terms is intent on rejecting even the laws required by the state as the foundation of the freedom of religious groups....[Theirs] is an unfair perspective that seeks to enjoy special freedoms for themselves only, leaving Shinto and Buddhism in their present state constrained by the existing laws and ordinances. It's unfair because, if, as this one faction of Christianity intends, the Religious Bodies Law were to be defeated, the laws and ordinances that have for several decades since the beginning of the Meiji period pertained to Shinto and Buddhism will remain

unchanged, and Christianity alone will be governed by Ministry of Home Affairs Ordinance 41 of 1899 relating to religions other than Shinto and Buddhism. If the opinion had been premised on an absolutely fair and just starting point, there is no way it would be simply a refusal to accept the Religious Bodies Law. It is entirely reasonable that there are those who criticize it as a movement very much degenerated into self-centred egotism.[34]

The implication is clear. Christians who make this sort of claim are interested only in their own welfare. Not only are they no longer suitable recipients of invitations to confer with policy makers, but the religion they espouse is not likely to have anything to contribute to the good of the nation. In the political climate of the late 1920s, as the democratic ideals of the Taisho era were increasingly subjugated to the coercive force of a state apparatus buttressed by the 1925 revised Peace Preservation Law, the message was clearly not just addressed to Christians informing them that the government considered their stance unacceptable. It also sounded a warning bell to other dissident voices that they, too, would be pilloried by the government if they were to step out of line. In the same document the government was equally scathing of the Buddhist voices who argued for continuation of the separate treatment of Christianity, pointing out that they came from 'a small portion of Buddhists who advocate absolute belief and narrow-mindedly posit the same old intolerant argument for discriminatory treatment of Christianity.'[35]

Clearly, there is little government love lost for Christianity. But the point to note here is that the ridicule was mutual. In light of the nature of the proposed legislation, the long sought after equality with other religions now became unpalatable to Christians, and the vituperative language cited above came after attacks by Christians on the Religious Bodies bill and its drafters. Some of the language used by Christians to attack the bill could at best be described as uncharitable, and is probably more accurately described as provocative. It is the language of personal invective. Uchimura Kanzô, for example, one of the elder statesmen of Japanese Christianity, asserted that the interference of politics in religion was 'foolish'. In particular, the Ministry's suggestion that those opposing the bill are ignorant of the nature of religion is a response to Uchimura's claim that,

> the people who drafted it [the bill] don't know a thing about religion. In my nearly 40 years of ministry, I have hardly ever met a bureaucrat or politician who knows anything about religion...[the drafters] are just outsiders who know nothing of God, spiritual matters, and the world to come.[36]

Uchimura's words could hardly have been more inflammatory when we remember that the committee that drafted the bill included Christian members.

In 1929 the government again tried to pass legislation controlling religious activity. In response, the churches in Japan set up an ecumenical special committee to respond to the Religious Bodies Bill[37] under the chairmanship of Yamamoto Hideteru, retired professor of church history at Meiji Gakuin. At the peak of the debate in February-March 1929 the committee investigated the attitude of 1240 Protestant churches and reported that in a limited period since the bill had been tabled, over two thirds (865) had registered their opposition to the bill.[38] The special committee concluded that 'the Ministry of Education says that the majority of churches support the proposed bill, with those opposing being but a few, but that is totally incorrect'.[39]

The 1930s

Within the space of less than two decades from the time Christian leaders had sat down with government leaders to address the declining moral state of the nation, and no more than three years after churches had endorsed rites of imperial succession, the church-state relationship had clearly become a confrontational one. But it was not only the state that Christians had now begun to alienate. Well before 1939, and even before Japan became seriously embroiled in conflict with China in 1937, the social context of legislation had changed in an important way. In 1899 and again in 1927, Christians had stood alongside spokespeople of other religions in opposing the government's legislative initiative. By as early as 1933, however, the Buddhist Association had decided that equating Christianity with Buddhism was not to their liking. De facto, the position they took was that of the government:

> Today, the changes and rumblings in the world of religion have become more violent. This is a point in time when we feel more than ever the urgency of boosting the spirit of the people...We believe that it is a matter of the utmost urgency that...religions be given their appropriate place in terms of the law.[40]

Six years later, under Prime Minister Hiranuma in January 1939, by which time domestic and international circumstances had changed dramatically, the government again put to the parliament a Religious Bodies bill. This time the bill was more succinct, simplified to just 37 clauses from the 130 of the 1927 Religions bill. Shinto had been excluded as a religious group, whereas the 1927 Religions bill had included, in addition to one chapter each on Shinto and Buddhism, a third on Christianity. The bill was passed on March 23, without dissent from inside the chamber or on the streets,[41] and promulgated the following month. The voice of opposition had faded. On the contrary, 'in

Christian circles, there was rejoicing that the word 'Christianity' appeared for the first time [in a bill passed into law] as a religious body'.[42]

To suggest that the spectre of the repressive military regime accounts for the neutralisation of Christian opposition to legislation which was unchanged in essence from that of a decade earlier is too simplistic. The argument of this chapter is that the deafening silence was as much of the Christians' own volition as enforced by the government of the day. Christians' eagerness to celebrate the recognition Christianity had been given as equal in social and legal status to the other two religions of Buddhism and Shinto, had blinded them to reality. And the reality was that by at last succeeding in placing Christianity on a par with other religions, the government had managed to position it to be shaped to the government's liking.

The government was able to use the confrontational approach taken by Christians to further isolate the Christian voice from the position of political influence it had held only 15 years earlier. Akiko Minato's suggestion that 1912 marked the height of Christian acquiescence to the government of the day clearly needs to be rethought.[43] 1912 may well have marked the high water in terms of Christian political influence, but 1939 and the ensuing years saw far greater cooperation with the government than thirty years earlier. Analysis of the post-war Christian experience suggests that Christians had failed to learn that acceptance by the wider society comes at a price, and that by becoming incorporated as part of the state apparatus in the 1910s and 1920s, Christians had left themselves with little room to manoeuvre in opposition to the state in the 1930s.

Conclusion

We thus observe a seesaw of church-state relations in the pre-war era which is repeated in the post-war period. In the mid-nineteenth century missionaries with notions of religion free from state interference arrived in a society where state use of religion was the centuries-old norm and Christianity had been outlawed for over 200 years. The uneasy relationship came to a head in the confrontation of 1899, only for the tension to dissipate in the mutual recognition of the 1910s and 1920s. Confrontation again becomes the key characteristic of the relationship from 1927 through the 1930s and 1940s, before the halcyon days of the Occupation in 1945–52. The post-Occupation period sees a reversion to the type of confrontation on the legal battle field which marked the late 1920s and 1930s.

How do we account for this seesaw of church-state relations? State policy alone is a partial but ultimately inadequate explanation. More fruitful is an understanding from the point of view of Christian identity.

The sense of guilt at both wartime acquiescence and post-war tardiness in admitting guilt, combined with the knowledge that their actions would be subject to the scrutiny of society around them, ensured that Japanese churches in 1989 did not want to be seen to be repeating their error of earlier periods. They were prepared to go on the political offensive as publicly as possible. In their desire to be seen to do the right thing, Japanese Christians succumbed to the temptation to engage in the constitutional debate at the expense of presenting a more identifiably Christian position. The home ground advantage had been ceded to the state, and it appears that on its own turf the state presented as an invincible opponent.

The presence of a guilty conscience for having cooperated with the war effort was a new element in the political awareness of the post-war Japanese church. Had Japanese Christians' awareness of their own history, an awareness which Yasuo Furuya identifies as arising in the 1970s,[44] led to greater consideration of events a little further back than the late 1930s, there is reason to think that the pre-war pattern of legal confrontation might not have recurred. The reality, however, appears to be that the issue of war guilt so dominated Christian historical consciousness that determination to ensure that the mistake of acquiescence to the state was not repeated became the paramount guide to behaviour.

Opposition to the state became a public platform in the 1970s and 1980s on which the churches could establish their credentials as no longer being tied to the state. Such opposition had several characteristics: it was public; it was intellectual; it ostensibly addressed the question of war guilt; and it maintained a sense of separation or purity. On all these counts, I would suggest that the church was out of step with the rest of Japanese society. Moreover, it chose the political realm, about which increasingly consumerist and materialist Japan cared little in the 1970s and 1980s, as the forum for asserting its influence. The church focused on sustaining its identity as Other than the surrounding society, and chose to do so by declaring its opposition to the state. It worked from an assumption of cultures as static, discrete and singular, rather than fluid, not clearly defined, and multi-faceted.[45]

In essence the point to realise here is that the Christian community in Japan in the post-war period seemed to have learnt little from its previous experience. Firstly, it emulated the nineteenth-century missionary insistence on self-separation from surrounding culture. Secondly, it imitated its own ultimately futile course of opposition to legislation of religion in the 1920s and 1930s. Thirdly, it adopted the pattern of using the post-war constitution as the basis for arguing against government initiatives. In doing so, it conceptually locked itself into the government's sphere of influence, just as it had wedded itself to the state more overtly in the 1910s and 1920s.

The Christian opposition to state attempts to legislate for control over religion in the 1920s and 1930s was a critical turning point in the relationship between church and state. The halcyon days of the immediate post-war period appear at first glance to indicate a return of Christianity to a privileged position comparable to that enjoyed forty years earlier. Analysis shows, however, that the position rested on the shifting sands of constitutional guarantees, a willingness to avoid discussion of past mistakes, and short-lived goodwill engendered by shared hardship during the war and reconstruction period. The re-emergence in the 1960s and beyond of the issue of the relationship between church and state, and particularly attempts to introduce legislation in that area, resulted in the church moving even further towards sustaining its identity by maintaining its distance from societal norms. Opposition to the state became the predominant mode of self-expression of the Christian identity to the surrounding society.

Seduced by the freedoms enshrined in the post-war Japanese constitution, Christians used it as the bedrock of their self-identity. They attempted to define and sustain an identity by using an institution of the state. By doing so it seems that they came perilously close to losing sight of both previous Japanese Christian experience and broader Christian history. As such, their experience offers a contemporary case study that appears to confirm the wisdom of the biblical injunction to eschew conformity with surrounding societal norms (Romans 12:2), lest one's Christian identity lose any distinctively Christian characteristics.

ENDNOTES

[1] The two relevant articles of the Constitution are Articles 20 and 89. Article 20 reads: 'Freedom of religion is guaranteed to all. No religious organization shall receive any privileges from the State, nor exercise any political authority. 2) No person shall be compelled to take part in any religious acts, celebration, rite or practice. 3) The State and its organs shall refrain from religious education or any other religious activity.' Article 89 reads: No public money or other property shall be expended or appropriated for the use, benefit or maintenance of any religious institution or association, or for any charitable, educational or benevolent enterprises not under the control of public authority.'

[2] The succession was completed with ascension rites in November 1990, which likewise consisted of two parts, although unlike the two parts of the funeral, which occurred on the same day, these two were separated by ten days. The first was the *sokuinorei*, or ascension itself, a public declaration of succession to the throne by the new emperor, and the second was the most contentious of all the ceremonies involved in the succession process, the *daijôsai*, or grand harvest festival.

[3] Clammer, John 2001, *Japan and its Others: Globalisation, Difference and the Critique of Modernity*, Melbourne, Trans Pacific Press, p. 168.

[4] Clammer, John 1997, 'Sustaining otherness: self, nature and ancestralism among contemporary Japanese Christians', *Japan Forum*, vol. 9, no. 2, p. 179.

[5] The most widely adduced New Testament point of reference in support of obedience to the state is Romans 13:1-7; justification for opposing the state is derived primarily from Acts 4:19 and 5:29. Relevant Old Testament sources include the warnings about the demands of civil authorities in 1 Samuel 8:10-17, and the altercations between Israelite rulers and religious spokesmen recorded in the pre- and post-exilic literature. For an introduction to some of the key thinkers on church-state relations, see Villa-Vicencio, Charles (ed.) 1986, *Between Christ and Caesar: Classical and Contemporary Texts on Church and State*, Grand Rapids, Eerdmans.

[6] Dohi, Akio and Tomura, Masahiro (eds) 1988, *Tennô no daikawari to watashitachi (Imperial successions and us)*, Tokyo, Nihon Kirisutokyôdan Shuppankyoku; Sasagawa,Norikatsu 1988, *Tennô no sôgi (Imperial Funeral Rites)*, Tokyo, Shinkyô Shuppansha; Tomura, Masahiro 1988, *Ima, X-dê o kangaeru (Thinking about X-Day Now)*, Tokyo, Kirisuto Shinbunsha; The Japan Baptist Convention, 1988a, *Tennô no daikawari ni sonaete: sonotoki kyôkai wa...(In Preparation for the Succession of the Emperor: What should the Church*

do?), Tokyo, The Japan Baptist Convention; The Japan Baptist Convention 1988b, *'Nakaya saiban' hanketsu kara tennôdaikawari e (From the Decision in the 'Nakaya Case' to the Succession of the Emperor)*, Tokyo, The Japan Baptist Convention.

[7] The condition was that religious freedom was 'limited to the extent that it does not hinder law and order, and does not oppose the duties of citizens.'

[8] See Articles 19 and 21 of the Constitution.

[9] Note that the translation 'attacking action' is also used for example by Taniguchi, Yasuhei 'The Post-War Court System as an Instrument for Social Change', DeVos, George (ed.) 1984, *Institutions for Change in Japanese Society*, Berkeley, CA, University of California, p. 32. The other two categories are 'party litigation' (*tôjisha soshô*) and 'people's litigation' (*minshû soshô*).

[10] Taniguchi, 1984, pp. 37-8.

[11] Taniguchi suggests several psychological barriers to litigation in Japan—see Taniguchi, 1984, p. 34. The suggestion that Japanese are inherently less litigious than other nations has been well refuted. See, for example, Haley, John O. 1978, 'The Myth of the Reluctant Litigant', *Journal of Japanese Studies*, vol. 4, no. 2, pp. 345-70.

[12] For a reasonably comprehensive introduction to several major legal and political issues in Japan in the 1960-80s, see Field, Norma 1993, *In the Realm of a Dying Emperor: Japan at Century's End*, New York, Vintage Books.

[13] Tomura, Masahiro 1990, *Sokuinorei to daijôsai o yomu (Interpreting the Sokuinorei and the Daijôsai)*, Tokyo, Nihon Kirisutokyôdan Shuppankyoku, pp. 169-70.

[14] The legal precedent of social consensus has had ongoing and wider implications in Japanese law. The most recent use has been in amendments to Japan's Labor Standards Law which passed through parliament on 27 June 2003. Under the revised legislation, dismissal of an employee will be deemed void if it is considered out of line with socially accepted norms of punitive treatment proportionate to the employee's misconduct. See Baker and McKenzie 2003-04, *Asia Pacific Legal Developments Bulletin*, vol. 18, no. 4, December 2003/January 2004, p. 12.

[15] Ramseyer, Robert 1992, 'When Society Itself is the Tyrant', *Japan Christian Review*, no. 58.

[16] Ramseyer, 1992, p. 78.

[17] Kumazawa, Yoshinobu and David L. Swain (eds) 1991, *Christianity in Japan, 1971-90*, Tokyo, Kyo Bun Kwan (The Christian Literature Society in Japan), p. 65.

[18] Kumazawa and Swain (eds) 1991, p. 66.

[19] See Tomura, 1990, p. 167.

[20] *Kenpô o mamoru kirisutosha no kai.*

[21] Hirayama, Shôji 1988, 'Kenpô o mamoru kirisutosha no kai' ('Christians For Defence of the Constitution'), *Nihon kirisutokyô daijiten (Encyclopedia of Japanese Christian History)*, Tokyo, Kyôbunkan, p. 494.

[22] Kagawa was appointed advisor by Prime Minister Prince Higashikuni immediately after the war, and was influential in having September 1945 declared a month of penitence.

[23] Sherrill, Michael J. 2001, *The Protestant Church and Japanese Society: 1950-2000*, Tokyo, Kirisutokyo.com, p. 9.

[24] Mombushô (Ministry of Education) 1927, *Ishin igo ni okeru kirisutokyô ni taisuru toriatsukai no hensen o joshi, kirisutokyô jogairon o bakusu (A Description of the Vicissitudes in the Treatment of Christianity Since the Restoration and a Refutation of the Theory of Christian Exception)*, Tokyo, Mombushô Shûkyôkyoku (Ministry of Education Religions Bureau), p. 1.

[25] The bill consisted of 54 clauses covering such matters as requirements for registration of religious organisations and acceptable religious activities. It was the subject of 48 amendments before being put to the parliament in February 1900. The bill was defeated, partly due to Christian responses to the draft legislation.

[26] Heihachiro Izawa 1988, 'Naimu shôrei daiyonjûichigo' ('Home Ministry Ordinance No. 41'), *Nihon kirisutokyô daijiten (Encyclopedia of Japanese Christian History)*, Tokyo, Kyôbunkan, p. 972.

[27] Dohi and Tomura (eds) 1988, pp.132-3.

[28] Dohi and Tomura (eds) 1988, pp.134-45.

[29] Dohi and Tomura (eds) 1988, p.134.

[30] Dohi and Tomura (eds) 1988, p.135.

[31] Dohi and Tomura (eds) 1988, p.140.

[32] Dohi and Tomura (eds) 1988, p.148.

[33] The Tokyo Asahi Shimbun ran a critical editorial on 14 February 1929 headed 'Reincarnation of the Religions Bill' while the Kokumin Shimbun of 17 February called it a 'retabling' of the Wakatsuki bill 'with minor amendments' and ran an article on 20 February entitled 'A wolf in sheep's clothing'. The Hôchi Shimbun of 19 February called it 'self-defeating' and on the following day warned that there was 'no room for optimism about the Religious Bodies Act—it won't get through parliament easily, and amendments are inevitable. See Nihon Kirisutokyô Tai Shûkyôdantaihôan Tokubetsu Iinkai (Japanese Christian Ad Hoc Committee on the Religious Bodies Bill) (eds) 1929, *Shûkyôdantaihôan ni taisuru shodaishimbun no shasetsu (Editorials of major newspapers relating to the Religious Bodies Bill)* Tokyo, no publisher.

[34] Mombushô (Ministry of Education) 1927, pp. 4-5.

[35] Mombushô (Ministry of Education) 1927, p. 4.

[36] Uchimura, Kanzô 1927, *Shûkyô hôan ni tsuite (Regarding the Religions Bill),* Tokyo, no publisher, p. 1.

[37] *Nihon Kirisutokyô Tai Shûkyôdantaihôan Tokubetsu Iinkai.*

[38] See Yamamoto, Hideteru 1929, *Shûkyô dantai hôan hantai kankei shiryô 'Kirisuto shinkyô no tasû wa hantai' (Materials Relating to the Opposition to the Religious Bodies Bill: Majority of Protestants Oppose Bill),* Tokyo, Nihon Kirisutokyô Tai Shûkyôdantaihôan Tokubetsu Iinkai (Japanese Christian Ad Hoc Committee on the Religious Bodies Bill).

[39] See Yamamoto, 1929. Significantly, two of the denominations with the largest number of objectors to the bill were the Salvation Army and the Holiness Church, both of which suffered the worst repression during World War II because of their continued opposition to government initiatives.

[40] Bukkyô Rengokai Honbu (Buddhist Federation Headquarters) 1933, *Shû kyôhô no hitsuyô naru riyû (Reasons Why A Religious Law is Necessary),* Tokyo, Bukkyô Rengokai Honbu (Buddhist Federation Headquarters), p. 2.

[41] Sasahara, Yoshimitsu 1988, 'Shûkyô dantaihô' (Religious Bodies Law) in *Nihon kirisutokyô daijiten (Encyclopedia of Japanese Christian History),* Tokyo, Kyôbunkan, p. 650.

[42] Sasahara, 1988.

[43] Minato, Akiko 1962, *Kirisutosha to Kokka (Christians and the State),* Tokyo, Seisho tosho kankôkai, p. 125.

[44] Furuya, Yasuo (ed.) 1997, *A History of Japanese Theology,* Grand Rapids, William B. Eerdmans.

[45] The result exemplifies the notion of Christ-against-culture spelt out by H. Richard Niebuhr in his classic 1951 work *Christ and Culture* (New York, Harper). This is the description which best fits the dominant Protestant attitude to Japanese culture right throughout the modern period. For a useful monograph-length discussion of the way in which Christian identity is formed, see Tanner, Kathryn 1997, *Theories of Culture: A New Agenda for Theology,* Minneapolis, Augsburg Fortress.

Section IV. The Future: Openness and Dogmatism

14. 'We already know what is good and just...'[1]: Idolatry and the scalpel of suspicion

Winifred Wing Han Lamb

Suspicion of religion and of religious believers is inherent in western atheism and it is not hard to find this reflected in philosophical thought. However, the 'hermeneutics of suspicion'[2] has been marginal in mainstream philosophy of religion which has concentrated on epistemological issues, inspired by what Merold Westphal has called 'evidential atheism'.[3] This critique of religious faith focuses on the alleged epistemological shortfalls in religious beliefs, pointing to its incoherence, unintelligibility and inadequate evidence.

While the theme of suspicion is muted in mainstream philosophy of religion, it is explicit and open in the work of Nietzsche, Freud and Marx but also in a less known work of David Hume, *The Natural History of Religion*.[4] Nietzsche was well aware of the epistemological objections to Christianity but he came to the realisation that his own atheism was evoked by something deeper than epistemological objections. His 'genealogical' investigation was inspired by suspicion about believers themselves and the extent to which such individuals are motivated by self-interest in their professions of faith. The focus is therefore on the integrity of believers and on the *very possibility of truthfulness in believing*. This is, of course a confronting critique for religious believers. How then can this 'atheism from suspicion'[5] open the way for dialogue between believers and their philosopher critics?

Dialogue and mutuality of engagement have not been notable characteristics in mainstream philosophy of religion. In fact philosophy has invariably set the agenda in both the content and approach taken in this enquiry. As Charles Taliaferro writes, philosophy of religion has often been characterised by 'aggressive critique on the one side and defence or accommodation on the other'.[6] How then can a more equitable exchange be created for religion to speak on its own terms?

Suspicion of believers is reflected in the statement quoted in the title: 'We already know what is good and just'. The full paragraph is found in Nietzsche's *Thus Spake Zarathustra* in which he describes a class of people, categorised as 'Pharisees' as follows: 'As those who say and feel in their hearts: "We already know what is good and just, we possess it also; woe to those who seek thereafter!'" These are closed-minded people that today we would call fundamentalists.[7]

The passage is part of Nietzsche's concentrated critique of Christianity which becomes progressively more vituperative in the course of his writing, but the condition he calls 'pharisaism' is a form of corrupt interiority which he extends beyond Christians to Jews and in fact, to all 'the good'. In other words, 'pharisaism' is intended as a general characterisation of the slave morality which Nietzsche both profiles so insightfully and attacks so violently. He seems quite unambiguous when he says, 'Pharisaism is not degeneration in a good man: a good part of it is rather the condition of all being good'.[8]

As noted above, Nietzsche's critique reflects the assumption within western philosophical thought that religious faith is a form of self deception which leads to epistemic closure. In other words, there is an underlying prejudice that all serious religious conviction has the seeds of fundamentalism. In his depiction of faith as self affirming illusion, Nietzsche represents Christians as psychologically diminished people who seek a packaged faith that they can control in order that they can live unchallenged with all that they believe and 'know'.

In this chapter, I will show (with particular reference to the Christian faith), that discomforting as suspicion is to believers, it can engender dialogue in at least two ways: first, by the mutuality, or a 'logic of implication' which suspicion itself introduces; second, by the insights which suspicion elicits from religion which serves religion by contributing to its self understanding. In addition, suspicion also increases general understanding by sharpening the differences between the interlocutors.

Here the notion of idolatry maps out the 'rhetorical space',[9] or the areas where engagement can be found. In other words, as far as Christianity is concerned, what philosophers like Nietzsche say about such interior corruption cannot be rejected outright since it resonates with what Christian faith itself characterises as idolatry. I use 'scalpel' as a metaphor for the incisive work which suspicion can do when religious believers confront suspicion and acknowledge the presence of idolatry in their beliefs and practices.

I will suggest that we can utilise this dynamic to open up dialogue with the serious religious sentiments with which suspicion resonates, not only in Christianity, but in any religious tradition which values a spirituality of inwardness. The paper will now fall into two parts. In the first part, I will outline the critique from suspicion in David Hume and in Nietzsche's profile of pharisaism. In the second part, I will consider Christian responses to critiques of this kind.

Nietzsche's critique

In his *Natural History of Religion*, Hume argues that religion originates from self-regarding human instincts, such as 'the anxious concern for happiness, the dread of future misery [and] the terror of death' and the 'unknown causes' of such deep emotion are objectified into the divine. Hume uses terms like 'superstition,' 'idolatry,' and 'polytheism' to describe the various ways in which religion is used to further those essentially self-regarding instincts.

While Hume showed a certain admiration for the lofty and noble ideals of religion, he advances his atheism with this challenging question: how could so much violence be done in its name.[10] Centuries later that question is echoed in the postmodern protest that the big stories of faith have given us as much terror as we can take.[11]

Hume's answer to his own question is challenging but illuminating to believers. He concluded that many religious people are able to live with the fundamental contradiction between the ideals of their faith and the violence which it produces because they have domesticated their religion into cosy ideas and 'comfortable views' which have lost all their challenge and edge. As he sees it, believers are so cocooned in their web of beliefs that they will use it to justify whatever they want. These people are in control of a religion that they use to advance their self interest.

With this in mind, Hume raises another question: how does this kind of domesticated religion fit in with religious worship? Does not worship of God require a letting go of self interest? Is not true worship a self-forgetful, non-calculating act? Hume therefore concludes that believers are simply psychologically incapable of worship and that what they call adoration and worship is nothing more than placation and flattery of the divine. An insurance policy against things going wrong.

In drawing the distinction between flattery and adoration, Hume anticipates Nietzsche who (as we shall see) represents religious piety as a form of restlessness borne of anxious self-preoccupation. Believing as he did that it was the philosopher's duty 'to squint maliciously out of every abyss of suspicion',[12] Nietzsche was convinced that his account would reduce faith to nothing more than the manifestation of psychological disease. His conclusion that Christianity is the most virulent form of the morality of *ressentiment* led Nietzsche to the broad conclusion that the Christian form of life is not only disingenuous and anaemic, but 'pharisaical' through and through.

Nietzsche's analysis of pity clearly illustrates the dynamics of Christian slave morality. For Nietzsche, what Christians consider to be virtues arise from weakness and low self esteem but they also show the 'cunning of impotence'[13] since in caring for another, they enjoy the taste of superiority and of being in the stronger emotional position. Pity is thus often 'obtrusive' and 'offends the sense of shame', hurting another's pride. Hence Nietzsche advises that 'unwillingness to help can be nobler than the virtue that rusheth to do so'.[14] In Nietzsche's characterisation, however, pharisaical Christians use pity as a covert revenge. Armed with their good deeds and acts of kindness, they parade as 'embodied reproaches' to those around them.

Nietzsche's representation of pharisaical moralism illuminates the dynamics of idolatry to show how failure of character breeds epistemic closure. Three personality traits structure pharisaical morality: self-enclosure, self-loathing and self-deception.

Firstly, self-enclosure. The pharisees hate new challenges. Nietzsche describes them as 'the beginning of the end' because they are unoriginal and 'cannot create'. By resisting visionaries like Zarathustra and Christ they 'sacrifice unto themselves the future...the whole human future'.[15] Since their spirit is 'imprisoned in their good conscience',[16] the pharisees are 'not *free* to understand' (my italics) new ideas. As Nietzsche judges, the Pharisees 'already know what is good and just'.

Secondly, Nietzsche insightfully suggests that pharisaical traits reflect a deep self-loathing. They speak of the person who is not content with himself, but who is always wishing that he were someone else: 'If only I were someone else...And yet—I am sick of myself!'[17]

Thirdly, the person who cannot bear himself also cannot bear to reveal who he is. But the dissembling of the pharisee works so well that duplicity passes over into self-deception, which flourishes within his lonely life. Nietzsche presents graphic descriptions of this squinting weak-willed individual who slinks about in dark places, continually brooding and machinating forms of underhand ascendency. The weak are consequently weighed down and 'exhausted' by their project of self-preservation: by thoughts about the next move and the next masking act. Such inauthenticity works itself into an art form and issues in a restlessness which Nietzsche describes as 'roving about'. Accordingly, the heart of the pharisee is a 'swampy ground' where 'worms of vengefulness and rancour swarm', in which 'the air stinks of secrets and concealments', and 'the web of the most malicious of conspiracies is being spun constantly'.[18]

The picture of Christians gets worse. Indeed, there is no doubt of Nietzsche's thorough hatred of Christianity when he wrote in *The Antichrist*,

> I call Christianity the one great curse, the one great intrinsic depravity, the one great instinct for revenge for which no expedient is sufficiently poisonous, secret, subterranean, *petty*—I call it the *one* immortal blemish of mankind...[19]

Christian response

Can Christianity respond to a critique of this kind, a critique which reduces it to suspicion and lies? We return to the points made earlier on how suspicion can engender dialogue.

We noted firstly that dialogue stems from the logic of suspicion itself, from what I have called a 'logic of implication'. This arises from the fact that suspicion is chiefly concerned with truth and with truthfulness in so far as it is driven by the desire to unmask what is false and inauthentic. If the author of suspicion seeks to expose the ways in which religion functions 'both to mask and to fulfil forms of self interest which cannot be acknowledged',[20] he or she must also accept their own vulnerability in this process. They must accept that the evasiveness of human consciousness extends to themselves. No one can claim self transparency and anyone is a potential target for unmasking.

This logic of suspicion unites and elicits insights which are both theological and philosophical. Christian biblical and theological thought does not hold back from pronouncing on the human capacity for self deception and the folly of any pretensions to self transparency. Foucault resonates with this awareness when he says 'it is not that everything is bad, but that everything is dangerous'.[21] And because of this there is always work to do in challenging pretensions to truth. This point of mutuality is rare in philosophy of religion but it is a good basis for dialogue, especially if it is framed by the sense of fragility of truthfulness which Foucault suggests.

The theologian, Karl Barth recognised the constructive role which suspicion plays against spiritual idolatry. He said that idols are 'No Gods' which trade the voice of truth for domesticated versions of it and arise from our desire to be comfortable and safe from the challenge of truth. The more domesticated and familiar, the less recognisable they are as idols. Barth therefore argued that Christians must listen to those prophetic voices from outside our comfortable spaces because they can reveal our idolatry and '[t]he cry of revolt against such a god is nearer the truth than is the sophistry with which men attempt to justify him'.[22]

Secondly, suspicion can challenge religious believers to respond in a way which deepens their self understanding. As John Caputo writes, such penetrating critique can serve a prophetic purpose, by 'holding the feet of religion to the fire of faith'.[23] In that sense, suspicion reminds religion of itself and of its prophetic potential.

In what follows, I will consider some areas of Christian theological thought which can be deepened by Nietzsche's profile of the Pharisee. Here, Nietzsche shows how self loathing feeds self deception and self enclosure. Imprisoned in his good conscience, the Pharisee creates a world impervious to challenge. The relationship between religious conviction and epistemic closure is indeed corroborated by what one finds in religious fundamentalism, but there are countervailing religious ideas on the issue. For example, the philosopher Kierkegaard was at pains to point out that faith is not epistemic certainty but an orientation of the self toward eternity, a passionate decision in the face of ultimate concern.[24]

Perhaps one of the most pointed warnings against the danger of self enclosure is found in Coleridge's well known aphorism. He writes: 'He who begins by loving Christianity better than truth, will proceed by loving his own sect or church better than Christianity, and end in loving himself better than all'.[25] This spiritual dynamic of faith is worth analysing. In the important distinctions that Coleridge makes between love of truth and love of Christianity and its specific forms, faith is clearly distinguished from idolatry. Further, according to Coleridge, faithfulness to truth must override faithfulness to Christianity because faith must be sought but never really found in the pharisaical sense. No Christian could claim that they 'already know what is good and just'. Neither can they claim to 'possess' it. Further, it follows that faith is a process of learning and must be protected from idolatry by self reflexivity and by interior vigilance.

So much about the nature of faith, but what about the claim that all 'the good' are Pharisees and that all one's efforts in the spiritual life are corrupted by instrumentality? This broad claim touches all spiritual aspirations everywhere. If the self is never free from itself then there can be no authentic spirituality. All religious devotion is sham and as Hume noted, worship is humanly impossible.

Yet, religion is not caught out by Nietzsche's observation about the ubiquity of the self. Indeed, most religious traditions recognise that instrumentality towards the divine leads to servility of the spirit. As Thomas Merton writes,

> If we remain in our ego, clenched upon ourselves, trying to draw down to ourselves gifts which we then incorporate in our own limited selfish life, then prayer does remain servile. Servility has its roots in self-serving. Servility, in a strange way, really consists in trying to make God serve our own needs...This fact of human nature is recognised and acknowledged at the beginning of prayer in order to rise above it.[26]

In the light of the above, Westphal points out that Merton's profound spiritual insight can explain why across religious traditions, the spiritual life is protected from the corrupting effects of instrumental self interest by what he calls 'terminal' activities, such as prayer, worship and meditation. These spiritual practices are designed to resist instrumentality by celebrating what Westphal calls 'useless (i.e. non instrumental) self-transcendence'.[27] They recognise Nietzsche's insight from the beginning, that while the self is ubiquitous, there are ways and means for devotees to reach that place of freedom where instrumentalism does not have the last word.

To argue categorically as Nietzsche does, that human beings are incapable of non-instrumentality is to be bound to the ultimacy of this logic and to a restricted view of human possibility. This is perhaps not surprising, given that instrumentality lies deep within the way we think and live. But it opens up the conversation on views of human nature and of the possibilities of the spiritual life. The Christian contribution to this discussion would refer to the theological notion of grace, to address Nietzsche's rich profile of the Pharisee who is forever weighed down by the exhausting project of inauthentic self representation. For as Jürgen Moltmann argues, grace pronounces 'the demonstrative value of [our] being'[28] to release us from the 'dreadful questions of existence'[29] that surround the instrumental approach to human worth.

However, suspicion can also divide the interlocutors. It can reveal the fact that they inhabit different worlds. For example, Dietrich Bonhoeffer, who read Nietzsche closely, bemoaned the prevalence of instrumental religion in the Christianity of his day. He identified it as the 'cheap grace'[30] which trades self-serving religion for the radical experience of self-surrendering discipleship. However, while agreeing with Nietzsche about the lure of self-affirming illusion in religion, Bonhoeffer maintains against Nietzsche that true freedom comes from self surrender to God. In answer to Nietzsche's analysis of the Christian life, Bonhoeffer puts forward the radical Christian understanding of power which challenges Nietzsche's understanding, not only of freedom, but also of weakness.[31] Clearly sharpened by his engagement with Nietzsche's psychological insights into the slavish uses of weakness, Bonhoeffer articulates a notion of 'Christian weakness' which is understood in relation to the imitation and discipleship of Christ. This 'weakness' is cultivated by the challenge of a courageous and robust character that constantly resists idolatry by self-reflexive learning. Thus Bonhoeffer starkly opposes a comfortable view of God with the Christ of the cross. He addresses Nietzsche's contempt for Christian ideas of redemption and his rejection of 'that wretched of all trees' with this statement of Christian distinctiveness: he writes:

> If it is I who say where God will be, I will always find there a [false] God who in some way corresponds to me, is agreeable to me, fits in with my nature. But if it is God who says where He will be…that place is the cross of Christ.[32]

Conclusion

It is clear that suspicion can provide a creative spur to religious self understanding.[33] Like a scalpel, it cuts deep into the religious conscience but it can be a source of insight which feeds continuing dialogue. It is also clear that suspicion can clearly show up profound differences between the parties but at least mutual understanding has been advanced. In this paper, I have tried to show that the notion of idolatry in both philosophy and theology provides a 'rhetorical space' for dialogue between faith and its interrogators and I have used the metaphor of the scalpel to indicate the cost of self reflexivity which is the price of fruitful dialogue.

ENDNOTES

[1] Nietzsche, Friedrich 1905, *Zarathustra*, Thomas Common (trans.), with an introduction by Elizabeth Forster-Nietzsche, New York, Macmillan, Third Part, LVI, # 26, p. 218. The full paragraph reads, 'As those who say and feel in their hearts: "We already know what is good and just, we possess it also; woe to those who seek thereafter!"'

[2] Paul Ricoeur describes this as the 'exegesis of the desires that lie hidden in...intentionality. See his (1970) *Freud and Philosophy: An Essay on Interpretation*, Denis Savage (trans.), New Haven, Yale University Press, pp. 457-58.

[3] Westphal, Merold 1993, *Suspicion and Faith: The Religious Uses of Modern Atheism*, Grand Rapids, Mich., Eerdmans.

[4] Hume, David 1956, *The Natural History of Religion*, H. E. Root, (ed.), London, Adam & Charles Black. I am indebted to Westphal for the discussion on Hume which follows.

[5] The phrase comes from Westphal, 1993.

[6] Taliaferro, Charles 1999, *Contemporary Philosophy of Religion*, Oxford, Blackwell, p. 3.

[7] Martin E. Marty characterises fundamentalists as those who look backwards and attempt to 'freeze' truth in some form. See his 1992, 'Fundamentalisms Compared,' *The 1989 Charles Strong Memorial Lectures*, Adelaide, Flinders University Press, p. 1. See also Lamb, Winifred Wing Han 1998, 'Facts That Stay Put: Protestant Fundamentalism, Epistemology and Orthodoxy,' *Sophia*, vol. 37, no. 2, pp. 88-110.

[8] Nietzsche, Friedrich 1977, *Beyond Good and Evil: Prelude to a Philosophy of the Future*, R. J. Hollingdale (trans.), London, Penguin, # 135, p. 82.

[9] Lorraine Code uses the notion to explore the effect of inequality in discussions. See her 1995 *Rhetorical Spaces. Essays on Gendered Spaces*, New York, Routledge.

[10] Hume, David 1956, *The Natural History of Religion*, H. E. Root, (ed.), London, Adam & Charles Black.

[11] Lyotard, Jean François 1981, *The Postmodern Condition: A Report on Knowledge*, Geoff Bennington and Brian Massumi (trans.), Minneapolis, University of Minnesota Press, p. 81.

[12] Nietzsche, *Beyond Good and Evil*, # 34, p. 47.

[13] Nietzsche, *On the Genealogy of Morals*, Kaufmann W. and Hollingdale R. J. (trans.) (New York, Vintage Books, 1967, I # 13, p. 40.

[14] *Zarathustra*, Fourth Part, LXVII, pp. 265-7.

[15] *Zarathustra* Third Part, LVI, # 26, pp. 218-9.

[16] *Zarathustra*

[17] Nietzsche, *On the Genealogy of Morals*, p. 122.

[18] Nietzsche, *On the Genealogy of Morals*.

[19] Nietzsche, 1990, *Twilight of the Idols/The Antichrist*, R. J. Hollingdale (trans.), London, Penguin, # 62, p. 199.

[20] Westphal, 1993, p. 14.

[21] Foucault, Michel 1983, 'On the Genealogy of Ethics: An Overview of Work in Progress,' Afterword to Hubert L. Dreyfus, Paul Rabinow, *Michel Foucault: Beyond Structuralism and Hermeneutics*, Chicago, University of Chicago Press, p. 231.

[22] Barth, Karl 1933, *The Epistle to the Romans*, Edwyn C. Hoskyns (trans.), New York, Oxford University Press, pp. 37-52. I am indebted to Westphal for his discussion on Barth in *Suspicion and Faith*, 1993, pp. 4-6.

[23] Caputo, John (ed.) 1997, *Deconstruction in a Nutshell: A Conversation with Jacques Derrida*, New York, Fordham University Press, p. 159.

[24] Kierkegaard described faith as being acquired on a daily basis 'through the infinite personal passionate interest'.See Kierkegaard, 1944, *Concluding Unscientific Postscipt*, David F. Swenson (trans.), Princeton, N.J., Princeton University Press, p. 53.

[25] Coleridge, Samuel Taylor 1825, *Aids to the Formation of a Manly Character*, London: Taylor and Hessey, p. 101.

[26] Merton, Thomas *Contemplation in a World of Action*, quoted in Merold Westphal, 1984, *God, Guilt and Death: An Existential Phenomenology of Religion*, Bloomington, Indiana University Press, p. 142.

[27] The phrase is discussed in Westphal, 1984, *God, Guilt and Death: An Existential Phenomenology of Religion*, pp. 138-51.

[28] The phrase is F. J. J. Buytendijk's and quoted in Moltmann, J. *Theology and Joy*, London, SCM Press, 1971, p. 42.

[29] Moltmann, 1971, p. 43.

[30] Bonhoeffer, D. 1959, *The Cost of Discipleship*, London, SCM, p. 35.

[31] There is a prejudice within modern atheism which equates Christianity with weak-willed conventionality and self-deceptive servility. Ludwig Feuerbach wrote, 'What distinguishes the Christian from other honourable people? At most a pious face and parted hair'. Feuerbach, L. 1980, 'Epigrams', *Thoughts on Death and Immortality*, Berkeley, University of California Press, p. 205.

[32] Bonhoeffer, D. 1986, *Meditating on the Word*, Cambridge, Cowley Publications, p. 45.

[33] For an extended discussion see Lamb, Winifred Wing Han 2004, *Living Truth and Truthful Living: Christian Faith and the Scalpel of Suspicion*, Adelaide: ATF Press.

15. The sacred and sacrilege — ethics not metaphysics

Eilidh St John

When I tell my colleagues in both the School of Philosophy and the School of Government that I am writing on blasphemy and sacrilege most of them meet me with blank stares and I have a distinct feeling that they think I have crawled out of the seventeenth century. And yet, in this world beset more each day with religious tension between faiths and between adherents of the same faith it becomes increasingly more urgent to find an adequate cross-cultural, multi-faith way of addressing questions of blasphemy and sacrilege. I haven't crawled out of the seventeenth century so there must be another explanation for this dichotomy of attitude. My teenage son has found the perfect explanation for any disputes or dichotomies which occur between us. He has learned some of the language of my world view so instead of shouting 'you don't understand me' and slamming out of the room he fixes me with his big brown eyes and says, 'either our paradigms are different, or *you* have made a category error'. Perhaps this is the explanation here. Either my paradigms are different from those of my colleagues or *they* have made a category error.

In discussing the issues of blasphemy and sacrilege perhaps a good place to start is with some definitions. The Australian edition of the *Collins Concise Dictionary* tells us that something is blasphemous if it 'involves impiety or gross irreverence towards God or something sacred'. It defines blasphemy narrowly as 'the crime which is committed if a person insults, offends, or vilifies the deity, Christ or the Christian religion'. *The New Shorter Oxford English Dictionary* provides a broader definition, namely 'profane talk of something supposed to be sacred'. To blaspheme is 'to show contempt or disrespect for (God or sacred things)'. Sacrilege it defines as 'originally the crime of stealing or misappropriating a sacred object or objects especially from the church. Later any offence against a consecrated person, or violation or misuse of whatever is recognised as sacred or under Church protection'. *Collins*, on the other hand, says that sacrilege is 'the misuse or desecration of anything regarded as sacred or as worthy of extreme respect' or an 'instance of taking anything sacred for secular use'. Whatever the variations in definition it is plain that both blasphemy and sacrilege involve the giving of offence to others, and they are, therefore, public as opposed to private or personal issues.

In a pluralistic society the idea of the sacred is one which appears to be fraught with difficulties. What is sacred to an indigenous person will not, on the face of it, be sacred to a Muslim, Jew or Christian, and obviously what is sacred to any of them will not be sacred to a person of no faith.

Immediately we can see two possible questions. Firstly, is it acceptable in a secular state to have as crimes behaviours towards God and matters related to God? In other words, is there a role for the expression of religious views or even the protection of religious views in public policy debate and formulation in a pluralistic liberal democracy? The second question is whether it is appropriate in a multicultural or pluralistic society to have state policy on matters which are so specifically focused on religion at all, but especially on one religion.

Liberal thought has tended to maintain that religion is too divisive to provide a constructive voice in public policy debates within democratic pluralistic societies. It is argued that the beliefs of various religious traditions are intimately bound up with views of the good, of right and wrong, which are not shared by others. Additionally, the argument goes, because such beliefs are not supported by publicly and universally accessible reasoning, they are likely to conflict with one another and with secular thought, thus threatening social stability.

Richard Rorty advocates privatising religion, 'making it seem bad taste to bring religion into discussions of public policy'[1] and Robert Audi argues that citizens should provide secular reasons for advocating public policies because 'conflicting secular ideas, even when firmly held, can often be blended and harmonised in the crucible of free discussion: but a clash of gods is like a meeting of an irresistible force with an immovable object'.[2] Although he has slightly modified his views in recent years John Rawls adopts a very similar position.

Writing of why it is inappropriate for universal truth claims about the essential nature and identity of persons to be made in determining a conception of justice John Rawls has this to say:

> as a practical political matter, no general moral conception can provide a publicly recognised basis for a conception of justice in a modern democratic state. The social and historical conditions of such a state have their origins in the Wars of Religion following the Reformation and the subsequent development of the principle of toleration, and in the growth of constitutional government and the institutions of large industrial market economies. These conditions profoundly affect the requirements of a workable conception of political justice: such a conception must allow for a diversity of doctrines and the plurality of conflicting, and indeed commensurable conceptions of the good affirmed by the members of existing democratic societies.[3]

An analogous kind of reasoning is applied when matters of sacrality are being discussed. It is thought that it is impossible to have a universal conception of the sacred because different faiths and different cultures regard different things as sacred. Conversely, in a pluralistic society, it is impossible to have a coherent view of what is sacrilegious for exactly the same reasons.

If a person adheres to a set of beliefs, a faith which holds a particularly well-defined God-head as the supreme or only God, and if attached to this strongly defined God there is a set of behaviours, artefacts and attitudes which belong only to that well-defined God, it is only logical that anything which falls outside the well-defined parameters, cannot be considered as sacred by the person of well-defined faith. It is this logic which allowed a pastor from a Pentecostal church in Hobart to refer to a statue of the Buddha which the Buddhist community had just installed in their grounds as a 'lump of metal'. It is this logic which allows devout Christians who enter their sacred places with due reverence, to climb Uluru. It is the same logic which allows American troops to enter mosques and Indian troops to enter the golden temple at Amritzah, and which allows secular tourists from everywhere to enter cathedrals and churches in Britain as if they were going to the fair.

This way of thinking about universal morality or universal sacrality is an error of reasoning amounting to a category error. What we need is to change our style of thinking.[4] This chapter, therefore, is about changing the style of thinking—ostensibly about what we choose to call 'the sacred'. This is such a fundamental change, however, that it brings with it a radical shift in our understanding of what it means to be human, in our perception of self, in our functioning in society and certainly in our understanding of what words like sacrilege, blasphemy and profanity might mean.

Concepts like the sacred have been misappropriated by organised religion. Such concepts apply universally to human beings and their exclusive attachment to systems of belief has caused a debilitating fragmentation in our understanding of reality, resulting in severe and near irreparable damage to the human psyche, to human society and to the environment which envelops our humanity. Current understandings of these concepts, coloured as they are by the dominating doctrines of the Judeo-Christian tradition are inadequate, or at best partial. This chapter is an attempt to restore them to what I consider to be their proper realm—human Being-ness.

I recognise that human Being-ness is a peculiar term. With it I am attempting to elucidate specifically the distinction between the profoundly and unalterably given nature of a human and the multifarious and ever changing ways each human has of being in the world for which I reserve the term human being. This distinction can be illustrated analogously, by contemplation of the difference between the 'I AM THAT I AM'[5] of Jewish Scripture and the statement 'I am a jealous God'. Robert Young maintains that this phrase indicates the essential unsearchableness of God rather than mere existence even though it is derived from *hayah*, the Hebrew verb *to be*.[6] I would use 'human Being-ness' to indicate, not the mere existence of human beings, but rather the essential, but as yet, not fully fathomed unity of being each human has in his/her intimacy with existence. Human Being-ness, therefore has much in common with Heidegger's *Dasein* in that 'the essential definition of this being cannot be accomplished by ascribing to it a 'what' that specifies its material content, because its essence lies rather in the fact that in each instance has to be its being as its own...'[7] This idea is borne out in the ancient Celtic I AM poems. Traditionally, the first of such poems is held to be the one composed by Amairgen, when his people the Milesians claimed Ireland as their own. It illustrates well this condition which I call human-Beingness.

> I AM the wind which breathes upon the sea,
> I AM the wave of the ocean,
> I AM the murmur of the billows –
> I AM the ox of the seven combats,
> I AM the vulture upon the rocks,
> I AM a beam of the sun,
> I AM the fairest of plants,
> I AM the wild boar in valour,
> I AM the salmon in the water,
> I AM a lake in the plain,
> I AM a world of knowledge,
> I AM the point of the lance of battle,
> I AM the God who creates the fire in the head.[8]

In this poem there is no dualism. There is only unity of being. It illustrates the ontological height, depth and breadth of the possibilities and realities of human-Beingness and it takes us in the direction of recognising the places where humans be as holy ground.

We can argue about whether or not 'Put off thy shoes from off thy feet, for the place whereon thou standest is holy ground'[9] is a literal verbal communication from Yahweh to Moses. Fascinating as the extensive discussions about the literal truth of scripture and its ratio-philosophical/theological interpretation may be, for the purposes of this chapter they do not really matter. What does matter here is that scripture tells us that human beings have, for a very long time had a conception of something called 'holiness' and for an equally long time they have been able to locate this thing called 'holiness' or 'the sacred' in the world. Scripture does not tell us that God said 'I am in a holy place' but rather that the place, in the world, where Moses stood was a holy place. Scripture can be seen, according to this understanding, not as the exclusive property of a particular religion or religious grouping, but rather as the accumulated liturgical-poetic responses of humanity to the experience of being human in the world.

This does not mean that scripture should be held to be less holy or sacred when seen in this light but I recognise that this does not coincide with the generally held view among believers and non-believers alike. For the most part, religious adherents claim that their holy books impart exclusive and literal knowledge of the divine, while those who do not accept the dogmas attached to religions tend also to eschew the sacred writings. It is my contention that as a consequence, both individuals and humanity as a whole are the losers. Such a position challenges the view that scripture and 'the sacred' are the exclusive province of religion. It is necessary therefore, to examine precisely what is meant when the word 'religion' is used. Such an examination shows that the meaning is anything but precise.

According to the *New Shorter Oxford English Dictionary* 'holy' refers to a thing or place kept, or regarded, as sacred or set apart for religious use or observance. Specifically, in Christianity it is a place or thing 'free from all contamination of sin and evil, morally and spiritually perfect'. 'Holy' can also refer to somebody 'specially belonging to, empowered by or devoted to God, or something pertaining to, originating from or sanctioned by God'. 'Sacred' is defined as 'consecrated to, or considered especially dear to a god or supernatural being' or 'set apart for or dedicated to a religious purpose and so deserving veneration and respect'.

In lexicological terms then, 'holy' or 'sacred' can be seen as both relating specifically to gods or God, and as set apart from, and capable of being contaminated by, human beings. This idea of the possibility of contamination seems to be conveyed in the command 'Put off thy shoes from off thy feet'. In other words, humans were being commanded not to bring the pollution of their everyday (mundane) life into the places where they could meet holiness or divinity.

All this may seem very basic. It certainly appears that everyone knows what 'sacred' means. Its application to designated places of worship and the rites of recognised religion and the somewhat more arcane sites and practices of indigenous culture and the relics and artefacts of both is unremarkable. Today, however, it is also used, literally or metaphorically, in many other contexts. In the West we have, at best, an ambivalent attitude to the whole category of religion and the sacred. In most of the western world, at least, religion and theology have become sidelined as the curious and peculiar pastimes of small ghettos of the idiosyncratically inclined.[10]

Those things which concern the inhabitants of these ghettos are seen, therefore, to be completely separate and different from the issues of 'real life'. This is particularly so in Australia where secular life is believed to be enshrined in the Constitution.[11] Philosophers, particularly, are susceptible to the ambivalences inherent in this debate. It is a suspicion of philosophers that theology is not nearly such a rigorous enterprise as philosophy, many seeing academic theology as thinly disguised apologetics for non-rational beliefs. In addition there is tentativeness among philosophers about words, and their meaning that makes questions about the nature of the sacred seem to be fraught with difficulty. In the words of F. E. Peters,

> Philosophers have been uneasy about language almost from the beginning. The sculptor may curse his stone or the painter his oils, but neither contemplates suing for divorce. The philosopher, on the other hand, lives constantly in the shadow of infidelity, now suspecting metaphor, now tautology, or occasionally succumbing to the ultimate despair, the fear that he is dealing with *nomina tantum*.[12]

Only words—this certainly seems to apply to 'religion' and 'sacred'. It appears that nowadays 'religion' can mean anything, everything and nothing. That religion has no value, that it is anachronistic, superstitious nonsense—that religious institutions are at best irrelevant, and at worst, conservative, backward-looking inhibitors of human progress, are common-place attitudes to be found in almost every discussion from talk-back radio to the academy. As well as the claims that religion means nothing there can also be detected attitudes that religion can mean anything and everything. Statements like 'I don't go to church any more because I am spiritually fulfilled by Tai Chi'—or Feng Shui, or bushwalking, or painting, or Amnesty International are commonplace. A further attitude toward religion can be characterised as the pragmatic approach, where religion is used somewhat cynically, especially by politicians, to engender particular patriotic fervour among a populace. The use of religious language at times of national threat is a case in point. The authenticity of such language must be questioned. How authentically Christian is it, for instance, to use the language of a religion whose founder preached peace and 'turning the other cheek', when sending young people off to war?

One of the aims of this chapter is to bring some clarification to our understanding of what constitutes the sacred in order to develop a philosophical understanding of what the sacred means in the context of human Being-ness, and determine what might constitute sacrilege or blasphemy in a secular and multicultural state.

Here I find myself in sympathy with the work of the German idealist philosopher Friedrich Schleiermacher. Schleiermacher set himself in sharp opposition to the intellectualism and moralism of the Age of Reason. He accused Enlightenment thinkers of misunderstanding and debasing religion, by confusing it with, and transforming it into, metaphysics and morality. By this process religion became the object of empirical scrutiny and was stripped of its completely unique and independent essence. It is this process, Schleiermacher claims, which discredited religion to the point where it was being considered an irrelevance. He tirelessly repeated his demands that a sharp distinction must always be made between religion and all metaphysics and all moralities.[13]

In order to make quite clear to you what is the original and characteristic possession of religion; it resigns, at once, all claims on anything that belongs either to science or morality. Whether it has been borrowed or bestowed it is now returned.

Schleiermacher makes a strong distinction between 'religion', with its questionable metaphysics and even more questionable morality, and what he calls 'piety', but what might equally be called 'reverence'. In his introduction to the first edition of Schleiermacher's *Collected Speeches on Religion*, Otto had this to say:

> Schleiermacher based his justified attack—though very exaggeratedly—on the complete rejection in the field of religion of knowledge and action, of 'metaphysics' and 'practice'…He wished to show that man is not wholly confined to knowledge and action, that the relationship of men to their environment —the world, being, mankind, events—is not exhausted in the mere perception or shaping of it. He sought to prove that if one experienced the environing world in a state of deep emotion, as intuition and feeling, and that if one were deeply affected by a sense of its eternal and abiding essence to the point where one was moved to feelings of devotion, awe and reverence—then such an affective state was worth more than knowledge and action put together.[14]

This is what Schleiermacher himself says on this matter of metaphysics, morality and piety:

> Only when piety takes its place alongside of science and practice, as a necessary, an indispensable third, as their natural counterpart, not less in worth and splendour than either, will the common field be altogether occupied and human nature on this side complete.[15]

Schleiermacher is more concerned with the essential experiences that give rise to the processes and his use of 'piety' as the attitude correlative to religion is a radical departure from the thinking which preceded him, and regrettably, much of that which followed him.

Schleiermacher's concern is to describe or redescribe that characteristic of human Being-ness, which gives rise to religion. To this extent he has no doubt about the validity of religion. His concern is that this characteristic has been misconstrued, distorted, contorted and neglected because people had been mistaken about its nature. His descriptions, therefore, do not seek to prove anything for he does not believe that there is anything to prove. He is merely describing a phenomenon which the 'cultured despisers' have misconstrued and therefore erroneously rejected.

Schleiermacher describes religion in a way which is new and radically different. This is because his perspective is different. Before Schleiermacher, theologians concentrated their attention on the object of religious activity—namely God and doctrines of God. Schleiermacher is not interested in furnishing new evidence for the existence of God, the independence of the soul, or immortality. Schleiermacher's focus is unequivocally, the subject that engages in religious activity, namely humanity. He identifies the essence of religion, not by a unique object, but by the uniqueness of the human faculty that operates in religious activity. He attempts to show that human understanding has three components: knowing, doing, and feeling, and that just as science is the legitimate expression of human knowing, and ethics is the legitimate expression of human doing, religion is the legitimate expression of human feeling.

Otto warns us that we should not be misled by the English word 'feeling'. Schleiermacher is not linking religion with a particular emotional attitude or a very personal and particular inner experience. He makes this clear with the use of three different German words: *Anschauungen* (intuitions), *Gefühle* (feelings), and occasionally *ahnden* (divining or surmise). Clearly Schleiermacher did not intend to associate religion with an emotional response nor did he seek to ground religion in a personal inner religious experience. 'Feeling' refers to a faculty of mind and not a mental category, and is, therefore, a metaphysical or ontological category rather than a psychological one. For Schleiermacher, the important factor is not that religion is the human response to 'being' or to 'power', but that it is a particular kind of response, which has been called 'religious response' to 'whatever' one considers divine. The object of that response is unimportant. What is important is the kind and quality of response. Viewed in this way it is possible for a person to reject any particular religion as a conglomeration of culturally conditioned manifestations and yet be a full participant in an authentic religious life.

Schleiermacher identifies a religious sphere to human life that is not a matter of belief, but of being, so that whatever else humans may be—physical, moral, mental, social, emotional—they are also religious. Human life is incomplete if the religious side is not developed, and human existence is understood incompletely if its religious facet is not considered. When J.N. Mohanty writes, 'Authentic religiosity experiences the world as intrinsically sacred'[16] he is making this same point—that when one lives authentically there is no definitive distinction between holy things and everyday things, between holy places and ordinary places.

The holy, the sacred, the numinous, can be characterised, according to this view of religion, not as Anselm had it as 'that than which no greater can be conceived' but rather as the Upanishads proclaim, the *ā-caryam,* [17] 'that in whose presence we must exclaim 'aaah!'

> This is the way It [Brahman] is to be illustrated:
> When lightnings have been loosened:
> aaah!
> When that has made the eyes to be closed –
> aaah! –
> so far concerning Deity (*devatā).*

As we go about our daily lives, ordinariness, routine and rational explanations prevail. We eat and drink because we need nourishment and hydration in order to survive, we build shelters as protection from life threatening elements and we indulge our sex drive because of the promptings of the 'selfish gene'. None of these responses are questioned or questionable in our scientific age. The explanation follows the behaviour as night follows day. But our 'religious' impulses are not given the same value. They are seen as a distortion of our other impulses rather than as a legitimate response to a legitimate prompting. The object of these impulses is of little significance here. What is interesting is that it cannot be disputed that human beings from the beginning of their history have recognised the 'aaah of things'.[18] Recognition of the 'aaah of things' has nothing to do with the characterisation of the 'aaah'. The characterisation is time and culture specific. The logic of the characterisation is simple if not simplistic. It goes something like this: 'The essence of the thing which elicits the "aaah" must logically be greater, more significant, more powerful, more beautiful, more loving, more sagacious, more valuable, than anything we know which does not elicit the "aaah". Let us, therefore, attribute to "the aaah of things" the superlatives of that which we value'.

Human beings are communicating beings and in order to communicate the experience of the 'aaah of things', it is necessary to clothe the ungraspable, the ineffable, the unconceptualised, in language and concepts which have some immediate rational meaning. The 'aaah of things' the *ā-caryam,* is that element of the Being-ness of human being which reveals to each individual his or her reality as part of something other than the routine ordinariness of finite, physical, empirically provable existence.

Here then is an explanation of how we can make sense of such concepts as sacrilege and blasphemy in a secular multicultural state. If we think about sacrality as emanating from objects which have been designated as sacred by groups or persons who claim to have jurisdiction in such matters we can develop one of two possible ways of thinking about the universal sacred. We can adopt the position, which seems to be the one adopted by Rawls of believing that what is sacred (or moral) is entirely relative—peculiar to specific groups and therefore not capable of being universalised. If such a position is taken then the appropriate response is surrender to the entirely relative, or the one taken by Rawls, of attempting to develop a universal concept which isolates the relativities and pursues a parallel path to universalities.

There is another way of looking at this issue. Sacredness or sacrality is not constituted by an object (a relic, an icon, a deity, a place or a person) in just the same way that love in not constituted by an object (the beloved person, thing or place). In a special sense it is not objective—it is not vested in objects.

Like love, sacrality or sacredness is a faculty—an orientation, an attitude. It is therefore subjective—the product of a subject. The subjectivity of the sacred does not mean, however, that the sacred or sacredness is necessarily and exclusively relative. Even though what is sacred for you is not necessarily sacred for me the 'subjective sacred' can be universalised because being a subject is a human universal.

When we recognise that the possession of the faculty for sacredness, like the possession of the faculty for love, is an indelible characteristic of what it means to be human we can respect the sacrality which others recognise without needing to accept the specifics of their sacred objects, or the idiosyncrasies of the system they adopt to identify the sacred.

By this process sacrality is transformed from a question of metaphysics into a question of virtue. The focus moves from the contestable arena of the nature of the sacred object to the less controversial domain of relationships. The question is no longer whether this or that object, person, place or practice is sacred. It is transformed into a question of what virtue is operating when subjects are engaging their faculty for recognition of the sacred.

What is a virtue? It has been argued that 'a virtue of a thing or being is what constitutes its value, in other words, its distinctive excellence...'[19] So virtue in human beings is both what makes them distinctively human and also what contributes to their excellence as human beings. A virtuous human being then might be one who has a disposition (given or acquired) to do what is good. Thinking of virtue in this way circumvents the relativist dilemma created by attempts to define the Good. There is no need to contemplate or know an Absolute Good or goodness-in-itself if the focus is on the subject rather than the object, or to put it another way if the focus is on the verb rather than the noun. Goodness ceases to be something which we must define and agree upon—it becomes something to be accomplished and virtuousness becomes transformed from a list of attributes to be acquired to a way of being—an endeavour to act for excellence in every situation.

What does this mean for the issue of sacrality and for the denial of sacrality—sacrilege? What is the virtue most applicable to this part of human-Beingness? If Schleiermacher and Mohanty are right and the sacred is not something to be defined but rather to be apprehended—'the aaah of things'—then the virtue associated with the sacred is the capacity for awe or an understanding that there is that which lies outside human control. Sacrilege then becomes a refusal to accept this understanding. The English word 'reverence' is the one which most nearly describes this 'sacred-centred' virtue. It is a word which has fallen into disuse probably because of overuse and misuse in a previous time. I am not arguing for a return to reverence by rote or formula, or to reverence without humour or criticism—that is a kind of inverted hubris—but I am arguing that to forget that one is only human or to deny the inevitable imperfection of being human is the attitude of mind which gives rise to the absence of the 'sacred-centred virtue' or sacrilege. Claiming to have absolute truths, claiming to know the mind of God either through scripture or experience, claiming to act on God's behalf is to fall into this understanding of sacrilege. Sacrilege thus ceases to be an attack on particular beliefs or artefacts and becomes an assault on human beings living up to the best they know. It becomes, not a crime against God or gods, but rather a crime against humanity because as the capacity for awe or reverence increases so too does the capacity for respecting the work and life of all human beings even in, or especially in their inevitable imperfection.

As a consequence of this understanding, determining whether a particular act or utterance is blasphemous or sacrilegious requires the asking of two new questions. Firstly it is necessary to ask whether that which is being 'attacked' is an example of human beings living up to their potential for awe. If the answer is affirmative then it becomes clear that the object or behaviour or person being attacked is sacred. The second enquiry concerns the accused but the question is no less straightforward. Was the 'attack' made in reverence; that is was it made in an attempt to live up to the possibility of excellence (not perfection) in human-Beingness, or was it made from a position of lack of virtue? Obviously, even such straightforward questions carry their own complexities and another paper is necessary to even begin such a project, but if these two questions become the criteria for assessing whether blasphemy or sacrilege have occurred the vexing questions of cultural relativism disappear while sensitivity to those things which people hold sacred is preserved and enhanced.

ENDNOTES

[1] Rorty, Richard 1994, 'Religion as a Conversation-Stopper', *Common Knowledge*, vol. 3, no. 1, p. 2.

[2] Audi, Robert 1989, 'The Separation of Church and State and the Obligations of Citizenship,' *Philosophy and Public Affairs*, vol. 18, p. 296.

[3] Rawls, John 1985, 'Justice as Fairness: Political not Metaphysical', *Philosophy and Public Affairs*, vol. 14, p. 310.

[4] 'Much of what we do is a question of changing the style of thinking'. Wittgenstein, Ludwig 1972, *Lectures and Conversations on Aesthetics, Psychology, and Religious Belief*, Cyril Barrett (ed.) Berkeley CA, University of California Press, p. 28.

[5] Exodus 3:14.

[6] Young, Robert 1979, *Analytical Concordance to the Holy Bible*, 8th. edn., Guildford, Lutterworth Press.

[7] Heidegger, Martin 1996, *Being and Time*, Stambaugh, Joan (trans.), Albany, State University of New York, p. H12.

[8] Quoted in O'Donohue, John 1997, *Anam ara*, London, Bantam Press, p.128.

[9] Exodus 3:4.

[10] This is so, even in the USA where church-going is more prevalent than in Australia. There, attendance at church can be seen to be much more about civic duty and pride than about genuine faith. See Bellah, Robert et al.1985, *Habits of the Heart: Individualism and Commitment in American Life*, Berkeley, University of California Press.

[11] 'The Commonwealth shall not make any law for establishing any religion, or for imposing any religious observance, or for prohibiting the free exercise of any religion, and no religious test shall be required as a qualification for any office of public trust under the Commonwealth.' Commonwealth of Australia Constitution Act (as amended 1986) section 116.

[12] Peters, F. E. 1967, *Greek Philosophical Terms: A Historical Lexicon*, New York, New York University Press, p. ix.

[13] Schleiermacher, Friedrich 1958, *On Religion: Speeches to its Cultured Despisers*, John Oman (trans.), New York, Harper and Row, p. 35.

[14] Otto, R. 'Introduction', in Schleiermacher, 1958, pp. xvii-ix.

[15] Schleiermacher, 1958, pp. 37-9.

[16] Mohanty, J. N. 2000, *The Self and Its Other: Philosophical Essays*, New Delhi, Oxford University Press, p. 42.

[17] Otto speculates on the derivation of the Sanskrit word *āšarya*, claiming that it may be a compound of two words *as* and *carya*. *Carya* meaning that which is done or is to be done and *as* being the primitive sound used to express awe—'the long protracted open vowel of wonder (ā oh, hā) combining with the sibilant, which in all languages is used to express or produce a terrified silence (cf. Hist! Sh! Sst!). An *āšarya* would not then be properly and primarily anything conceptual at all, not even a 'marvel', but simply 'that in the presence of which we must exclaim 'ās! ās!' 'If this interpretation is correct, we can detect in this word just the original 'shudder' of numinous awe in the first and earliest form in which it expressed itself, before any figure of speech, objective representation, or concept had been devised to explicate it…' Otto, R. 1950, *The Idea of the Holy, an inquiry into the non-rational factor in the idea of the divine and its relation to the rational*, John W. Harvey (trans.), London, Oxford University Press, p. 191.

[18] Otto, R. 1950, pp. 191-2.

[19] Comte-Sponville, André 2002, *A Short Treatise on the Great Virtues: The Uses of Philosophy in Everyday Life*, London, Random House, p. 2.

16. Resolving disputes over Aboriginal sacred sites: Some experiences in the 1990s

Hal Wootten

The material in this chapter arises out of some practical experiences of the way the Australian state has negotiated claims for the protection of Indigenous 'sacred' places that were threatened by private or public claims to exploit or remake the landscape in pursuit of wealth or public safety or amenity. For many readers this topic will bring to mind the unhappy experience of the Hindmarsh Bridge affair, where such a conflict dragged out through inquiries and litigation over some seven years and left behind bitter recrimination about the genuineness of Indigenous claims, the appropriateness of processes for evaluating them, and the proper role of experts such as anthropologists in those processes.[1] It is unfortunate that this particular dispute is so dominant in public perceptions of such conflicts, and continues to frustrate the development of more appropriate procedures for their resolution, because it is not typical of the outcomes of Australian Government intervention, as my experiences will show.

In early April 1992 I was asked by the then Federal Minister for Aboriginal and Torres Strait Islander Affairs, Mr Tickner, to prepare a report for him in relation to an application by some Alice Springs Aboriginals seeking the protection, under the *Aboriginal and Torres Strait Islander Heritage Protection Act*, 1984, of some sites that would be destroyed by the construction of a dam, which the Northern Territory Government was planning in the Todd River above the town. For me it was to be the start of nearly a decade's involvement in 'the negotiation of the sacred' in a quite literal sense: the endeavour to find terms and conditions for resolving conflicts between Aboriginal claims for respect of the special significance that certain areas of land had for them, and claims to exploit those areas for private gain or public utility.

The first application referred to me arose out of a dispute between some Alice Springs Aboriginals, represented by the Central Land Council, and the Northern Territory Government, which was proposing to build a major dam for flood mitigation purposes on land that had particular significance for the Aboriginals, or, as was said in common parlance, contained sacred sites. The Territory Government claimed that a major benefit of the dam would be to save the lives of Aboriginals who might otherwise drown in the Todd River when a flood reached town. Undoubtedly some of the Alice Springs townspeople saw the dam as a potential site for water-based recreation, but the Territory Government strongly resisted the suggestion that it would be so used.

My report was to be the principal basis of the Minister's decision whether or not to protect the site, and under the legislation he could not act until he had received and considered my report. Because a lot of time had been used up in fruitless attempts to get an agreed settlement, the last interim declaration the Minister could make would expire in a little over a month, and the Northern Territory Government's bulldozers were ready to commence work immediately it expired. So I, a secular non-Aboriginal lawyer, had about a month to come to an understanding of the Act; the nature of the significance Aboriginals attached to land and, in particular, that Aboriginal women in Alice Springs attached to parts of the upper Todd River; the reasons why the NT Government had decided to build a flood mitigation dam at this particular place; and everything relevant to the Minister's weighing the desirability of the dam against the desirability of protecting the sites. There was no standing machinery for the implementation of the Act, and I made inquiries and wrote the report unassisted by any staff.

As it turned out, this was to be the first of four appointments as a rapporteur to the Minister. Later I dealt with challenges to BHP's mining of a site at Iron Knob in South Australia, to the recreational and pastoral use of Boobera Lagoon in northern NSW, and to some of the mining proposed in the Century Mine project in the Queensland Gulf. In each case my first task was to see if there was a possibility of an agreed solution that would relieve the Minister of the need to make an invidious decision, and then, if no settlement was possible, to collate the materials and considerations relevant to a wise decision. Mercifully in the other three cases I did not face such an acute time constraint as I did at Alice Springs.

That such conflicts involved the 'sacred' on one side at least is acknowledged in the common designation of such areas as 'sacred sites', although a community that seems willing enough to acknowledge the sacredness of sites at an abstract level may become sceptical of their genuineness when particular claims are advanced, or reluctant to concede that their protection should override the pursuit of wealth or projects conceived in the public interest. Recognition of the need to provide legal protection for Indigenous heritage came late to Australia, and initially was often conceived as underpinned by the requirements of archaeological and anthropological scholarship rather than by respect for Indigenous values, beliefs and feelings. In other words it was directed to the concerns of non-Aboriginal, rather than Aboriginal people, about the preservation of sites and relics.[2]

The *Aboriginal and Torres Strait Islander Heritage Protection Act*, 1984, was framed as a last resort measure, enabling Aboriginals to seek Commonwealth protection only if State or Territory law did not provide effective protection for a significant Aboriginal area, that is, 'an area of particular significance to Aboriginals in accordance with Aboriginal tradition'. This is the terminology of the Act, which does not use the word 'sacred'.

Sacredness and significance

The category of the 'sacred', and the items assigned to the category, are constructs of the culture that uses the term. One could not expect that it would translate with ready equivalence between cultures as different as the modern, capitalist, predominantly secular culture of mainstream Australia (which itself would contain many differences of interpretation), and the cultures of Aboriginal groups or individuals.[3] Had the Aboriginal heritage legislation followed popular terminology and required decisions as to whether sites were 'sacred', it would have been very difficult to apply. However the problem has always been avoided. Although the early legislation did use the term 'sacred site', it defined it to mean 'a site that is sacred to Aboriginals *or is otherwise of significance according to Aboriginal tradition*'.[4] The *Aboriginal and Torres Strait Islander Heritage Protection Act*, 1984 drops the word 'sacred' entirely, but retains the requirement that the particular significance arise out of 'Aboriginal tradition', which is defined to mean 'the body of traditions, observances, customs and beliefs of Aboriginals[5] generally or of a particular community or group of Aboriginals, and includes any such traditions, observances, customs or beliefs relating to particular persons, areas, objects or relationships'.

As a result there has been no need to debate whether sites are 'sacred', and the phrase 'particular significance', while susceptible to a number of different interpretations, has not, so far as I am aware, given rise to any difficulties. In my Boobera Lagoon report, for example, I noted that the phrase had been discussed by some members of the High Court in the Tasmanian Dam case (*Commonwealth v Tasmania* (1983) 46 ALR 625), and went on to say that

> the remarks of the judges support the view that 'particular' is directed only to the existence of a distinguishing characteristic, not to a particular level of significance.

> In seeking a distinguishing characteristic, two possibilities have been pointed out. The area might have particular significance for Aboriginal people in contrast to its significance to other people, or it might have particular significance in contrast to the significance which all land or waters have for Aboriginals. On either view, it is clear that Boobera Lagoon has particular significance at least to the Aboriginal people associated with the Toomelah Boggabilla area.

Comparing the incommensurable

Underlying my task in each case was the question: 'How does one measure the value of protecting an Aboriginal site against the value of some proposed activity that threatens it?' Or to put it crudely, 'How much is one prepared to pay to protect an Aboriginal site?' That in essence is what the Minister has to do at the end of the inquiry, unless an agreement can be brokered. There is invariably a price tag to protection, and the currency in which the price has to be paid varies—it may be money, perhaps in the form of lost GNP or revenue or export earnings; it may be in jobs or other opportunities foregone; it may be in the loss of the chance of water-based recreation for people living in a hot, dry climate, as in the Boobera Lagoon case, or it may be, as the Northern Territory Government was suggesting in my first assignment, in terms of lives that would be lost.

Of course it will not be the Minister, or the rapporteur who advises him, who will pay the direct price—they will not lose the profits or get drowned. The burden may fall on a private company, a government, individuals or some form of community interest. But the responsibility is the Minister's and there will usually be a political price to pay, and for both the Minister and rapporteur there may be other forms of unpleasantness. After the Alice Springs dam was stopped, I had to suffer the misrepresenting of my report and the traducing of my character under Parliamentary privilege by the Northern Territory Ministers of the day, with the Minister for Transport and Works saying, 'I tell Mr Tickner, Mr Wootten and the Leader of the Opposition that they will be hounded. Despite the fact that they will be long gone from the public arena, I will hound them next time there is a flood that causes damage or loss of life. Wherever they might be, whether it is in one year's time or 10 years time, I will ensure that they are reminded of this little charade, this shameful exercise, perpetrated on the people of the Northern Territory.' So far 12 years have passed uneventfully, and I sometimes wonder if I have the powers of the sacred sites to thank, but I still keep an eye on the Alice Springs weather reports.

I have not heard anyone advocate that all Aboriginal sites should be preserved intact, whatever the consequences, although I have encountered the view that sites should never be given special protection against lawful activities, because, it is argued, this would amount to racial discrimination. Once you put these extreme views aside, you become involved in a balancing of interests, a negotiation. Consistent with this, the Act requires the report to deal on the one hand with the particular significance of the area to Aboriginals and the nature and extent of the threat to it, and on the other hand with the effect of protection on the proprietary or pecuniary interests of other persons.

How do you balance one against the other? A philosopher might say that the conflicting interests are of such radically different kinds that one cannot weigh one against the other; they are simply incommensurable. However lawyers, and others responsible for bringing disputes to an end, learn to be pragmatic. In a recent paper to the Academy of the Humanities, I compared the pursuit of truth by historians and by courts. Historians have the luxury of dealing in provisional truth. They never have to make a final decision, they can decline to make a decision at all. Courts necessarily have a quite different approach, which is not to pursue truth for its own sake, but to respect it as one factor among a number in their task of putting an end to disputes as justly as possible. In essence a court does not and cannot say to parties 'These findings are the truth about your dispute'. It can only say, 'This is the closest we can get to the truth following a just and practicable procedure and with the time and resources available. We hope we got it right, but whether it's right or wrong, it is the basis on which you have to conduct your affairs for the future. Stop arguing and get on with life.'[6]

It is the same with the protection of a site. The competing interests may be incommensurable, but a decision has to be made or the bulldozers will roll. A failure to make a decision amounts to a decision that the site will not be protected.

How then does one go about weighing the contesting claims? The conflicting interests may be logically incommensurable, but reasonable people make choices between incommensurable things every day. Popular wisdom says that apples and oranges are not commensurable, but few people would have difficulty in choosing between ten apples and one orange, or between a good apple and a bad orange, or an apple worth a dollar and an orange worth a cent, and a dietician may give you other information that facilitates a choice.

This example illustrates two points. One is that finding out more about the objects of comparison may make choice easier, although it won't necessarily do so. The other is that you may be able to find criteria by which very different things can be compared. In our capitalist society money is often invoked to play this role. Market economists, for example, tend to think that everything can be given a monetary value. I once heard an economist making a case for nuclear power add in so many hundred thousand dollars for each life that would be lost, assuring his audience that he had an actuarial basis for what he was doing. And I believe the Australian Bureau of Agriculture and Resource Economics has calculated that it would be cheaper to move the inhabitants of low-lying Pacific Islands to Australia than cut the consumption of greenhouse gas producing fossil fuels. I have not seen an attempt to put a money value on a sacred site, although questions sometimes arise as to whether Aboriginals will accept monetary compensation for interference with a site, and opposing interests are quick to argue that willingness to accept financial compensation would show that the claim of significance is not *bona fide*.

The role of the rapporteur

So what does a rapporteur do? I preface my answer with the observation that in exercising any legal power or function under Australian law, one is constrained by some basic features of our legal system. We are a community that accepts the rule of law. Any exercise of power must find its authority in the law, and be carried out within the limits of the conferred power and in accordance with any conditions or requirements attached to it. A power or function is conferred for a particular purpose, which is either expressly stated in the law or inferred from the nature of the law, and it can't be used for any other purpose. In exercising the power, all relevant factors, and no irrelevant factors, must be taken into account. Again, what factors are relevant may be expressly stated in the law, or inferred from its purpose.

A power to make a decision that may adversely affect someone's interests must also be exercised in accordance with the principles of natural justice, unless legislation otherwise provides. This means particularly that the person exercising the power should not be biased, or reasonably open to the suspicion of bias, and should give a fair hearing to anyone whose rights may be affected.

The role of the rapporteur is thus a quasi-judicial one; he or she must be independent and give a fair hearing to all interests affected and report fairly to the Minister, not omitting anything that is relevant to be taken into account, or giving weight to anything that is not relevant. The functions of the Minister and the rapporteur are thus confined within a procedural mould and cannot be exercised arbitrarily.

As a rapporteur I had to subject both sides of the balance to scrutiny and evaluation. Scrutinising and evaluating Aboriginal beliefs is an invidious task, particularly for a non-Aboriginal person. It is not surprising that people—any people—would resent having what are essentially religious beliefs scrutinised, particularly by someone who does not share those beliefs, or even the cultural framework within which they exist. It is not surprising that women may be reluctant to have their beliefs, especially gender-restricted beliefs, evaluated by a man. And it is certainly to be expected that many Aboriginals may resent having their beliefs evaluated by members of the dominant community that dispossessed them. These conflicts were among issues considered by Elizabeth Evatt when she was appointed to review the Act in 1995, and she made recommendations designed to mitigate or eliminate them, which the present Government has not adopted.[7]

For my part, I simply had to live with these problems, and do what I could to minimise their effects. Over and above the resentment of intrusion on their privacy and the inner sanctum of belief that might be felt by anyone whose beliefs are subjected to scrutiny, I have observed three specific things causing hurt or anger to Aboriginal people in these applications. One is scepticism of their veracity or *bona fides*, another is the ridiculing of their beliefs (a deplorable feature of the Coronation Hill dispute), and a third is the presumption of arguing that a belief is in some sense 'disproved' by showing that people have flouted it without incurring adverse consequences. It must be particularly galling to Aboriginals that these hurts are so frequently offered by the most ignorant and bigoted of white Australians, who are secure in a sense of their own intellectual superiority that is not obvious to anyone but themselves.

In coming to grips with the Aboriginal claim, a rapporteur will usually have the benefit of at least one anthropological report as well as direct input from Aboriginal people themselves. Sometimes a report may be obtained by one or more interested parties and then offered adversarially to the rapporteur. In less contentious cases there may be agreement on retaining a particular anthropologist to report. Sometimes there is complaint that anthropologists should not be used, but competent anthropologists are of enormous value. Their professional knowledge enables them to provide a context for the claim, and to cast light on its plausibility and its significance. In addition their linguistic and fieldwork skills enable them to collate evidence from Aboriginals that would take an inordinate time for the rapporteur to collect, if indeed it were possible. Sometimes the anthropologist may have worked in the relevant community for a long time.

The Alice Springs Dam Case

In the Alice Springs Dam case I found that there was undisputed and long authenticated evidence of the beliefs in question. The sites in question derived their significance from two Dreaming tracks that converged in the area. One was the path of Two Women whose mythical journey started far to the southwest in Pitjantjatjara country, the other the path of a group of Uncircumcised Boys who travelled from the area of Port Augusta to the north coast of Australia. Women from distant lands and tribal groups who shared the Two Sisters story had on several occasions travelled to Alice Springs to support the claim of the Arrernte women, who put their views forcibly to me in a large meeting from which all other men were excluded. They confided to me, for transmission to the Minister, 'secret women's business' that would normally never be disclosed to men.

With the co-operation of the Northern Territory Solicitor-General, who represented the Territory Government, and acted throughout with the utmost professionalism and good sense, arrangements were worked out for handling the 'secret women's business'. It was agreed that it could be revealed to the Minister and myself, as the women had volunteered, and supplied to the Northern Territory Government on the basis that the details would be confidential to a female anthropologist employed by the Government. Fortunately in the Territory the parties were accustomed to devising ways of dealing with confidential material in land claims, and one of the problems on which the Hindmarsh Bridge application later foundered was thus avoided.

Investigating the claim was a novel and moving experience for me. I recorded some of the problems I wrestled with in the following section of the report, which was frequently quoted from during the subsequent Hindmarsh Bridge disputation:

> 7.1.9 To reveal these beliefs to anyone not entitled to know them under Aboriginal tradition (including other Aboriginals and even people of the opposite sex in the same community) is itself a kind of desecration, and it has been done reluctantly and painfully on the basis that it is necessary to prevent the destruction of important sites. I feel a personal obligation to respect the confidentiality of the information given to me. Moreover, I would not wish my report to be the vehicle for the public trivialisation and ridicule of Aboriginal beliefs in the media by uncomprehending people, a situation which was such a shocking feature of the debate over Coronation Hill.

> 7.1.10 It is difficult for those of us who have grown up in Western European culture to appreciate the nature of the attachment to and concerns about such areas on the part of Aboriginals. Our perceptions of values which we categorise as spiritual, religious, sacred, traditional, and political are shaped by our own culture and do not necessarily fit with categories or with concerns in Aboriginal culture. This is exemplified by the absence from the English language of any word corresponding to what we unhappily translate as 'the Dreaming'. The anthropologist's report in this case stresses, for example, that our division between sacred and secular realms does not correspond to traditional Aboriginal ideas. The Western notion of knowledge as objective and scientifically based does not square with the Aboriginal notion of knowledge, which in the fields with which we are concerned, derives from authoritative statement by a person who, in terms of traditional authority, was qualified to define the knowledge.

> 7.1.11 Western civilisations have long been accustomed to the notion of traditions as being recorded and authenticated in written texts, and more recently to their being interpreted and their correctness tested in a rationalist manner in the light of the results of historical and scientific inquiry. It is not easy for those who have grown up and been formally and informally educated in this culture to understand and empathise with traditions communicated by oral narrative, song, art and dance, and having an authority quite independent of historical, scientific and rationalist scrutiny.

7.1.12 One way in which Aboriginals stress the importance of sites in the area is by voicing the belief that destruction of the sites would lead to devastating social consequences and particularly consequences to all women, including non-Aboriginal women, and to relations between the sexes. While I refer to this as an indication of the degree of importance attached by Aboriginals to the sites, I warn against the tendency of Europeans to trivialise Aboriginal beliefs by treating such fear of consequences as their essence.

7.1.13 I can assure the curious that the confidentiality is not because the information would be found titillating, shocking or even particularly interesting by Western standards. It simply lacks significance in Western culture, and I could not claim to appreciate its significance to Aboriginals. The issue should not be whether, judged by the norms and values of our secular culture or our religions, the sites are important, but whether they are important to Aboriginals in terms of the norms and values of their traditional culture and beliefs. In other words the issue is not whether we can understand and share the Aboriginal beliefs, but whether, knowing they are genuinely held, we can therefore respect them.

It became clear to me that there were strongly and widely held beliefs that would be severely affronted by interference with the sites, that a significant number of women would suffer great anxiety because they believed that apocalyptic consequences would follow, and that many Aboriginals saw the matter as a test case of white Australia's respect. But should this prevail against the building of a dam that would not only protect the town from flood damage, but save lives of people who might otherwise be drowned in floods, as a number of Aboriginals had been in the past?

I found the issue easier to resolve than I had feared. It is not possible to go into the matter fully here, but a detailed examination of the dam proposal showed that by normal engineering standards the dam was uneconomic, returning over its life less than 33 cents in material terms for every dollar spent, and that there were other ways of reducing flood damage to the town. The case for the dam therefore rested heavily on its potential for saving lives. However investigation showed that there had been seven drownings in 20 years, and most of these, probably all, could have been prevented by relatively simple steps that could be implemented in the future. I asked rhetorically whether anyone who had $20 million to spend on saving Aboriginal lives would use it on building this dam.

On receipt of my report the Federal Minister prohibited the building of the dam.

Mining at Iron Knob

The next matter referred to me involved a claim to protect an area from mining at BHP's mine at Iron Knob in South Australia, a step that would sterilise millions of dollars worth of iron ore. The Aboriginal people in the area had lived an urbanised life for some time, and when the elderly Aboriginal woman who had instigated the claim died, there was no local person who could speak authoritatively to it. With financial assistance from BHP, which acted throughout in a very sympathetic and co-operative fashion, senior traditional Aboriginal men and women from other tribes far to the north were brought to Iron Knob. Although they had never visited the area before, they knew of the country in detail through songs and dances that recorded the stories attached to a Dreaming track that passed through Iron Knob on the way to their own country. They were immediately able to recognise and explain the mythical significance of the various features of the landscape.

For reasons that are too complex to go into here, this case would have presented me with a difficult balance to draw up, but the matter took a surprising twist. The BHP manager became committed to the importance of preserving Aboriginal culture, offering money for books, films, dancing companies, and visits by local to more traditional peoples. The Aboriginal people were grateful and impressed, but still unable to agree to the destruction of the site. The impasse was broken when the manager offered to dig up the sacred site and install it on land the company would provide for a cultural centre at Whyalla. I expected this proposal to get no support, as the actual location of the site seemed critical to its significance, but to my surprise the proposal was immediately embraced by the leading Aboriginal spokeswoman, and a deal was done. Some of the men, however, seemed uneasy, and I was not unduly surprised to learn a few years later that the Aboriginals had regretted their decision and persuaded the company to leave the site undisturbed.

Boobera Lagoon

In May 1995 I was appointed rapporteur in relation to Boobera Lagoon, an old path of the MacIntyre River in New South Wales near the Queensland border. According to the mythology of the local Aboriginal people, the Lagoon was made by and is now the resting place of a local version of the Rainbow Serpent, a being that appears in Aboriginal mythology in many places. There was no doubt about the genuineness of the claim, which had long been documented by anthropologists and consistently pursued by local Aboriginals whenever an opportunity had arisen over the years. The most acute among many issues was that the Lagoon had become a major waterskiing site, providing the only water-based recreation for the inhabitants of the hot, dry, dusty Goondiwindi area, but one that the Aboriginals found offensive and disrespectful to what they treasured as a sacred place. Also at issue was the effect of cattle depastured around the Lagoon, most acutely where a Travelling Stock Route bordered the Lagoon. Apart from spiritual desecration, the Aboriginals were concerned that both the waterskiing and the cattle were causing serious environmental damage to the Lagoon.

The matter proved difficult. The Aboriginals had been fighting for the protection of the Lagoon for many years, and although they were quite happy to share its enjoyment with non-Aboriginals who treated it respectfully, they would not condone waterskiing or continued environmental damage. The non-Aboriginal side was no less intransigent. The local authority managing the Travelling Stock Route would not even agree to watering cattle with water pumped into troughs from the Lagoon, a procedure that would have allowed its bank to be fenced off. One could not but feel sympathy for the water-skiers who had been using the Lagoon for many years and had come to regard it as a major feature of family and community recreation for which no substitute was available. There are many aspects canvassed in my report in the course of weighing up the competing claims, but in the end I recommended that waterskiing be banned and arrangements made to keep travelling stock off the Lagoon bank.

The recommendation was to have a chequered history. My report had been commissioned by the Labor Minister, Robert Tickner, but by the time I presented it in August 1995 the Government had changed and Senator Herron, a Queensland Liberal, was the Minister. Although I believed that my report made a persuasive case for banning the waterskiing and taking other steps to protect the Lagoon, I held out little hope of a positive outcome, particularly given that the move was opposed by the Deputy Prime Minister who held the adjoining Federal seat.[8] Several years passed with no decision announced, although I did hear a report of a white-headed man in a Commonwealth car calling in at Boggabilla Hotel to seek directions to Boobera Lagoon. Then under Ministerial rearrangements the Aboriginal Heritage Section was transferred on 17 December 1998 to the Department of the Environment, and Mr Herron, I am told, breathed a sigh of relief. However the Prime Minister decreed that he must deal with the matter before handing it over. To everyone's surprise he banned the waterskiing, softening the blow with a grant of $5 million to construct a new waterskiing site near Goondiwindi. There were a number of postponements, but ultimately the new site was constructed and quiet descended on the Lagoon. It is a declared Aboriginal place under NSW law, and is now managed by a committee with a majority of Aboriginal members. They are gradually negotiating increased protection from cattle damage around the lagoon, and on recent inquiry I was told that the only blight on their satisfaction was that the $5 million to build the new waterskiing site was taken out of Aboriginal Heritage Protection Funds.

Mining in 'blackfella country'

About the Century Mine negotiations, there is little to say. The Carpentaria Land Council made an application under the Act for the protection of some sites within the proposed mining lease, but there was never a real problem. The Company was determined that sites would not become an issue and was willing to make whatever concessions were necessary on that score, as well as anxious to lay the foundations for the future operation of the mine in a way that would bring real benefits to the local communities. The parent company was Applera Corp-Celera Genomics Group (CRA), and one sensed that the disastrous experience of Bougainville Copper was never far from the minds of its executives. Many matters were negotiated, but I believe the real underlying issue was that many Aboriginals, including Murrandoo Yanner, the influential Director of the Carpentaria Land Council, still saw and treasured the Gulf as essentially 'blackfella country', and did not want its character changed by the intrusion of a major mine. The issue was summed up for me by an incident at a Darwin seminar when Tracker Tilmouth, the very able and entrepreneurial Director of the Central Land Council, was waxing lyrical about the successful enterprises of the Council and the opportunities available in business partnerships. When he finished, Murrandoo stood up and asked, 'Well Tracker, they are all fine things, but when do you get time to be a blackfella?'

That seems to me the dilemma that every Aboriginal faces. How do you remain a blackfella while engaging with what the modern world has to offer? What are you prepared to forgo to hang on to the things that you find essential to your identity? To the extent that I am a bleeding heart, my heart bleeds for the individual Aboriginals who every day have to make painful decisions and compromises in the course of finding a satisfying and dignified place in an alien society that took over their country, long excluded them from participation, but today impatiently expects them to accept whatever place is offered them or rapidly find their own.

Some reflections

One thing that I found striking in all the applications with which I dealt was the peaceful and law-abiding way in which Aboriginals pressed their claims, and their capacity to be understanding of their opponents. The only occasion in which the question of violence was raised was in relation to Boobera Lagoon. As I described in my report, the Aboriginals of the area had a long history of pressing their claims lawfully and constructively whenever the opportunity arose, and no one could have credibly predicted violence on their part. It was white residents who predicted that if a declaration were made prohibiting water-skiing, water-skiers would resort to violence and defy it, and that the white community would also react vindictively against Aboriginals, for example by refusing them employment. Two members of Parliament hinted at the same thing when, in opposing protection, they expressed their fear that it might 'lead to a worsening of the already fragile relations'. The supposition in all these submissions was that the threat of white violence was a reason for refusing the

Aboriginal claim, a view that I rejected, although I did recommend a strategy of community public relations to head it off.[9]

The reaction of the Aboriginal community was stoic. The submission on their behalf read:

> Any racial violence which flows from the granting of the declarations will merely be a continuation of what they have had to tolerate since the beginning of European occupation. Concern about the possibility of racial violence should not sway the Minister away from making the declarations. To do so would be a grave injustice to Aboriginal people. It would be a continuation of what is already perceived to be a flawed system biased against Aboriginal people. It would be the law succumbing to intimidation from those prepared to threaten violence by the use of illegitimate force to obtain their ends.

This was a view with which I agreed, and one that in my view the state must be prepared to stand up for in negotiating the sacred in a multicultural community.

The Australian state on whose behalf I was acting is essentially secular. Although its Constitution was expressly adopted in humble reliance on the blessing of Almighty God, it gave no powers or privileges to God or God's representatives or adherents and expressly forbade the Commonwealth from establishing any religion, imposing any religious observance, prohibiting the free exercise of any religion, or requiring any religious test for any Commonwealth office or public trust. As it happens, my personal outlook is secular, although I hope respectful and understanding of other views, but even if I had not been, it would have been my duty to act in a manner becoming the secular agent of a secular state. From this secular viewpoint, the beliefs of Aboriginal claimants, whether sacred in character or not, were not something to be judged as right or wrong, or as better or worse, or more or less credible, than other beliefs, but something to be respected, not merely as an expression of their liberal right to different views, but as part of their human identity. It may well be that it is easier for a secular state to negotiate the sacred, than it would be for one committed to a particular view of the sacred as the official and correct one.

ENDNOTES

[1] An independent scholarly account of the events remains to be written. A factual summary can be found at the beginning of the judgment of Justice von Doussa of the Federal Court in *Chapman v Luminis Pty Ltd*, 21 August 2001, which ended the litigation. As to the resultant consideration of law reform, see endnote 4.

[2] For example, in the Northern Territory the *Native and Historical Objects and Areas Preservation Ordinance 1955* was enacted to protect 'prescribed objects'. A prescribed object was defined as 'an object relating to the Aboriginal natives of Australia which is of ethnological or anthropological interest or value' (s. 3). Six years later the Ordinance was amended to prohibit interference with 'any place used by Australian Aboriginal natives as a ceremonial, burial, or initiation ground' (s. 9H). Another 17 years

went by before there was an attempt in the Territory to give general legislative protection to sites of significance according to Aboriginal tradition (*Aboriginal Sacred Sites Ordinance 1978*). The first legislation in Western Australia vested control of sites in the Western Australian Museum (*Aboriginal Heritage Act 1972*).

[3] There are no doubt levels of generalisation at which one might speak of *an* Aboriginal culture, but in pre-invasion Australia there were many distinct Aboriginal groups, and thereafter dispossession, contact with different aspects of Western society, education, opportunity and many other pressures for cultural change and adaptation have operated, and continue to operate, differentially on groups and individuals.

[4] *Aboriginal Land Rights (Northern Territory) Act 1976* (Commonwealth), *Aboriginal Sacred Sites Ordinance 1978*, (Northern Territory). The former Act remains in force; the latter is superseded by the *Northern Territory Aboriginal Sacred Sites Act 1989*, which continues to use the same definition. Other examples of legislative broadening of the concept included 'sites and items of sacred, ceremonial, mythological or historic significance to the Aboriginal people', *Aboriginal Heritage Act 1979* (South Australia), and places and objects 'which are or have been of sacred, ritual or spiritual or ceremonial significance to persons of Aboriginal descent' (*Aboriginal Heritage Act 1972* (Western Australia).

[5] 'Aboriginal' is defined as 'a member of the Aboriginal race of Australia, and includes a descendant of the indigenous inhabitants of the Torres Strait Islands'.

[6] Wootten, Hal 2003, 'Conflicting Imperatives: Pursuing Truth in the Courts' in I. McCalman and A. McGrath (eds) *Proof and Truth*, Academy of the Humanities, Canberra.

[7] In October 1995, following unfortunate events in the Hindmarsh Island Bridge application, the then Labor Minister for Aboriginal and Torres Strait Islander Affairs asked Elizabeth Evatt AC to report on operation of the Act. In her *Review of the Aboriginal and Torres Strait Islander Heritage Protection Act 1984* (August 1996) she made a number of recommendations to amend the Act. In December 1996, the Government having changed, the new Liberal Minister announced the Government's intention to make wide-ranging changes to the Act 'designed to prevent another Hindmarsh Island saga'. Very few of the Evatt recommendations were reflected in the government's subsequently issued proposals, which were considered by the Parliamentary Joint Committee on Native Title and the Aboriginal and Torres Strait Islander Land Fund, but remained contentious, and no legislation has resulted.

[8] Lowitja O'Donohue described Senator Herron as 'a Minister without influence or purpose', *The Australian* 17 November 1997, p. 10.

[9] My recommended strategy was not adopted. Instead, as I have already noted, opposition was deflected by applying $5 million of funds allotted for Aboriginal heritage protection to provide an alternative site for the waterskiers.

Bibliography

Adams, C. 1995, in 'Kufr', John L. Esposito (ed.), *The Oxford Encyclopedia of the Modern Islamic World*, New York, Oxford University Press.

Amnesty International, 1996, *Report on Pakistan (ASA 33/10/96)*, London <www.thepersecution.org/ai/amnst196.html>.

Anderson, Ingrid and Pamela Rose 1978 ,'"Who the Hell Does She Think She Is?' interview with Mary Whitehouse', *Poly Law Review*, vol. 3, no. 2, pp. 13-18.

Arad, Y., Y. Gutman and A. Margolit 1981, *Documents on the Holocaust*, Jerusalem, Yad Vashem.

Arnot, Hugo (ed.) 1785, *A Collection and Abridgement of Celebrated Criminal Trials in Scotland*, Edinburgh.

Asmar, Christine 1992, 'The Arab-Australian Experience', in M. Goot and R. Tiffin (eds), *Australia's Gulf War*, Carlton, Melbourne University Press.

Audi, Robert 1989, 'The Separation of Church and State and the Obligations of Citizenship,' *Philosophy and Public Affairs*, vol. 18, no. 3, pp. 259-96.

Baker and McKenzie 2003-04, *Asia Pacific Legal Developments Bulletin*, vol. 18, no. 4, December 2003/January 2004.

Barnes, John (ed.) 1981, *Portable Australian Authors: Joseph Furphy*, St Lucia, University of Queensland Press.

Barth, Karl 1933, *The Epistle to the Romans*, Edwyn C. Hoskyns (trans.), New York, Oxford University Press.

Bartlett, R. 1993, *The Making of Europe: Conquest, Colonisation and Cultural Change 950-1350*, Princeton, Princeton University Press.

Baudrillard, Jean 1990, *Revenge of the Crystal: Selected Writings on the Modern Object and its Destiny, 1968-1983*, Sydney, Pluto Press.

Baur, J. 1992, 'Lutherische Christologie', in H. C. Rublack (ed.), *Die lutherische Konfessionalisierung in Deutschland*, Gütersloh, Gern Mohn.

Beer, Robert 1999, *An Encyclopedia of Tibetan Symbols and Motifs*, Boston, Shambala.

Bellah, R. 1970, 'Religious Evolution', *Beyond Belief: Essays on Religion in a Post-Traditional Society*, New York, Harper & Row.

—— 1967, 'Civil Religion in America', *Daedulus*, no. 96, pp. 1-21.

Bellah, R. et al. 1985, *Habits of the Heart: Individualism and Commitment in American Life*, New York, Harper & Row.

Bentley, James 1985, *Restless Bones: The Story of Relics*, London, Constable & Co Ltd.

Berger, P. 1969, *A Rumour of Angels: Modern Society and the Rediscovery of the Supernatural*, New York, Doubleday.

—— 1967, *The Sacred Canopy: Elements of a Sociological Theory of Religion*, Garden City, Doubleday.

Berger, P. and T. Luckmann 1966, *The Social Construction of Reality: A Sociological Treatise in the Sociology of Knowledge*, Garden City, Doubleday.

Bergmann, Werner and Juliane Wetzel 2003, 'Manifestations of anti-Semitism in the European Union, First Semester 2002', *Synthesis Report, on behalf of the European Monitoring Centre on Racism and Xenophobia*, Vienna.

Beyer, P. 1994, *Religion and Globalization*, London, Sage.

Blakeney, Michael 1981, 'Sequestered Piety and Charity—A Comparative Analysis', *Journal of Legal History*, no. 2, p207.

Bloch, M. 1989, *Feudal Society: Volume I The Growth of Ties of Dependence*, L. A. Manyon (trans.), London, Routledge.

Bonhoeffer, Dietrich 1959, *The Cost of Discipleship*, London, SCM.

—— 1986, *Meditating on the Word*, Cambridge, Cowley Publications.

Bouma, G. 1999, 'Social Justice Issues in the Management of Religious Diversity in Australia', *Social Justice Research*, vol. 12, no. 4, pp. 283-95.

Bradney, Anthony 2000, 'Faced by Faith', in Peter Oliver, Sionadh Douglas Scott, and Victor Tadros (eds) *Faith in Law: Essays in Legal Theory*, Oxford, Hart Publishing.

Brown, P. 1995, *Authority and the Sacred: Aspects of the Christianisation of the Roman World*, Cambridge, Cambridge University Press.

—— 1982, 'Society and the Supernatural: A Medieval Change', in P. Brown (ed.), *Society and the Holy in Late Antiquity*, Berkeley, University of Californian Press.

—— 1977, *Relics and Social Status in the Age of Gregory of Tours*, Berkshire, University of Reading.

Bukkyô Rengokai Honbu (Buddhist Federation Headquarters) 1933, *Shûkyôhô no hitsuyô naru riyû*, Tokyo, Bukkyô Rengokai Honbu (Buddhist Federation Headquarters).

Butler, John 1995, *The Quest for Becket's Bones: The Mystery of the Relics of St Thomas Becket of Canterbury*, New Haven, Yale University Press.

Byrd, Vickie C., Nancy R. Johnson, and Kathie A Hamilton 2003, *Tibet: Treasures from the Roof of the World,* Orange County C.A., Bowers Museum of Cultural Art.

Calabresi, Guido 1985, *Ideals, Beliefs, Attitudes and the Law,* Syracuse, N.Y., Syracuse University Press.

Caldwell, D. 2002, 'Something major is happening. Are we witnessing the beginnings of an Islamic Reformation?' <http://www.beliefnet.com/story/92/story_9273_1.html?rnd=94>

Callois, R. 1939, *L'Homme et la Sacre,* Paris, Gallimard.

Caputo, John 1997, *The Prayers and Tears of Jacques Derrida: Religion Without Religion,* Bloomington and Indianapolis, Indiana University Press.

——(ed.) 1997, *Deconstruction in a Nutshell: A Conversation with Jacques Derrida,* New York, Fordham University Press.

Castell Hopkins, J. 1896, *The Sword of Islam or Suffering Armenia,* Brantford, the Bradley-Garretson Co. Ltd.

Cazeaux, C. (ed.) 2000, *The Continental Aesthetics Reader,* London, Routledge.

Clammer, John 2001, *Japan and its Others: Globalisation, Difference and the Critique of Modernity,* Melbourne, Trans Pacific Press.

—— 1997, 'Sustaining otherness: self, nature and ancestralism among contemporary Japanese Christians', *Japan Forum,* vol. 9, no. 2, p. 179.

Cobbett, W., Howell T. B. et al. (eds) 1809-1828, *A Complete Collection of State Trials [State Trials],* 34 vols, vol. 13, London.

Code, Lorraine 1995, *Rhetorical Spaces. Essays on Gendered Spaces,* New York, Routledge.

Cole, Tim 1999, *Selling the Holocaust: from Auschwitz to Schindler, How History is Bought, Packaged, and Sold,* New York, Routledge.

Coleridge, Samuel Taylor 1825, *Aids to the Formation of a Manly Character,* London, Taylor and Hessey.

Comte-Sponville, André 2002, *A Short Treatise on the Great Virtues: The Uses of Philosophy in Everyday Life,* London, Random House.

Coombe, G. 1975, [1926] *A Tibetan on Tibet: being the travels and observations of Mr Paul Sherap (Dorje Zödba) of Tachienlu; with an introductory chapter on Buddhism and a concluding chapter on the Devil Dance,* Kathmandu, Ratna Pustak Bhandar.

Crouzet, D. 1990, *Les Guerriers de Dieu. La violence au temps des troubles de religion,* Seysell, Champ Vallon.

Davis, E. 1999, *Techgnosis: Myth, Magic and Mysticism in the Age of Information*, London, Serpent's Tail.

De Beer, E. S. (ed.) 1981, *The Correspondence of John Locke,* 8 vols, Oxford, Clarendon Press.

De Coulanges, F. 1900, *The Ancient City*, Boston.

Delany, Joseph F. 2003, 'Sacrilege', *New Advent Catholic Encyclopaedia,* <http://www.newadvent.org/cathen/13321a.htm>, viewed 16 January 2006.

Denning, A. D. 1949, *Freedom Under the Law*, Hamlyn Lectures 1st series, London.

Dohi, Akio and Tomura, Masahiro (eds) 1988, *Tennô no daikawari to watashitachi (Imperial successions and us),* Tokyo, Nihon Kirisutokyôdan Shuppankyoku.

Dowman, Keith 1997, *The Sacred Life of Tibet*, London, Thorsons.

Dunne, John 1978, *The Way Of All The Earth,* South Bend Indiana, University of Notre Dame Press.

Durkheim, E. 1965 [1915], *The Elementary Forms of the Religious Life*, J. W. Swain (trans.) New York, Free Press.

—— 1953, *Professional Ethics and Civic Morals*, Westport, Greenwood Press.

—— 1974, *Sociology and Philosophy.* New York, Free Press.

—— 1973, 'Individualism and the Intellectuals', R. Bellah (ed.) *Emile Durkheim on Morality and Society*, Chicago, University of Chicago Press.

Eagleton, T. 1990, *The Ideology of the Aesthetic*, Oxford, Basil Blackwell.

Ekvall, Robert B. 1964, *Religious Observances in Tibet: Patterns and Function*, University of Chicago Press, Chicago.

Eliade, Mircea 1974, *The Myth Of The Eternal Return: Or, Cosmos And History,* Princeton, Princeton University Press.

Ernst, C. 1987, 'Islamic Concept', in M. Eliade, (ed.), *The Encyclopaedia of Religion,* New York, Macmillan Publishing House.

Esack, F. 2002, *On Being a Muslim: Finding a Religious Path in the World Today*, Oxford, One World.

Esposito, J. L. and John O. Voll 2001, *Makers of Contemporary Islam*, New York, Oxford University Press.

Eternal Reefs 2005, *Eternal Reefs*, viewed 28 September 2005, <http://www.eternalreefs.com/>

Evans, Richard 2001, *Telling Lies About the Hitler: the Holocaust, History and the David Irving Trial*, London, Verso.

Evans-Pritchard, E. 1937, *Witchcraft, Oracles and Magic Among the Azande*, Oxford, Clarendon Press.

Evatt, Elizabeth AC 1996, *Review of the Aboriginal and Torres Strait Islander Heritage Protection Act 1984*, <http://www.austlii.edu.au/au/special/rsj-project/rsjlibrary/evatt/toc.html>

Feuerbach, L. 1980, *Thoughts on Death and Immortality*, Berkeley, University of California Press.

Field, Norma 1993, *In the Realm of a Dying Emperor: Japan at Century's End*, New York, Vintage Books.

Finch, Henry Leroy 2001, *Simone Weil And The Intellect Of Grace*, New York, Continuum.

Finkelstein, Norman 2000, *The Holocaust Industry*, London, Verso.

Fisher, A. and H. Ramsay, 2000, 'Of Art and Blasphemy', *Ethical Theory and Moral Practice*, vol. 3.

Francke, Auguste H. 1998 [1907], *A History of Western Tibet, One of the Unknown Empires*, New Delhi, Motilal Banarsidass.

Fraser, J. G. 1923-7, *The Golden Bough: A Study in Magic and Religion*, London, Macmillan.

Ford, H. A. J. and W.A. Lee, 1983, *Principles of the Law of Trusts*, Sydney, Law Book Co.

Foucault, Michel 1983, 'On the Genealogy of Ethics: An Overview of Work in Progress', Afterword to Dreyfus, Hubert L. and Rabinow, Paul *Michel Foucault: Beyond Structuralism and Hermeneutics*, Chicago, University of Chicago Press.

Furuya, Yasuo (ed.) 1997, *A History of Japanese Theology*, Grand Rapids, William B. Eerdmans.

Garber, Zev 2002, 'America Attacked and Zion Blamed—Old-New Antisemitism: *Fatwa* Against Israel', Editorial viewpoint, *Shofar*, vol. 20, issue 2.

Gardner, Paul 2003, 'The New Threat: Global Antisemetism', *Australian Jewish News*, no. 16, p. 19.

Geary, Patrick 1978, *Furta Sacra: Thefts of Relics in the Central Middle Ages*, Princeton University Press, Princeton.

Gelder, Ken and Jane M. Jacobs 1998, *Uncanny Australia,* Melbourne, Melbourne University Press.

Gellner, E. 1994, *Conditions of Liberty: Civil Society and its Rivals*, Penguin Books.

Glock, C. 1962, 'On the Study of Religious Commitment', *Religious Education, Research Supplement*, vol. 57, no. 4, pp. S98-110.

Goody, J. 1961, 'Religion and Ritual: The Definitional Problem', *British Journal of Sociology*, no. 12, pp. 142-64.

Granet, M. 1975 [1922], *The Religion of the Chinese People*, M. Freedman (trans.), Oxford, Basil Blackwell.

Grattan, Michelle (ed.) 2000, *Reconciliation: Essays on Australian Reconciliation*, Melbourne, Black Inc.

Guttenplan, D. D. 2001, *The Holocaust on Trial*, New York, W.W. Norton.

Habermas, J. 1999, 'A Conversation About God and the World' in J. Habermas and E. Mendieta (eds) *Reason and Religion*, Cambridge, Polity.

Hakim-Murad, Abdal 1997, 'British and Muslim?' lecture given to a conference of British converts to Islam, 17 September 1997, viewed 11 August 2005, <http://www.masud.co.uk/ISLAM/ahm/british.htm>

Haley, John O. 1978, 'The Myth of the Reluctant Litigant', *Journal of Japanese Studies,* vol. 4, no. 2, pp. 345-70.

Hall, Dawn (ed.) 1997, *Tibet: Tradition & Change*, Albuquerque, The Albuquerque Museum.

Hand, S. (ed.) 1989, *The Levinas Reader,* Sarah Richmond (trans.), Oxford, Basil Blackwell.

Harland, Marion 1897, *Under the Flag of the Orient: the Thrilling Story of Armenia*, Philadelphia, Historical Publishing Company.

Hassan, R. 2003, *Faithlines: Muslim conceptions of Islam and Society,* Karachi, Oxford University Press.

—— 2002, 'On Being Religious: A Study of Christian and Muslim Piety in Australia', *Australian Religion Studies Review*, vol. 15, no. 1, pp. 87-114.

Haug, W. F. 1987, *Commodity Aesthetics, Ideology and Culture*, New York, International General.

Heckel, M. 1992, 'Religionsbann und landesherrliches Kirchenregiment', H. C. Rublack (ed.) *Die lutherische Konfessionalisierung in Deutschland*, Gütersloh, Gerd Mohn.

—— 1989, 'Zur Historiographie des Westfälischen Friedens', K. Schlaich (ed.) *Martin Heckel Gesammelte Schriften: Staat, Kirche, Recht, Geschichte*, Tübingen, J. C. B. Mohr. I.

—— 1984, 'Das Säkularisierungsproblem in der Entwicklung des deutschen Staatskirchenrechts', G. Dilcher and I. Staff (eds) *Christentum und modernes Recht. Beiträge zum Problem der Säkularisation*, Frankfurt a. M., Suhrkamp.

Hefner, R. 2000, *Civil Islam: Muslims and Democratisation in Indonesia*, Princeton, Princeton University Press.

Heidegger, M. 1996, *Being and Time,* Juan Stanbaugh (trans.), Albany, State University of New York.

Heihachiro Izawa 1988, 'Naimu shôrei daiyonjûichigo' ('Home Ministry Ordinance No. 41'), *Nihon kirisutokyô daijiten (Encyclopedia of Japanese Christian History),* Tokyo, Kyôbunkan.

Hill, Mark 2001, 'Judicial Approaches to Religious Disputes', in Richard O'Dair and Andrew Lewis (eds), 2001, *Law and Religion,* Oxford, Oxford University Press.

Hirayama, Shôji 1988, 'Kenpô o mamoru kirisutosha no kai' ('Christians For Defence of the Constitution'), *Nihon kirisutokyô daijiten (Encyclopedia of Japanese Christian History),* Tokyo, Kyôbunkan.

House of Lords Select Committee on Religious Offences 2003, *Religious Offences in England and Wales – First Report* [HL Paper 95-I, Session 2002-03], viewed 11 August 2005, <http://www.parliament.the-stationery-office.co.uk/pa/ld200203/ldselect/ldrelof/95/9501.htm>

Horner F. 1843, *Memoirs and Correspondence,* Leonard Hunter (ed.), 2 vols, London.

Hume, David 1956, *The Natural History of Religion*, H. E. Root (ed.), London, Adam & Charles Black.

Hunter, Michael 1992, '"Aikenhead the Atheist": The Context and Consequences of Articulate Irreligion in the Late Seventeenth Century', in Michael Hunter and David Wootton (eds) *Atheism from the Reformation to the Enlightenment*, Oxford, Clarendon Press.

Huntington, Samuel P. 1996, *The Clash of Civilizations and the Remaking of World Order*, New York, Simon & Schuster.

—— 1993, 'The Clash of Civilizations', *Foreign Affairs*, vol. 72, no. 3, pp. 22-49.

Huntington, John and Dina Bangdel 2003, *Circle of Bliss*, Chicago, Serindia Publications.

Ibrahim, S. 1996, *Egypt, Islam and Democracy*, Cairo, AUC Press.

James, W. [1902], *The Varieties of Religious Experience*, 1957, New York, Collier; 1985, London, Penguin

—— 1979, *The Will to Believe, and Other Essays in Popular Philosophy,* Cambridge Mass., Harvard University Press.

The Japan Baptist Convention 1988a, *Tennô no daikawari ni sonaete: sonotoki kyôkai wa...(In Preparation for the Succession of the Emperor: What should the Church do?)*, Tokyo, The Japan Baptist Convention.

—— 1988b, *'Nakaya saiban' hanketsu kara tennôdaikawari e (From the Decision in the 'Nakaya Case' to the Succession of the Emperor)*, Tokyo, The Japan Baptist Convention.

Jones, Peter 1990, 'Respecting Beliefs and Rebuking Rushdie', *British Journal of Political Science*, vol. 20, no. 4, pp. 415-37.

Kamali, M. 2001, 'Civil Society and Islam: A Sociological Perspective', *European Journal of Sociology,* vol. 42, vol. 3, pp. 457-82.

Kant, I. 1987, *Critique of Judgement* [1790], W. S. Pluhar (trans.), Indianapolis, Hackett Publishing Company.

Kantorowicz, E. 1957, *The King's Two Bodies: A Study in Medieval Political Theology,* Princeton, N. J., Princeton University Press.

Khadduri, M. 1984, *The Islamic Conception of Justice*, London, The John Hopkins University Press.

Kierkegaard 1944, *Concluding Unscientific Postscipt*, David F. Swenson (trans.), Princeton, N.J., Princeton University Press.

King, P. 1976, *Toleration,* London, Allen and Unwin.

Kircher, Athanasius (ed.) 1677, *China Illustrata*, apud Jacobum á Meurs, Amstelodami.

Klein, N. 2001, *No Logo*, London, Harper Collins.

Klug, Brian 2003, 'The collective Jew: Israel and the new anti-Semitism', *Patterns of Prejudice*, vol. 37, no. 2.

Koestler, A. 1964, *The Sleepwalkers: A History of Man's Changing Vision of the Universe*, Harmondsworth, Penguin.

Kohler, Lotte and Hans Saner 1992, *Correspondence Hannah Arendt and Karl Jaspers 1926-1969,* New York, Harcourt Brace.

Kumazawa, Yoshinobu and David L. Swain (eds) 1991, *Christianity in Japan, 1971-90*, Tokyo, *Kyo Bun Kwan* (The Christian Literature Society in Japan).

Lamb, Winifred Wing Han 2004, *Living Truth and Truthful Living: Christian Faith and the Scalpel of Suspicion,* Adelaide: ATF Press.

—— 1998, 'Facts That Stay Put: Protestant Fundamentalism, Epistemology and Orthodoxy,' *Sophia*, vol. 37, no. 2, pp. 88-110.

Laqueur, Walter 1971, 'The Jewish Question today: Between Old Zionism and New Anti-Semitism', *Encounter*, vol. 37, no. 2, p. 52.

Larner, Christina 1981, *Enemies of God: The Witch-hunt in Scotland*, Chatto & Windus, London.

—— 1984, 'The Crime of Witchcraft in Scotland' *Witchcraft and Religion: The Politics of Popular Belief*, in Alan Macfarlane (ed.) Blackwell, New York.

Lawyers Committee for Human Rights 2002, *Fire and Broken Glass: The Rise of Antisemitism in Europe*, New York and Washington, DC.

Levinas, Emmanuel 1989 [1984], 'Prayer without Demand' Sarah Richmond (trans.), Seán Hand (ed.), *The Levinas Reader*, Basil Blackwell, Oxford.

Levy, L. 'Blasphemy', in M. Eliad (ed.), *The Encyclopaedia of Religion*, New York, Macmillan Publishing House.

Lewis, B. 1993, *Islam and the West*, New York, Oxford University Press.

Llewellyn, Nigel 1991, *The Art of Death: Visual Culture in the English Death Ritual c.1500-c.1800*, London, Reakton in association with Victoria & Albert Museum.

Luckmann, T. 1967, *The Invisible Religion: The Problem of Religion in Modern Society*, New York, Macmillan.

Luhmann, N. 1982, *The Differentiation of Society,* S. Holmes and L. Charles (trans.), New York, Columbia University Press.

L'Hôpital, M. de. 1824-5, *Oeuvres Completes de Michel de L'Hôpital*.

Locke, John 1981, *The Correspondence of John Locke*, E. S. de Beer (ed.), 8 vols, Clarendon Press, Oxford.

Lopez Jr., Donald S. 1998, *Prisoners of Shangri-La: Tibetan Buddhism and the West*, University of Chicago Press, Chicago.

Lyotard, Jean François 1981, *The Postmodern Condition: A Report on Knowledge*, Geoff Bennington and Brian Massumi (trans.), Minneapolis, University of Minnesota Press.

Macaulay, T. B. 1915, *The History of England, from the Accession of James the Second*, Charles Harding Firth (ed.), 6 vols, Macmillan, London.

Maddox, M. 2002, *Indigenous Religion in Secular Australia,* Parliament of Australia, Parliamentary Library Research Paper 11, 1999-2000.

Manderville, J. 1964, *Travels of Sir John Mandeville, with three narratives in illustration of it, The Voyage of Johannes de Plano Carpini, The Journal of Friar William de Rubruguis, The Journal of Friar Odoric*, New York, Dover Publications.

Manzoor, S. P. 1995, 'Desacralisng Secularism', *The American Journal of Islamic Social Sciences,* vol. 12, no. 4, pp. 545-59.

Marr, D. 1999, *The High Price of Heaven*, St Leonard's, Allen & Unwin.

Marty, Martin E. 1992, 'Fundamentalisms Compared,' *The 1989 Charles Strong Memorial Lectures,* Adelaide, Flinders University Press.

Marx, K. 1967 [1867], *Capital: A Critique of Political Economy, vol. 1, The Process of Capitalist Production,* S. Moore and E. Aveling (trans.), New York, International Publishers.

Mason, Keith 1990, *Constancy and Change: Moral and Religious Values in the Australian Legal System,* Sydney, Federation Press.

Mayer, Arno 1990, *Why Did the Heavens not Darken?: The 'Final Solution' in History,* New York, Pantheon Books.

Mehmet, O. 1990, *Islamic Identity and Development,* London, Routledge.

Mellick, J. D. S. 1982, *Portable Australian Authors: Henry Kingsley,* St. Lucia, Queensland University Press.

Metz, Johan Baptist 1980, *Faith in History and Society,* New York, Seabury Press.

Meyer, P. 1997, *Religion and Globalization,* London, Sage Publications.

Minato, Akiko 1962, *Kirisutosha to Kokka (Christians and the State),* Tokyo, Seisho tosho kankôkai.

Moaddel, M. and K Talattof 1999, *Contemporary Debates in Islam: An Anthology of Modernist and Fundamentalist Thought,* New York, St Martin's Press.

Modrak, D. M. 1981, 'An Aristotelian Theory of Consciousness?' *Ancient Philosophy,* vol. 1, no. 2, pp. 160-70.

Moltman, J. 1971, *Theology and Joy,* London, S. C. M. Press.

Mombushô (Ministry of Education) 1927, *Ishin igo ni okeru kirisutokyô ni taisuru toriatsukai no hensen o joshi, kirisutokyô jogairon o bakusu (A Description of the Vicissitudes in the Treatment of Christianity Since the Restoration and a Refutation of the Theory of Christian Exception,* Tokyo, Mombushô Shûkyôkyoku (Ministry of Education Religions Bureau).

Mohanty, J. N. 2000, *The Self and Its Other: Philosophical Essays,* New Delhi, Oxford University Press.

Mottahedeh, R. 1980, *Loyalty and Leadership in an Early Islamic Society,* Princeton, Princeton University Press.

Muller, F. M. 1893, *Introduction to the Science of Religion,* London, Longman, Green.

Mullin, Glen H. and Jeff Watt 2003, *Female Buddhas. Women of Enlightenment in Tibetan Mystical Art,* Clear Light Publishers, Santa Fe.

Murphy, Andrew R. 1997, 'The Uneasy Relationship between Social Contract Theory and Religious Toleration', *The Journal of Politics,* vol. 59, no. 2, pp. 368-92.

New South Wales Law Reform Commission 1992, *Blasphemy: Discussion Paper*, viewed 11 August 2005, <http://www.lawlink.nsw.gov.au/lrc.nsf/pages/DP24TOC>

—— 2004, *Blasphemy: Report*, viewed 11 August 2005, <http://www.lawlink.nsw.gov.au/lrc.nsf/pages/r74toc>

Niebuhr, H. Richard 1951, *Christ and Culture*, New York, Harper.

Nietzsche, F. 1979, 'On Truth and Lies in a Nonmoral Sense', D. Breazeale (trans. and ed.), *Philosophy and Truth: Selections from Nietzsche's Notebooks of the Early 1870s*, Atlantic Highlands, Humanities Press.

—— 1967, *On the Genealogy of Morals*, W. Kaufmann and R. J. Hollingdale (trans.) New York, Vintage Books.

—— 1977, *Beyond Good and Evil: Prelude to a Philosophy of the Future*, R. J. Hollingdale (trans.), London, Penguin.

—— 1990, *Twilight of the Idols/The Antichrist*, R. J. Hollingdale (trans.), London, Penguin.

—— 1905, *Zarathustra*, Thomas Common (trans.), New York, Macmillan.

Nihon Kirisutokyô Tai Shûkyôdantaihôan Tokubetsu Iinkai (Japanese Christian Committee on the Religious Bodies Bill) (eds) 1929, *Shûkyôdantaihôan ni taisuru shodaishimbun no shasetsu (Editorials of major newspapers relating to the Religious Bodies Bill)*, Tokyo, no publisher.

Nirenberg, D. 1996, *Communities of Violence: Persecution of Minorities in the Middle Ages*, Princeton N. J., Princeton University Press.

Norris, P. and R. Inglehart 2003, 'Islamic Culture and Democracy: Testing the Clash of Civizations Thesis', *Comparative Sociology,* vol. 1, no. 3-4, pp. 235-63.

Novack, G. 1965, *The Origins of Materialism*, New York, Pathfinder Press.

Novick, Peter 2000, *The Holocaust in American Life*, New York, Houghton-Mifflin.

O'Dair, Richard and Andrew Lewis (eds) 2001, *Law and Religion,* Oxford, Oxford University Press.

O'Donohue, John 1997, *Anam ara*, London, Bantam Press.

Ogilvie, M. H. 1992, 'Church Property Disputes: Some Organizing Principles' *University of Toronto Law Journal,* vol. 42, pp. 377-393.

O'Rorke, Imogen 2001, 'Skinless wonders...', *The Observer,* Sunday May 20 2001, viewed 28 September 2005, <http://observer.guardian.co.uk/review/story/0,,493200,00.html>

Otto, Rudolf 1950, *The Idea of the Holy: an inquiry into the non-rational factor in the idea of the divine and its relation to the rational,* John W. Harvey (trans.), London, Oxford University Press.

Padoa-Schioppa, A. 1997, 'Hierarchy and Jurisdiction: Models in Medieval Canon Law', A. Padoa-Schioppa (ed.), *Legislation and Justice,* Oxford, Oxford University Press.

Pal, Pratapaditya 2003, *Himalayas: An Aesthetic Adventure*, Chicago, Art Institute of Chicago in association with the University of California & Mapin Books.

—— 2001, *Desire and Devotion, Art from India, Nepal and Tibet: In the John and Berthe Ford Collection*, London, Philip Wilson Publishers.

Parsons, T. 1999, 'Christianity and Modern Industrial Society', B. S. Turner (ed.) *The Talcott Parsons Reader,* Oxford, Blackwell.

—— 1960, 'Some Comments on the Pattern of Religious Organization in the United States', *Structure and Process in Modern Societies*, New York, Free Press, pp. 385-421.

Peters, F. E. 1967, *Greek Philosophical Terms: A Historical Lexicon,* New York, New York University Press.

Pickering, W. 1984, *Durkheim's Sociology of Religion*, London, Routledge and Kegan Paul.

Pipes, D. 2002, *Militant Islam Reaches America*, New York, Norton.

Polo, Marco 1982, *The Travels*, Penguin, Harmondsworth.

Popkin, R. H. 1999, 'Introduction', J. E. Force and R. H. Popkin (eds) *Newton and Religion: Context, Nature, and Influence*, Dordrecht, Kluwer Academic Publishers.

Ramadan, T. 1999, *To be a European Muslim*, Leicester, The Islamic Foundation.

—— 2001, *Islam, the West and the Challenges of Modernity*, Leicester, The Islamic Foundation.

Ramseyer, Robert 1992, 'When Society Itself is the Tyrant', *Japan Christian Review,* no. 58, p. 78.

Ramsey, A. W. 1999, *Liturgy, Politics, and Salvation: The Catholic League in Paris and the Nature of Catholic Reform, 1540-1630*, Rochester NY, University of Rochester Press.

Rawls, John 1985, 'Justice as Fairness: Political not Metaphysical', *Philosophy and Public Affairs,* vol. 14, no. 2, pp. 223-51.

Rhie, Marilyn M. and Robert A. F. Thurman 1991, *Wisdom and Compassion*, London, Thames & Hudson.

Richardson, James T. 2004, *Regulating Religion: Case Studies from Around the Globe,* Kluwer Academic Publishers.

Ricketts, C. E. F. 1990, 'An Anti-Roman Catholic Bias in the Law of Charity?', *The Conveyancer and Property Lawyer,* no. 34, pp. 66-86.

Ricoeur, Paul 1970, *Freud and Philosophy: An Essay on Interpretation,* Denis Savage (trans.), New Haven, Yale University Press.

Ridge, Pauline 2004, 'The Equitable Undue Influence and Wills', *Law Quarterly Review,* no. 120, pp. 617-39.

—— 2003, 'The Equitable Doctrine of Undue Influence Considered in the Context of Spiritual Influence and Religious Faith', *University of New South Wales Law Journal,* no. 26, 1, pp. 66-86.

—— 2003, 'Legal and Ethical Matters Relevant to the Receipt of Financial Benefits by Ministers of Religion and Churches', *Griffith Law Review,* no. 12, 1.

—— 2002, 'McCulloch v Fern', *Journal of Contract Law,* no. 18, p. 138.

Rinpoche, Guru 1987, *The Tibetan Book of the Dead: The Great Liberation through Hearing in the Bardo,* Boston, Shambala.

Roberts, K. 2004, *Lovemarks: The Future Beyond Brands,* New York, Power House Books.

Rorty, Richard 1994, 'Religion as a Conversation-Stopper', *Common Knowledge,* vol. 3, no. 1, pp. 1-6.

Rutland Suzanne D. and Sophie Caplan 1999, *With One Voice: the History of the New South Wales Jewish Board of Deputies,* Sydney, Australian Jewish Historical Society.

—— 1992, 'The Jewish Experience', in Murray Goot and Rodney Tiffen (eds) *Australia's Gulf War,* Melbourne, Melbourne University Press.

Sasagawa, Norikatsu 1988, *Tennô no sôgi (Imperial Funeral Rites),* Tokyo, Shinkyô Shuppansha.

Sasahara, Yoshimitsu 1988, 'Shûkyô dantaihô' (Religious Bodies Law) in *Nihon kirisutokyô daijiten (Encyclopedia of Japanese Christian History),* Tokyo, Kyôbunkan.

Schleiermacher, Friedrich 1958, *On Religion: Speeches to its Cultured Despisers,* Oman, John (trans.), New York, Harper & Row.

Schilling, H. 1989, 'Sündenzucht und frühneuzeitliche Sozialdisziplinierung: Die calvinistische, presbyteriale Kirchenzucht', in Emden vom 16. bis 19. Jahrhundert, G. Schmidt (ed.), *Stände und Gesellschaft im Alten Reich,* Stuttgart, Franz Steiner Verlag.

Seidler, M. J. 2002, 'Pufendorf and the Politics of Recognition', I. Hunter and D. Saunders (eds) *Natural Law and Civil Sovereignty: Moral Right and State Authority in Early Modern Political Thought,* Basingstoke, Palgrave.

Sellick, R. G. 2002, *Venus In Transit: Australian Women Travellers, 1788-1930,* Fremantle, Fremantle Arts Centre Press.

Seshadri, Sudha 2004, 'Buried in the Sky: Some Parsi Zoroastrians Are Having a Hard Time Accepting Changes to Traditional Death Rituals', *Science & Theology News,* viewed 28 September 2005, <http://www.be-liefnet.com/story/152/story_15243.html>

Shairani, H. M. (ed.) 1954, *An Account of the Rise and Progress of Mahometanism, with the Life of Mahomet, And a Vindication of him and his Religion from the Calumnies of the Christians,* Lahore, Orientalia.

Sherrill, Michael J. 2001, *The Protestant Church and Japanese Society: 1950-2000,* Tokyo, Kirisutokyo.com.

Smith. W. R. 1907, *Lectures on the Religion of the Semites,* London, A. and C. Black.

Stanner, W. 1967, 'Reflections on Durkheim and Aboriginal Religion', M. Freedman (ed.) *Social Organization: Essays Presented to Raymond Firth,* London, Frank Cass.

Stark, R. and Glock, C. 1968, *American Piety and the Nature of Religious Commitment,* Berkeley, University of California Press.

Stern, S. and E. Seligmann (eds) 2002, *The End of Tolerance?* London, Nicholas Brealey.

Strelein, Lisa 2000, 'Dealing With Unfinished Business: A Treaty For Australia', *Public Law Review,* vol. 11, no. 4, pp. 261-5.

Stubbe, Henry 1954, *An Account of the Rise and Progress of Mahometanism, with the Life of Mahomet, And a Vindication of him and his Religion from the Calumnies of the Christians,* E. Hafiz Mahmud Khan Shairani (ed.) Orientalia, Lahore.

Susin, Luiz Carlos 2000/2 'A Critique Of The Identity Paradigm', *Concilium.*

Swatos, W. H. Jr. (ed.) 1998, *Encyclopedia of Religion and Society,* Hartford Institute for Religion Research, Hartford Seminary, Walnut Creek, Altamira Press, <http://hirr.hartsem.edu.ency/Sacred.htm>.

Taliaferro, Charles 1999, *Contemporary Philosophy of Religion,* Oxford, Blackwell.

Tamney J. 2001, *Resilience of Conservative Religion*, New York, Cambridge University Press.

Taniguchi, Yasuhei 1984, 'The Post-War Court System as an Instrument for Social Change', in George DeVos (ed.), *Institutions for Change in Japanese Society*, Berkeley, CA, University of California.

Tanner, Kathryn 1997, *Theories of Culture: A New Agenda for Theology*, Minneapolis, Augsburg Fortress.

Tatz, Colin 2003, *With Intent to Destroy: Reflecting on Genocide*, London, Verso.

—— 1994, 'Reflections on the Politics of Remembering and Forgetting', The First Abraham Wajnryb Memorial Lecture, Macquarie University, 1 December 1994, Centre for Comparative Genocide Studies.

—— 1982, *Aborigines and Uranium and Other Essays*, Heinemann.

Thomasius, C. 1705, 'Ob Ketzerei ein straffbares Verbrechen sei? (An haeresis sit crimen)', 'Vom Recht evangelischer Fürsten in Mitteldingen oder. Kirchenzeremonien' (*De jure principis circa adiaphora*, 1695), Thomasius C. (ed.), *Auserlesene deutsche Schriften Erster Teil*, Halle, Renger, 1.

—— 1701, *De crimine magiae / Von dem Verbrechen der Zauber- und Hexerey*. Halle, Renger.

—— 1701, Dreyfache Rettung des Rechts Evangelischer Fürsten in Kirchen-Sachen, Frankfurt a.M.

Thomasius C. (ed.) 1705, *Auserlesene deutsche Schriften, Erster Teil*, Halle, Renger.

Thomson, Thomas and Cosmo Innes (eds) *The Acts of the Parliament of Scotland*, 1814-1875, 12 vols, Edinburgh.

Tibi, Bassam 2002, 'A Plea for a Reform Islam', *The End of Tolerance?* in Susan Stern and Elisabeth Seligmann (eds) London, Nicholas Brealey.

Tomura, Masahiro 1988, *Ima, X-dê o kangaeru (Thinking about X-Day Now)*, Tokyo, Kirisuto Shinbunsha.

—— 1990, *Sokuinorei to daijôsai o yomu (Interpreting the Sokuinorei and the Daijôsai)*, Tokyo, Nihon Kirisutokyôdan Shuppankyoku.

Trusen, W. 1992, 'Rechtliche Grundlagen des Häresiebegriffs und des Ketzerverfahrens', Menchi S. S. (ed.), *Ketzerverfolgung im 16. und frühen 17. Jahrhundert*, Wiesbaden, Otto Harrassowitz.

Turner, B. S. 1983, *Religion and Social Theory: A Materialist Perspective*, London, Heinemann Educational Books.

Turner, Ian (ed.) 1968, *The Australian Dream*, Melbourne, Sun Books.

Tylor, E. B. 1891, *Primitive Culture: Researches into the Development of Mythology, Philosophy, Religion, Language Art and Custom*, London, J. Murray.

UNDP, 2002, *The Human Development Report*, New York, Oxford University Press.

Uchimura, Kanzô 1927, *Shûkyô hôan ni tsuite (Regarding the Religions Bill)*, Tokyo, no publisher.

Vergote, Antoine 1995, 'Debate Concerning the Psychology of Religion', *International Journal for the Psychology of Religion,* vol. 5, pp. 119-24.

Vidal-Naquet, Pierre 1992, *The Assassins of Memory*, New York, Columbia University Press.

Villa-Vicencio, Charles (ed.) 1986, *Between Christ and Caesar: Classical and Contemporary Texts on Church and State*, Grand Rapids, Eerdmans.

Wach, J. 1949, *Sociology of Religion,* Chicago, University of Chicago Press.

Waghid, Y. 1996, 'In Search of a Boundless Ocean of New Skies: Human Creativity is a Matter of Amal, Jihad and Ijtihad', *The American Journal of Islamic Social Sciences,* vol. 13, no. 3, pp. 353-62.

Welsch, W. 1997, *Undoing Aesthetics*, A. Inkpin, (trans.) London, SAGE Publications.

Westphal, Merold 1993, *Suspicion and Faith: The Religious Uses of Modern Atheism,* Grand Rapids, Mich., Eerdmans.

—— 1984, *God, Guilt and Death: An Existential Phenomenology of Religion,* Bloomington, Indiana University Press.

Wistrich, Robert S. 2002, *Muslim Anti-Semitism: A Clear and Present Danger,* The American Jewish Committee.

—— c1991, *Antisemitism: The Longest Hatred,* New York, Pantheon.

—— 1985, *Anti-Zionism as an Expression an Expression of Antisemitism in Recent Years,* Jerusalem, Shazar Library, Institute of Contemorary Jewry.

Wiesel, Elie 1985, *Against Silence: the Voice and Vision of Elie Wiesel*, Irving Abrahamson (ed.), New York, Holocaust Library, 3 vols.

Williams, John Alden 1994, *The Word of Islam*, Austin, Texas.

Wittgenstein, Ludwig 1974, *Philosophical Investigations,* Oxford, Blackwell.

—— 1972, *Lectures and Conversations on Aesthetics, Phsychology and Religious Belief,* Cyril Barrett (ed.), Berkeley, C.A., University of California Press.

Wokler, R. 2000, 'Multiculturalism and Ethnic Cleansing in the Enlightenment', in P. G. Ole and R. Porter (eds), *Toleration in Enlightenment Europe,* Cambridge, Cambridge University Press.

Wootten, Hal 2003, 'Conflicting Imperatives: Pursuing Truth in the Courts' in I. McCalman and A McGrath (eds) *Proof and Truth,* Canberra, Academy of the Humanities.

Wright, Stephen and Jean Saye-Adams 2000, *Sacred Space*, London, Harcourt.

Wylie, Turrell 1964-1965, 'Mortuary Customs at Sa-Skya, Tibet.' *Harvard Journal of Asiatic Studies,* vol. 25, pp. 229-42.

Yamamoto, Hideteru 1929, *Shûkyô dantai hôan hantai kankei shiryô 'Kirisuto shinkyô no tasû wa hantai' (Materials Relating to the Opposition to the Religious Bodies Bill: Majority of Protestants Oppose Bill),* Tokyo, Nihon Kirisutokyô Tai Shûkyôdantaihôan Tokubetsu Iinkai (Japanese Christian Ad Hoc Committee on the Religious Bodies Bill).

Young, Robert 1979, *Analytical Concordance to the Holy Bible,* 8th edn., Guildford, Lutterworth Press.

Acts and cases

Aboriginal Heritage Act 1972

Aboriginal Heritage Act 1979 (South Australia)

Aboriginal Heritage Act 1972 (Western Australia)

Aboriginal Land Rights (Northern Territory) Act 1976 (Commonwealth)

Aboriginal and Torres Strait Islander Heritage Protection Act, 1984

Aboriginal Sacred Sites Ordinance 1978 (Northern Territory)

Allcard v Skinner (1887) LR 36

Attorney-General for New South Wales v Grant (1976) 135 CLR

Barry v Butlin [1838] 2 Moo 480; 12 ER 1089

Blake v Associated Newspapers Ltd [2003] EWHC 1960

Bosch v Perpetual Trustee Co [1938] AC 463

Chapman v Luminis Pty Ltd (2001)

Chennells v Bruce (1939) 55 TLR 422

Church of the New Faith v Commissioner for Pay Roll Tax (Vic) (1983) 154 CLR

Commonwealth v Tasmania (1983) 46 ALR 625

Extension of Charitable Purpose Act 2004 (Cth)

Family Provision Act 1982 (NSW)

Gay News Ltd. and Lemon v United Kingdom [Eur Comm HR] 5 EHRR 123 (1982)

Gilmour v Coats [1949] AC 426

Hackett v Public Trustee [2 May 1997] ACT SC (Unreported, Higgins J)

Hall v Hall (1868) LR 1 P & D 481

Hartigan v International Society for Krishna Consciousness Inc. [2002] NSW SC 810 (Unreported, Bryson J)

Hugenin v Baseley (1807) 14 Ves Jr 273, 288.

Illuzzi v Christian Outreach Centre (1997) Q ConvR

Islamic Council of Victoria Inc v Catch the Fire Ministries Inc [2003] VCAT 1753
(21 October 2003),viewed 11 August 2005, <http://www.aust-
lii.edu.au/cgi-bin/disp.pl/au/cases/vic/VCAT/2003/1753.html>

*Islamic Council of Victoria v Catch the Fire Ministries Inc (Anti Discrimination –
Remedy)* [2005] VCAT 1159 (22 June 2005), viewed 11 August 2005,
<http://www.austlii.edu.au/cgi-
bin/disp.pl/au/cases/vic/VCAT/2005/1159.html>

Islamic Council of Victoria v Catch the Fire Ministries Inc (Final) [2004] VCAT
2510 (22 December 2004), viewed 11 August 2005, <http://www.aust-
lii.edu.au/au/cases/vic/VCAT/2004/2510.html>

Johnson v Buttress (1936) 56 CLR 113

Lyon v Home (1868) LR 6 Eq 655

Maguire v Attorney General [1943] IR 238

McCulloch v Fern [2001] NSW SC 406 (Unreported, Palmer J)

Morley v Loughnan [1893] 1 Ch 763

Native and Historical Objects and Areas Preservation Ordinance 1955

Nock v Austin (1918) 25 CLR 519

Northern Territory Aboriginal Sacred Sites Act 1989

Nottidge v Prince (1860) 2 Giff 246; 66 ER 103

Parfitt v Lawless (1872) LR 2 P & D 462, 474 (Lord Penzance)

Pell v *National Gallery of Victoria* [1998] 2 VR 391

Permanent Trusteee Co Ltd v Fraser (1995) 36 NSWLR 24

Quek v Beggs (1990) 5 BPR [97405]

Racial and Religious Tolerance Act 2001 (Victoria), viewed 11 August 2005,
<http://www.austlii.edu.au/au/legis/vic/consol_act/rarta2001265/>

R v Chief Metropolitan Magistrate, ex parte Choudhury [1991] 1 QB 429

R v Gott (1922) 16 Cr App R 86

R v Hetherington (1841) 4 State Trials ns 563

R v *Regina and Foote* 15 Cox CC 231 (1883)

Scandrett v Dowling (1992) 27 NSWLR 483

Taylor's Case (1676) 1 Vent. 293 (KB), 86 ER 189

The Local Spiritual Assembly of the Baha'is of Parramatta Ltd v Haghighat (2004)
Aust Torts Reports 81-729

Tyrrell v Painton [1894] P 151

United States v Kuch [1968] 288 F Supp 439

Whitehouse v Gay News, Whitehouse v Lemon [1979] AC 617; [1979] 2 WLR 281; [1979] 1 All ER 898 (HL)

Winter v Crichton (1991) 23 NSWLR 116

Other sources

Amateau, Albert 2005, 'Chinese takeover of Tibet protested at art opening', *The Villager*, Thursday, 3 March 2005, viewed World Tibet News (WTN) 18 September 2005, <http://www.tibet.ca>

Anon., 1900, *History of Modern Anatomy*, viewed 28 September 2005, <www.fact-index.com/h/hi/history_of_modern_anatomy.html>

Anon., 1926, '...The Realm of the Devil Dancers.' *New York Times*, 25 July 1926.

Anon., 1930, 'Made from Human Bones.' *New York Times*, April 1930, pp. 25.

Cahill, Desmond, 'Religion and Social Cohesion in Australia: an interim report', presented at the *Academic Colloquium, 'After September 11: Religion, Diversity and Cohesion in the Global Neighbourhood*, 13-14 September 2002, RMIT, Melbourne.

Carlson, P. 'UFOs? When Penguins Fly! Sedona Exposes Those Amazing Extra-terrestrials', *The Washington Post*, 10 November 1998, p. BO2.

Centre of Research on Anti-Semitism, 'Anti-Semitism Study in the Spotlight', *Newsletter*, no. 26, Centre of Research on Anti-Semitism, December 2, 2003.

Channel 4 2005, The Anatomists: The Anatomy Act, *Channel 4*, viewed 28 September 2005, <http://www.channel4.com/science/microsites/A/ana-tomists/ethics1.html#act>

Christies, *Indian and Southeast Asian Art*, 25 March 2004.

Coren, Michael ' "Blaming it on the Jews": Antisemitism is an old, never-ending story', *Sun Media* (Toronto), 20 July 2002.

Corr, R. 2000, 'Asians, Muslims and "Authentic Australians": Neoracism Down Under', paper presented at *Challenges of Immigration and Integration in the European Union and Australia*, Centre for European Studies, The Australian National University.

Daly, Martin 'Trial cut short as Roche admits guilt', 'News', *Sydney Morning Herald*, 29-30 May 2004, p. 4.

Evans-Pritchard, Ambrose 'Jews face resurgence of hate in Europe', *The Age* (Melbourne), 31 May 2002.

Fray, Peter 'Europe cultivates the ugly flower of prejudice', *The Age* (Melbourne), 22 June 2002.

Fray, Peter *The Age* (Melbourne), 22 June 2002.

Harding, Vanessa 2005, 'An Interview with Vanessa Harding' *The Great Plague; Channel 4 history programme transcript*, viewed 28 September 2005, <http://www.channel4.com/history/microsites/H/history/e-h/harding.html>

James, Dianna, 'How can we sing our own songs in a strange land?', Locations of Spirituality: 'Experiences' and 'Writings' of the Sacred, Humanities Research Centre, Old Canberra House, The Australian National University, 26-27 October 2002, viewed 16 January 2006, <http://www.anu.edu.au/hrc/conferences/conference_archive/2002/LocationsofSpirituality_abstracts.php>.

Jefferies, Stuart, 'The naked and the dead', *The Guardian*, Tuesday March 19, viewed 28 September, 2002, <http://education.guardian.co.uk/higher/arts/story/0,,670045,00.html>

Jones, Jeremy *October 2002 to September 2003 Report*, Executive Council of Australian Jewry, 2003.

Maitland Mercury, 14 September 2001, p. 14.

Melchior, Rabbi Michael Speech to the Subcommittee on Near East and South Asian Affairs of the United States Senate Committee on Foreign Relations, 15 October 2003.

Neely, Paula Kripaitis, '17th Century Jamestown Burials: Tell Tales of Stressful Beginnings', Press Release, viewed 28 September 2005, <http://www.apva.org/apva/burial.pdf>

Pellach, Peta 'Interfaith Dialogue and the Issue of Israel', paper presented at the 16th *Annual Conference of the Australian Association of Jewish Studies*, Melbourne, 16-17 February 2004.

Schoenfeld, Gabriel Editorial comment, 'Israel and Anti-Semitism', *Commentary*, June 2002.

Sotheby's 1997, *Indian and Southeast Asian Art*, Wednesday September 24.

Space Service Inc. 2005, Memorial Spaceflights, viewed 28 September 2005, <http://www.spaceservicesinc.com/MemorialSpaceflights/intro.asp>

Uniting Church in Australia, *Code of Ethics and Administrative Practice*.

William, Michael 2002, 'Journeying with Respect', 'How can we sing our own songs in a strange land?', Locations of Spirituality: 'Experiences' and 'Writings' of the Sacred, Humanities Research Centre, Old Canberra

House, The Australian National University, 26-27 October 2002, viewed
16 January 2006, <http://www.anu.edu.au/hrc/conferences/confer-
ence_archive/2002/LocationsofSpirituality_abstracts.php>

Index

faith
distinguished from idolatry, 174
as manifestation of psychological
disease, 171
faithfulness
to Christianity, 174
to truth, 174
Family Provision Act, 1982, 9
family provision legislation, 139, 140, 142
'Final Solution', 84
fitra, 52, 53, 61
'flaw in the nation-building process', 43, 45
Forrest River Massacres, 87
Forty Days at Musa Dagh, 83
free speech, 2, 32
freedom of speech, 4
functional specialisation, 120

Gay News, 4, 31, 35, 38
Geneva Convention, 36
genocide, 21, 79, 81
Armenian, 79–80, 82–83
German Empire 113
Gibson, Mel, 32
Giotto, 32
Golden Temple, Amritsar, 181
Gott, John William, 35
gift-giving, 135
relevance in a multicultural society, 133
gifts,
inter vivos, 133, 134
legal restraints upon, 133, 134, 140–142
motivated by religious faith, 133, 134,
139, 141
negotiating the sacred in law, 135
testamentary, 9, 10, 133–139
globalisation, 99
God
existence of, 186
place of in civil and political matters, 33
understandings of, 39
'Goodness and Kindness' program, 26
Gordon-Cumming, Constance, 46
Grueber, Father John, 93
Gulf War (1990–91), 17, 18

Hanson, Pauline, 19
Hansonism, 19
Hare Krishna community, 136
Hashem Aghajari affair, 122
Haug, Wolfgang Fritz, 100, 101
heresy, 7, 110, 111, 115
Heritage Bookshop, 20
Himmler, Heinrich, 79
Hindmarsh Bridge case, 11, 191, 198
Hiromachi, Kozaki, 156
Hitler, 21, 47, 80
Holocaust, the, 6, 23, 80, 81, 84, 85
denial, 19, 20,
denialism, 82–86
holocaust, 80
House of Lords Select Committee on
Religious Offences, 31
holy, the, 186
'human Being-ness', 181–190
human bones,
as art objects, 92, 95
trafficking in, 92
in Western art history, 94
Human Development Index, 127
humanism, sacralisation of, 58
Hume, David, 10, 169–171
Huntington, Samuel, 17, 27

Ibn Khaldoun, 55
idolatry, 170, 176
ijtihad, 56, 61
Imperial Rescript on Education, 157
In the Will of Thomas Walsh, 138
incommensurable, comparing the, 194–195
indigenous religions, 11
individualism, 104
Indonesia, 129
injustice, 46
institutional differentiation, 120
instrumentalism, 175
intolerance, 9, 76
Iran, 128, 129
Iron Knob, mining at, 199–200
Irving, David, 85
Irving v Lipstadt & Penguin Books, 85–86
Islam, 3

in Australia, 24, 123
  secular intellectuals, 57
  secular model in Turkey, 57
mystical experiences, 74
mysticism, 99

Nakaya Case, 152
Nasr Hamed Abu Zeid affair, 122
nation-building process,
National Viewers' and Listeners'
  Association, 35
Native Title legislation, 11
'nature mysticism', 74
Nazi Germany, 21, 79, 84
Nefesh ha' Hayyim, 39
negotiating the sacred, 104, 191
  in law, 133–145
  in a multicultural society, 43–50
  the role of the state, 11
negotiation in a pluralistic society, 12
New Advent Catholic Encyclopaedia, 71, 72
New South Wales Council of Christians and
  Jews, 25
New South Wales Law Reform Commission,
  116
New South Wales Jewish Board of
  Deputies, 17
Nietzsche, 10, 169, 170
  critique of religion/Christianity, 171–172
  Christian response to, 173–175
No Logo, 103
Noonkanbah Station, 86
Northern Territory Government, 191, 192,
  197

'obdurate believers', 9, 141, 142
objective standards, 140–143
offence, 2
One Land, One Law, One Culture, 47
One Land, One Law, One People, 47
One Nation, 19
Oslo Accords, 18

Pakistan, 129
  blasphemy in, 123
  Christians, 123

Islamisation in, 122
Oxford University Press in, 123
Pauline Hanson's One Nation, 20
Peace of Westphalia, 113
Pell, Bishop George, 4, 35
People's Republic of China, The, 95
Peres, Shimon, 83
performance and the profane, 120
pharisaical moralism, 172
'pharisaism', 170–172
philosophers and language, 184
Pietists, 114
piety, 185
'Piss Christ', 4, 35
'plastination', 95–96
pragmatism, 67
prayer, 10
probate undue influence, 134, 137, 138
property, 69
proprietary or pecuniary interests, 194
Protestant church, 111
Protestant Ethic, 99
Protestantism, 6
Professional Ethics and Civic Morals, 68, 70

Qadr, 51
Qur'an, 53, 56, 60

Racial and Religious Tolerance Act, 2001, 40
Rainbow Serpent, 200
Ramadan, Tariq, 57
Ramseyer, Robert, 151
rapporteur, role of, 196–197
rationality, 100
Rawls, John, 180, 187
religio, 104
religion
  and blasphemy, overview, 121–123
  and society, 68
  as cultural right, 2
  as deep grammar of society, 69
  as institution, 102
  as social solidarity, 67
  coexistence with capitalism, 104
  Durkheim's definition of, 67
  freedom of, 3, 8, 9

www.ingramcontent.com/pod-product-compliance
Lightning Source LLC
Chambersburg PA
CBHW061244270326
41928CB00041B/3410